# Fashioned from Penury

**Studies in Australian History**

Series editors:
Alan Gilbert, Patricia Grimshaw and Peter Spearritt

# FASHIONED FROM PENURY

## Dress as Cultural Practice in Colonial Australia

*Margaret Maynard*

DEPARTMENT OF ART HISTORY, UNIVERSITY OF QUEENSLAND

**CAMBRIDGE**
UNIVERSITY PRESS

For my father, Bob Louttit

Published by the Press Syndicate of the University of Cambridge
The Pitt Building, Trumpington Street, Cambridge CB2 1RP, UK
40 West 20th Street, New York, NY 10011–4211, USA
10 Stamford Road, Oakleigh, Melbourne 3166, Australia

© Cambridge University Press 1994

First published 1994

Printed in Hong Kong by Colorcraft

*National Library of Australia cataloguing in publication data*
Maynard, Margaret.
Fashioned from penury: dress as cultural practice in
colonial Australia.
Bibliography.
Includes index.
1. Costume – Australia – History – 18th century. 2. Costume –
Australia – History – 19th century. [3.] Aborigines,
Australian – Costume and adornment. 4. Convicts –
Australia – Costume. 5. Great Britain – Colonies – Australia.
6. Australia – Social life and customs. I. Title. (Series:
Studies in Australian history (Cambridge, England)).
391.00994

*Library of Congress cataloguing in publication data*
Maynard, Margaret.
Fashioned from penury: dress as cultural practice in colonial
Australia / Margaret Maynard.
(Studies in Australian history)
Includes bibliographical references and index.
1. Costume – Australia – History – 18th century. 2. Costume –
Australia – History – 19th century. 3. Australian aborigines –
Costume. 4. Prisoners – Australia – Costume. 5. Great Britain –
Colonies – Australia. 6. Australia – Social life and customs.
I. Title. II. Series.
✓ GT1590.M39 1994
391'.00994 – dc20
93–37953
CIP

*A catalogue record for this book is available from the British Library.*

ISBN 0 521 45310 0 Hardback

# Contents

# Illustrations

# Acknowledgements

I would like to extend my grateful thanks to the many people who have so willingly assisted me in the preparation of this book. Teachers, librarians, museum curators and friends are too numerous to list individually. I am especially grateful to my first teacher and mentor Stella Mary Newton and to Judith Allen, Gail Reekie, Karen Finch, Marion Fletcher, Kylie Winkworth, Birgit Culloty, Judith McKay, as well as Don Baker who read an early draft. Institutions who have given their special support include the Western Australian Museum, the National Trust of Victoria, the Powerhouse Museum, the National Gallery of Victoria, the David Jones Archive, the Swan and Guildford Historical Society, the London Museum, and the John Oxley, LaTrobe, Allport, Mortlock, Fryer and Mitchell Libraries.

I am extremely indebted to the University of Queensland for two special project grants which enabled me to travel around Australia to see a number of costume collections in situ and consult their curators. I am grateful too for the hospitality of the Humanities Research Centre, Canberra, for giving me the peaceful opportunity to finalise this manuscript in 1992.

Special thanks go to Richard Maynard who was endlessly supportive and never doubted that the project would finally be completed.

# Glossary

NB. Terms used in the nineteenth century did not always have the modern meaning.

**batiste:**  fine cotton or linen fabric.

**beaverteen:**  twilled cotton fabric with a looped pile.

**beef boots:**  thigh boots.

**bell-topper:**  top hat.

**bloomers:**  women's baggy, knee-length trousers.

**blucher boots:**  strong leather half-boots or high shoes.

**bowyang:**  thong or strap worn below the knee.

**buffon:**  a projecting covering of gauze or linen for women, worn at the breast.

**cambric:**  fine white linen or cotton fabric.

**caraco/caracao:**  short jacket worn by working women.

**chemise:**  women's loose undergarment, like a shift; often sleeveless.

**china crepe:**  silk gauze.

**coatee:**  short coat, usually worn by children.

**crinoline:**  wide, stiff petticoat, usually extended with wires or hoops.

**drugget:**  coarse fabric of wool or woollen mix.

**duck:**  strong linen or cotton fabric, untwilled; lighter than canvas; used for sailors' trousers.

**durant:**  long-lasting woollen fabric.

**fall fronts:**  loose fronts to trousers, preceding the fly front.

**fichu:**  light, triangular piece of fabric worn at the neck or about the shoulders.

**fleshings:**  tights, as worn by actors.

**frock:**  a loose-fitting male garment, often used for work; a smock.

**frockcoat:**  man's close-fitting coat, usually double-breasted, extending to the knees.

**fustian:**  thick twilled linen or cotton fabric.

**gingham:**  patterned cotton fabric, usually in stripes or checks.

**gorget:**  decorative metal throat-piece deriving from armour, worn by military officers.

**gurrah:**  plain, coarse Indian muslin.

**jabot:**  ornamental lace frill worn on the breast.

**jean:**  durable twilled cotton fabric.

**jumper:**  loose jacket or shirt reaching to the hips; usually of coarse fabric.

**kersey:**  lightweight wool mix fabric.

**leghorn:**  plaited straw used for hats.

**linsey-woolsey:**  coarse fabric of linen and wool mix.

**mantua:**  a gown.

**moleskin:**  strong twilled cotton fabric.

**musquito:**  probably a net fabric.

**ottoman:**  heavy fabric of silk and wool; a shawl made from this.

**pantaloons:**  men's narrow trousers.

**pelerine:**  a short cape.

**peplum:**  short overskirt.

**petticoat:**  usually an outer garment for working women, like a skirt; also a capacious undergarment worn with crinoline.

**pilot cloth:**  thick blue woollen fabric.

**sac suit:**  loose-fitting, man's suit.

**shoddy:**  inferior woollen cloth.

**skeleton/skelton suit:**  young boy's suit, with the trousers buttoned to the jacket.

**slops:**  coarse, loose-fitting, readymade garments.

**stays:**  corsets.

**stuff:**  common woollen fabric.

**teagown:**  loose gown worn in the afternoons.

**thread hose:**  stockings.

**ticking:**  heavy linen or cotton fabric.

**tournure:**  small waist pad or bustle.

**watchcoat:**  heavy overcoat.

**wideawake:**  a general term used for a broad-brimmed hat.

**worsted:**  fine woollen fabric.

# INTRODUCTION

Virginia Woolf, in *A Room of One's Own* (1929), writing about the values of women as opposed to those made by men, said in passing: 'Speaking crudely, football and sport are "important": the worship of fashion, the buying of clothes "trivial"'.[1] Woolf's words have an ominous ring for anyone seriously contemplating the study of dress. They seem to sound a special warning to those investigating Australia and its dressing habits. In a country where national pride centres on the mythology of war, sporting heroes and flag poles, the cultural blindness about fashion and the belief that dress is 'women's business' has been especially pronounced.

Whilst many Australians today are interested in fashion, it is a common perception that they are not stylish dressers. Dame Edna Everage's sequined gowns and sparkling bracelets seem to encapsulate, quite succinctly, cultural beliefs about the nation's 'style'. Australia has no substantial tradition of haute couture or fine garment manufacturing and it would be a challenge to think of any fashionable women who have made the world's 'best dressed' list. Australian men have had the reputation of somehow existing outside fashion, and thinking about their clothes for as long as it takes to put on their stubbie shorts, thongs and a towelling hat.

Economic rationalist thinking about the importance of appearance in the corporate workplace has certainly inflected Australian dress practices since the 1980s, but the myth that Australian dress is classless and therefore thoroughly uninteresting persists. Robert Treborlang, in his satire *How to Survive Australia* (1985), entitles his chapter on the democratic nature of Australian clothing 'How Not to Dress'.

Yet lurking beneath the perceived 'dullness', 'stylelessness' and sometimes even 'vulgarity' of the nation's clothing lies a fascinating history that throws new light on a number of areas of historical debate in both penal and colonial society. Why then has the subject received practically no critical attention? Whilst current proliferating interests in popular culture and gender studies are effectively challenging some of the long-held myths about Australian cultural practices, dress has yet to gain full academic credibility.

From the vantage point of the 1990s, our perceptions of what constitutes an 'Australian' dress are deeply coloured by the nationalistic developments in the arts during the previous decades. At this time innovative designers like Jenny Kee and Linda Jackson burst onto the Australian market purveying ideas rather than classic style. In 1983 Jackson launched her Bush Couture label. Both Kee and Jackson produced high-quality clothing which celebrated the local environment, using Aboriginal designs and indigenous images such as wattle flowers, eucalypt leaves and koala bears. Their preoccupation with local imagery was matched by products of the Australian film industry which also played a key part in popularising an imagined view of colonial dressing.

The colourful styles produced by Jackson, Kee and, later, Ken Done seemingly marked the coming of age of local designer clothing, which had begun to emerge some time before, in the early 1950s. Nowadays tourists who purchase a Ken Done T-shirt or an Akubra hat accept them as quintessentially Australian. Yet from the 1970s onwards the use of indigenous symbols, or the reworking of an imagined colonial past into an Australiana dress cult (especially through the use of archetypal forms of masculine attire) was the self-conscious sign of a intensely commercialised and manufactured identity.

In fact the R. M. Williams hat, Driza-bone coat or some other tourist commodity gives little idea of the subtle constituents of an 'Australian' form of dress. Indeed, its characteristics were being formulated from the time of first settlement and were located in a network of social practices rather than simply at the level of style. There are some isolated colonial examples of the use of local floral motifs painted or stitched on garments, such as the wedding gown of Edith Cowan painted with tiger lily motifs in the Western Australian Historical Society collection. Yet the characteristics of an 'Australian' dress extend well beyond mere motifs.

It is tempting to regard clothing primarily as utilitarian, but dress functions on many levels and serves a number of purposes that extend beyond this. Nor are clothes simply a passive reflection of a culture. As Philippe Perrot says, 'everywhere, underneath the practical rationalization of consumption and behaviour in dress, are hidden meaning and social value'.[2] Clothing makes culturally visible the historical constraints and imperatives experienced by individuals and social groups. It serves as an arena for the public signalling of notions of morality and social stratification and can be a marker of sexual differences or ambiguities. Power relations, whether of class, race, age or sex, are constantly being negotiated through the practice of dress and its corollary, fashion.

Indeed, dress is a form of unspoken language, even though its signs have no fixed interpretation but a multiplicity of meanings. Through processes of decoding, dress discloses information about the most intimate aspect of lives and relationships, and the most delicate of perceptions about class. Moreover, the adornment and ornamentation of the body, linked to associated bodily activity, can be a visible sign of the workings of regulatory disciplines, privileges and the 'microphysics' of modern patriarchal power, as proposed in the writings of Foucault.[3] Whilst Foucault has been criticised for remaining silent on the disciplines that engender and formulate the feminine body, clearly dress and behaviour are crucial to the ways in which both sexes are culturally enacted.[4]

In Australia these processes took place in ways that do not necessarily match Eurocentric theoretical models, for they had specific local resonances. Indeed the study of dress in Australia opens up fresh perspectives on the nature of changing interactions between the dominant culture and the periphery. It highlights and extends our knowledge of the workings of penal discipline, of economic and cultural imperialism, racism, ethnicity, urbanisation, the formation of social classes, organisation of labour, and the definitions and ordering of masculinity and femininity. In essence, the subject amounts to far more than straightforward economic or technical history, or the study of manners. At any one time, then, dress can be located within a number of current discourses, which may include those addressing beauty, sexuality, class, ethnicity and economics. The orthodox view that there is some simple, causal link between clothes, women and the trivial cannot be sustained and tends to obscure the complexities of dress history.

It is surprising then that, almost without exception, the subject is neglected in Australian histories of the colonial period. Political decisions, deeds of civic importance and economic matters are privileged over what seem to be more personal matters of fashion and clothing supplies.[5] Perhaps for mainstream historians the apparent intimacy of clothing presents, as Virginia Woolf implies, a terrain ostensibly too 'domestic', too 'mundane' or too 'picturesque' to warrant rigorous inquiry. Many recent Bicentennial publications demonstrate a newfound interest in popular culture, including references to dress. Yet concerns with clothing remain simplistic and summary, showing little sign of grappling with the intrinsic issues of the subject itself.[6] By contrast, the manufacture of cloth and clothing and the economic opportunities for women in these trades have fared a little better in Australian histories, especially women's history.[7] But there has been no attempt, even in these texts, to link the garment trades with the artefacts of dress and its theoretical discourses.

Dress is a disturbing subject, partly because of its personal nature and its troubling associations with sexuality and the body. It threatens the stability of segregated zones, lying as it does uneasily and ambiguously at the junction between the realm of the public and that of the private.[8] Dress is not simply a matter of the social being displaced onto the separate entity of the body. As Sawchuk points out, dress, as a form of inscription, operates at the level of the body, constructing differences which produce the social body as 'a textured object with multi-dimensional layers, touched by the rich weave of history and culture'.[9]

It is partly the very intimacy of dress, and its inherent ambiguities, that have prevented it from being regarded as a serious historical discipline, with theoretical and critical credibility. Dress studies are further disparaged by the myth that clothes are merely 'women's business'. There is a long philosophical history of associating fashion and the decorative with the fickle and instinctual culture of women. Despite certain repositionings of attitude toward style and the gender order in post-modern dressing, the view that the ornamental nature of fashion is trivial, non-cerebral and suited to women's interests remains entrenched. In the historiography of Australia such views, and the absence of serious attention to dress, have been especially marked. The silences over the subject, linked as they are to the silences over women and their historical experiences, warrant further scrutiny.

In Australia those few authors who have directed their interests toward clothes have produced general surveys of fashion only. The major emphasis has been placed on pictorial imagery and the texts are often somewhat trivial and ill documented.[10] The linear and chronological evolution of fashion (essentially minority dressing) has been accorded centrality, ignoring fundamental issues relating to the dress of the major proportion of Australia's population. Two books which are notable exceptions to these more common fashion or pictorial surveys are Cedric Flower's *Duck and Cabbage Tree: A Pictorial History of Clothes in Australia* (revised edition 1984), and Marion Fletcher's *Costume in Australia, 1788–1901* (1984).

The lack of serious literature on the history of Australian clothing is reflected to some extent in the history of Australian collections of dress. These collections have come about more through accident than design; they are unrepresentative, and the holdings for the first half of the nineteenth century are quite sparse. The majority of items that do survive from these early years are unprovenanced. For this reason the small, quite ordinary pink and white cotton infant's gown of John Marsden, who died in 1803, has a significance beyond its intrinsic worth because it is the earliest provenanced Australian garment we have.[11]

Dress of the fashionable elite dating from about the 1860s, and especially the decoratively styled and visually appealing clothing of women, is well represented in major institutions such as the Powerhouse Museum, the Art Gallery of South Australia, the Victorian National Trust and to some extent the National Gallery of Victoria, as well as in historical societies such as those of Queensland and Western Australia. Within some of these cultural institutions there has been an inclination to link high art with fashionable dress.[12] Thus the prevailing notion that the value of dress is due to its decorative nature, or to the fine silk and embroidered textiles of which it is constructed, has plagued acquisitions in Australia as it has in many European collections. Partly as a result of this, there has been a tendency to bypass common clothing in favour of such stylish or prestige items.[13] As a consequence, the material evidence of the early dress of Australia, men's dress and the common dress of working people is, with some exceptions, practically nonexistent.

The inadvertent survival or collection of certain categories of garment has imperceptibly created cultural perceptions about dressing in the past. In this regard, fashionable garments which have been kept are often of imported origin and do not necessarily reflect local dressmaking or craft skills. These selectively preserved items tend to be unrepresentative, confirming historians' view of colonials as slavishly anglophile. At the other end of the spectrum a substantial amount of men's penal clothing survives, much of it parti-coloured uniforms rather than less colourful items.[14] These penal clothes are exceptionally significant for both British and Australian history, as no prison uniforms of the nineteenth century survive in Britain. Yet because striking costumes have been collected in preference to other drab blue or grey transportation garments, a spectacularly harsh view of convict life is historically sustained within the structuring of the national past.[15]

Australia has no specific museum devoted to dress. In some instances, like the Queensland Museum and the Museum of Victoria, costume is almost never displayed; sometimes, as at the Art Gallery of South Australia, costume falls within the unsuitable and broadly defined province of a Curator of European and Australian Decorative Arts. Holdings in galleries and museums remain virtually uncatalogued, and items of dress are not easily accessible to the scholar. Although many of these garments are likely never to be provenanced, there is still a wealth of material for the researcher in Australia's costume collections.

This study hopes to stimulate interest in a neglected area of cultural heritage by opening up the possibilities of dress and bodily adornment as a rich new site for both theoretical and material investigation. It does not merely examine clothing at the level of style. Rather it considers the purposes served by clothing, and the variable messages encoded in all facets of the dress of men and women in Australia. The attire of every section of penal and colonial society is examined, including convicts, emancipists, Aborigines, town and country dwellers, settlers and travellers. The study sets out to probe how the meanings of dress and related behaviour were constituted across all classes, ages and conditions in colonial society, without privileging the evolution of fashion for the minority elite.

The chief sources are diaries, letters, novels, official records, trade accounts, surviving garments and visual images. Letters and diaries describing dress in the colonies, like those of Katie Hume on the Darling Downs and Rachel Henning in North Queensland, some of which date from the earliest years of settlement, are lively, if prescriptive, texts; they often illuminate social aspirations but disguise actualities. There are no locally printed fashion magazines except for a Sydney edition of the *Lady's Magazine* in the mid-1830s, until the shortlived trade magazine *The Butterfly* (Hobart and Launceston) of 1869–70. Crucial information culled from Australian newspapers is therefore limited to textual advertisements and short journal articles until the advent of regular fashion illustration in newspapers in the 1870s. Thus much information about the period has to be prised from terse official records, statistical compilations and official memoirs. These are the accounts of the rulers and not the ruled. The clothes and experiences of the underclasses remain elusive and conjectural throughout the century.

In the early decades we have few images to rely on as a source of dress information. Unlike Britain, where miniature painting and portraiture were traditional art practices, Australian oil and engraved portraits are uncommon until the late 1840s and, as one would expect, are mostly representations of the elite. Visual traces of the poor and criminal classes are negligible, or carefully reconstructed to suit the preferences and proclivities of potential viewers. Artistic convention encouraged the depiction of 'curiosities' or ethnographical 'species', which included Aborigines, but convicts and settlers are seldom painted or engraved in any detail during the early years of settlement. We have only minute glimpses of them almost lost in topographical drawings and watercolours, blending into what were so often picturesque responses to an unfamiliar landscape.

The limitations of all these sources need to be noted. With the advent of the photographic record there are extensive new documents to examine. Whilst photographs give a sense of immediacy to the appearance of clothing as worn, they too are frequently unprovenanced, unreliably dated and unrepresentative. Most problematic are surviving garments themselves, which rarely reflect the dress of colonial society as a whole. Many items, usually of middle-class origin, languish limply in tissued museum drawers as sad and sometimes faded reminders of grand society balls or weddings, or perhaps worn out and stained from use. The precise agency and experiences involved in the wearing of these individual items of dress may never be entirely known.

What this book proposes is that, despite close links to Britain, colonial Australians dressed and behaved in distinctive ways. Today we freely acknowledge that many Queenslanders dress quite differently from people who live and work in Melbourne. We also accept that Australians frequently look different from Europeans. Such distinctions existed for both sexes throughout the colonial years, and in many cases were evident even from the time of first settlement. The distinctions were a product of factors which were specific to the region: social and environmental conditions, economic structures, demographic patterns, industrial development, and factors of class. In addition, women's dress of all social levels was constrained by substantially different elements and practices to that of men. Throughout the period people found it difficult to correlate appearance with the precise definition of class. The issue manifested itself in the early years of settlement and continued to be contentious all through the colonial years; it was reformulated by the economic and demographic changes of the gold-rush period, and affected again by the austerities of the 1890s depression.

All through the century, dress was implicated in the ways whereby various social organisations were empowered, overtly or less obviously, to control the lives and behaviour of Australians. Yet the disciplining of bodies and the ordering and fabrication of appearances from the penal period onward took place through small everyday mechanisms, techniques, technologies, procedures and levels of application that were specific to Australian society.

In the late twentieth century, dress remains of considerable economic and social significance to Australia, although its international character and aesthetic now predominates. The political implications of appearance, including clothing, are undeniable in the global society of the mass media. The bodies and attire of both men and women are commodified, and both sexes are drawn into capitalism's preoccupation with fashion and its mythology of desire. Yet garments do not merely cover the body. They inscribe upon it signs of ownership and gender, the wearer's occupation, age, financial position, ethnicity, and power. In addition, clothes are the material evidence of current preoccupations with appearance that speak of constantly changing relationships between the body and the performing self. Dress practices continue to be located at the core of the production and consumption of commodities. They still signify today, as they did in the nineteenth century, the constant, ever-changing human struggle for status and identity.

# PART I

# Penal Dress, 1788–1840

# 1

# IRREGULAR PATTERNS: GOVERNMENT AND THE SOCIAL ORDER

The circumstances of dressing were extraordinary in the early penal settlements of Australia. In its formative years New South Wales had no capitalist class, no free labourers and, initially, no free settlers. There was practically nothing to replace the complex network of supplies, shopping and marketing facilities and secondhand dealers that serviced the demand for clothes in Britain in a period of rising consumerism.[1] Whilst the country's original inhabitants were to be systematically dispossessed, what was at first virtually a military prison was to be transformed, within a single generation, into a fully organised capitalist society.

Clothes represent a fundamental human need for warmth and protection. Dress is also one of the primary cultural practices that represent and categorise sexual and other social differences. Adequate attire, like food, is thus crucial to the well-being and functioning of most cultures at both the utilitarian and the symbolic levels. Conversely, the lack of garments can have a severely detrimental effect on relationships and the fundamental ordering of the social hierarchy.

The supply of clothes to early Australia was haphazard. From first settlement Europeans of all classes suffered from shortages and inadequacies of dress that affected their labour, their well-being and their sense of social positioning. At times shortages of clothes placed the stability of the settlements in jeopardy. Official mechanisms of control that might otherwise have operated through the regulation of appearance were rendered largely ineffectual. These problems, unique to the colonies, were a combined result of the uncertain economy, the uninterest of the British government, irregularity of shipments, speculative trading, and the lack of encouragement to local industries.

Convicts suffered the most from inadequate clothing and were at times disaffected by this to the point of rebellion. In 1820 Governor Macquarie considered the situation to be potentially dangerous. He warned the Secretary for the Colonies, Earl Bathurst, that if garments were not forthcoming, the consequences would be alarming.[2] Rebellion did not occur, but the incident serves to highlight the close relationship between dress and the maintenance of discipline in the early penal settlements.

For the duration of the transportation period, the British government supplied and administered the dress of most of Australia's inhabitants, including convicts, civil and military officials, some settlers and many Aborigines. It did not supply civil personnel or their families, or later gentrified landowners, who formed part of the settlement's small, fashionable elite, or those convicts who had the means to clothe themselves. These groups remained largely independent of this official supply system, although they too were subject to the vagaries of shipping.

The extent to which the British government was responsible for clothing provisions should have resulted in a substantial degree of dress regulation within the penal settlements. This did not occur. The growth of complex mechanisms of panoptic surveillance and related practices which acted to produce the disciplined, docile body, as charted by Foucault in *Discipline and Punish*, was somewhat tempered in the colonies by local circumstances and the irregular functioning of supplies. In the settlements of New South Wales and Van Diemen's Land clothing issues were so unpredictable that the ordering of the social hierarchy was confounded. Class differentiation, one of the primary functions served by dress, was not always clear. A confusion about dress and its signals commenced that continued throughout the nineteenth century.

Although the standing of the elite was largely determined by indicators of wealth expressed by their dress and demeanour, it was for the most part difficult to distinguish the appearance of convicts from free working settlers. In Britain working clothes in rural and urban areas were extremely diversified and subject to subtle regional and occupational variations.[3] But in Australia an almost inadvertent dichotomy existed until the 1830s between the self-appointed elite and the lower social grouping of tradespeople, convicts, farmers and poor settlers.

For convicts, the problems of clothing commenced from the time of first settlement when they were subjected to the misery of appallingly inadequate dress issues. The difficulties were to continue in one way or another until the end of the transportation period and even beyond.[4] The government was both unsystematic and parsimonious in providing clothing, and there was seldom sufficient for convict needs. What clothes were supplied made it difficult to distinguish the appearance of free workers from most categories of transportees.[5] This caused particular problems when convicts were assigned to settlers; inevitably, it jeopardised the maintenance of discipline and stability in the fledgling colony.

John Hirst contends that New South Wales was a free society in the making, practically from the time of first settlement.[6] Whilst this notion has recently been the subject of some revision, the lack of difference between the appearance of convict and settler in the first decades of settlement might lead to the assumption that this independence did exist. Yet this was an inadvertent freedom. Some categories of convict confined to barracks did wear uniforms at times; those who were assigned to settlers did not, and they often failed to receive regular dress issues. Apparent freedom existed because of the ad hoc nature of supplies and the government's inability effectively to manage and regulate clothing issue.

From the 1790s governors sought to impose various kinds of uniform dress on convict men and women that differed from the standard issue. These attempts to introduce uniforms corresponded to rigorous procedures in the British and Continental prison systems where architectural design and management of prison inmates, including the use of clothing, were progressively deployed to survey, categorise, punish and supervise the conduct of prisoners.[7] Clear categories of uniform dress were never satisfactorily enforced in the penal colonies, even after 1820 when penal discipline became increasingly militarised. New South Wales was on the cusp between the old and new penal systems, and local circumstances obstructed this kind of regulation.[8] John Steven, giving evidence to the Select Committee on Secondary Punishments in 1832, described a continuing laxity in maintaining distinctive forms of convict dress. By that period, he noted, the wearing of uniforms had fallen into disuse.[9]

In the first years of settlement convicts and free working-class inhabitants all wore very similar kinds of clothes. The First Fleet convicts were issued with a two-year supply of government clothing, consisting of basic, readymade slops.[10] The term slops comes from the Dutch word 'slabbe' for seamen's wide breeches, but by this time it meant coarse, loose-fitting readymade dress. Convict slops, uniformly similar in appearance, probably resembled the drab prison clothing worn at the time in some English county prisons but were in effect standard working-class clothes.[11] Convict men were issued with short jackets, check frocks, trousers, check shirts and tall crowned hats, and the women jackets, petticoats (skirts), kerchiefs, caps and hats.

Ravenet, a Spanish artist who visited Port Jackson in 1793, made a rather arch wash drawing of *The Convicts of New Holland* which, although falling within the conventions of traditional costume books, conforms well with these written accounts (Plate 1). Here the male convict wears a practical dark jacket, perhaps brown or blue, cut to a serviceable length using the minimum amount of cloth. Above the petticoat of his companion is the thigh-length wrapping jacket, or so-called bedgown, which was worn by working women of the time, with various regional differences, throughout Europe.

Convict men looked very similar to naval ratings or Marines, who had an undress uniform of leather caps, white or check shirts and thread hose trousers.[12] Unfortunately no detailed study of Marine clothing exists for this period, and it is impossible to be certain what various ranks of Marines would have worn. Like naval uniforms, Marine dress at this time was being subjected to many changes as it was gradually transformed into the rigid uniform categories of the nineteenth century. We do know, however, that full dress uniform for a Marine officer in 1783 consisted of a brilliant red coat with silver epaulettes, gorget, laced black hat and white breeches and waistcoat.[13]

Only in such an outfit would the Marines have been clearly distinguishable from the transportees. Fox's assertion that in the early settlement there was one group 'whose clothing demanded obedience, the other yielding it' cannot be entirely supported.[14] Setting up the first camp in rough and often wet conditions, the Marines were at times

**1**   Juan Ravenet, *The Convicts of New Holland*, 1793, wash drawing (Dixson Galleries, State Library of NSW).

as ragged and ill-clothed as their charges. Reconnoitring overnight near Port Jackson in 1788 they looked like a 'gang of travelling gypsies'.[15]

Any degree of initial standardisation in slop clothing issued to convicts was soon erased by the erratic nature of incoming Commissariat supplies. As well, the extremely harsh living conditions caused considerable wear and tear on garments, especially shoes, all of which affected the appearance and well-being of both the transportees and Marines. There was little protection from sun or rain. Neither the first huts of cabbage-tree palm and clay nor the early brick dwellings were waterproof or durable.

Many convicts (and Marines too) had brought their own clothing and effects to Australia. This for a time prevented shortages but also added further to the disordered appearance of the early settlement. Within the British penal system an established hierarchy of convict uniforms was progressively introduced, enabling prisoners to be readily identified and thus subject to regulatory punishments and rewards. In the colonies, the lack of a distinguishing dress meant that discipline was difficult to maintain; patterns of behaviour were laid down in terms of informal dress codes that have cast their long shadows into the twentieth century.

The introduction of the assignment system brought more difficulties in terms of control. Convict tradesmen, who mostly lived in towns and had the greatest facility for purchasing liquor, could not be regulated by publicans because they were not identifiable by their dress.[16] There were instances of transportees being supplied with military uniforms when stocks of dress ran especially low.[17] Although the uniforms were dyed black, officials regarded this situation as undesirable from a disciplinary point of view. In Hobart, where clothing issue was particularly irregular, convicts who could afford it simply purchased ordinary clothing or wore jackets, caps and trousers of kangaroo skin obtained from stock-keepers. Hobart prisoners and ticket-of-leave men were officially forbidden to wear items made of skins in 1822.[18]

## Convict Uniforms

Despite the problems associated with convict dress supplies and lack of control over the activities of transportees, various governors sought in different ways to classify adult convicts and their degree of criminality through imposing categories of uniform penal clothing. These attempts at ordering the appearance of prisoners are recorded from the first years of settlement.

The introduction of a uniform for all convicts was first seriously suggested by Governor Phillip. He proposed the idea at much the same time that the Walworth transport contractor William Richards Jun. was recommending convicts wear what seems to our view an almost clownish blue and white uniform with green jackets for the voyage out to Australia.[19] In 1791, and again in 1792, Phillip, harassed by supply difficulties as well as by convicts bartering and misusing clothing, suggested the need for a distinctive convict uniform. He asked that dress for both men and women be made of the same fabric so that, 'by introducing one stripe of a different colour from the rest, prevent what is intended for the convict being sold to the soldier or the settler: and such a distinguishing mark should be put on everything intended for the use of the convicts'.[20]

Striped cloth was common in working-class dress and some convict dress for women was certainly striped, like the jackets and petticoats supplied to women transportees in 1789 by George Whitlock, contractor.[21] But Phillip was suggesting something different— a particular and distinguishing stripe woven into fabric destined for all convict use.

Phillip's idea of introducing uniforms was substantially different from other contemporary views about prison dress espoused by British reformers like John Howard. Ostensibly his concern with this kind of clothing had little to do with Howard's concern to humiliate prisoners or to enforce cleanliness as a path toward moral virtue. Neither was escape an issue in his prison without walls. Phillip's reasons were determined by practical necessity of the kind that led charitable institutions to use distinct dress for their inmates; that was to prevent clothes entering local pawnshops.[22] It was also intended as a way of establishing and maintaining a clear difference between convict, Marine and free inhabitant. The precise history of Phillip's striped uniform is not known. The government made some attempt to follow his suggestion in 1793, during Grose's period of office, but the material woven with a large bright stripe, although ordered, never seems to have reached the settlement.[23] The sense of discipline and order which such a uniform would have imposed was never achieved.

## Men's Uniforms

The problem of distinguishing convicts by their dress continued to occupy successive governors, and many requests were made for types of convict men to be classified by garments of an obviously different colour and quality from the working clothes of free settlers. For instance in 1793 thirty suits of men's clothing of 'a better sort' were despatched to New South Wales for 'trusty' convicts, although no special dress was considered necessary to grant as a favour to convict women.[24] These women were mostly engaged in domestic service or acting as homemakers, so the value of their labour could not be as readily defined in terms of production as were the often heavy, labouring tasks assigned to the men.[25] Thus for women, the absence of a system of either reward or punishment, couched in terms of dress, contributed to their lack of visibility. Perhaps more significantly, it reveals the lack of value placed on their labour.

In 1801, overseers were given coatees of blue cloth and pantaloons of grey to separate them from other males in blue jackets and trousers of duck or gurrah.[26] Form-fitting pantaloons (or very narrow trousers for half-dress or informal occasions) were the dress of the well-to-do man at this date. Trousers with their fall fronts and looser cut were more characteristic of sailors and labourers. The difference in the dress of overseers was thus one of cut rather than of colour. The notion, if not always the practice, of separating the dress of overseers and indeed cooks and wardsmen from public convicts was maintained well into the 1830s.[27] A watercolour of *Mitchell's Pass* in 1832 (Plate 2) shows a group that includes soldiers and labouring convicts; the latter are variously clothed in blue, yellow and grey garments, and some are in chains. An overseer on the left is distinguished by his waistcoat and also his authoritative hat.

As this watercolour shows, the colour of convict dress was quite variable. By the late 1790s there are increasing references to convict men being regularly issued with

**2** *Mitchell's Pass, Blue Mountains*, 1832, watercolour (Mitchell Library, State Library of NSW).

grey and blue garments, and the colour continued to be used for some convict service in the 1830s and even later. Blue clothing cannot be considered as a convict uniform as convict men were frequently issued with other colours. In 1810, for instance, men at public labour were given one red jacket, a pair of pantaloons and a blue shirt.[28]

Blue was traditionally the colour of working-class fabrics. Woad or logwood dyes were cheap, and occupational dress of the late eighteenth and early nineteenth centuries was often made of blue fabric. Indeed, the custom of wearing blue singlets and jeans, which still persists, has its origins in these working-class garments, but today it has quite different connotations. Blue was also worn by free working men in colonial towns and rural areas well into the 1820s and 1830s and assumed as a fashionable colour for the more affluent classes. It was commonly worn by the middle ranks and professional urban classes in Australia, as in Europe, until it was superseded in the 1840s and 1850s by grey, brown and black suits.

This brings us to a strange contradiction. The use of blue by all classes made it more difficult to determine convict status within the penal settlements. Yet Governor Hunter categorically asserted, in his evidence to the Select Committee on Transportation in 1812, that convicts could be recognised by their dress. It must be assumed he was thinking of the generally inferior quality of convict clothing, its poor fit, or some other significant exterior marks of which there are now no records. For men the most obvious sign of public convict status was the short government jacket, which marked out transportees from those free settlers or emancipists who could afford well-fitted, tailored frockcoats.[29] Yet the short jacket was equally the sign of a working man and not merely a convict uniform, thus compounding the difficulty in identifying transportees.

It seems clear that any differentiation that did exist in convict clothing must have been in the quality and fit of garments, not simply colour. This conclusion is at odds with Linda Young's contention that in establishing uniformity in penitential punishments, the colour, rather than the cut, of the convict suit was the most obvious indication of the wearer's status.[30] As well as this, in implying that the short jacket was a juvenile garment representing a 'cutting down to size', Young has failed to recognise the working-class origins of the short coat. Nor were convict side-buttoning trousers, sometimes worn over leg irons, necessarily intended to resemble a small boy's skelton suit, as she suggests. These so-called overalls were quite different from boilersuits today; they were a penal version of a traditional outer garment that could be pulled over other trousers for protection. In 1832 Deputy Commandant Laidley requested that 'trousers for convicts may be made to button at the sides like overalls, the prisoners finding it impractical to draw the common trousers over their leg irons'.[31] These side-buttoned overalls worn by convicts are clearly shown in Earle's lithograph of *A Government Chain Gang* in 1830 (Plate 3).

The manner in which the long coat of the gentleman differed from the short convict or working jacket is demonstrated with great clarity in Sophia Campbell's remarkable watercolour *The Costume of the Australasians* c.1817 (Plate 4). It seems that for Sophia Campbell, Australasians were all men. In this image, which includes soldiers from the newly arrived Northamptonshire Regiment of Foot (and almost certainly Macquarie's aide-de-camp on the left), convicts are wearing blue, yellow and brown suits with cropped jackets.[32] There is one exception, a man with a short but well-fitted blue jacket with white facings on the sleeves and lapels; he is clearly not a convict. His higher status is defined by such features as his ruffled neckerchief, his high collar, and his walking stick. The convict on the extreme right appears to be wearing a leather cap with flaps. These were standard convict issue, and a number survive in museums all around Australia. Their flaps and ties are a curious vestigial reminder of the eighteenth-century cocked hat.

**3**  Augustus Earle, *A Government Chain Gang*, 1830, lithograph (Mitchell Library, State Library of NSW).

**4**  Sophia Campbell, *The Costume of the Australasians*, c.1817, watercolour (Private Collection).

The matter of the appearance of convicts is not as straightforward as this illustration might suggest. Gentlemen convicts mixed freely in certain circles and could have little social contact with lower-class convicts.[33] According to Samuel Marsden, the influential Senior Chaplain of New South Wales, many wore fine boots and coats and lived like men of fashion.[34] Marsden, acknowledging the existing problems of status, sought a clear demarcation between himself and both emancipists and convicts, requesting that imperious gentlemen convicts be forced to wear nothing but common clothing.

Ticket-of-leave men were not readily distinguishable either. Indeed, in evidence given to Bigge, the wealthy John Jamison of Regentville recorded that the 'unblushing' style of dress assumed by many convicts resulted in confusion for both strangers and lower classes of people. He noted that it gave them 'such false notions of their real state that they frequently pass the superior officers of the Colony without paying the least respect'.[35] Settlers like Jamison had an imperative need to sustain social definition through clothing and they were deeply concerned at any perceived disruption of the social order. Macquarie's recognition of emancipists (by 1821 ex-convicts made up the largest group of free inhabitants of New South Wales) enabled a widening number to seek access to the settlement's upper social circles. The fledgling colony was a prickly society in which necessity forced everyone—bond, free and freed—to mix closely in everyday life. Any sign of equality demonstrated in dress was anathema to the local 'exclusive' set.

Even so, officials had great difficulty in sustaining social regulation regarding dress; the polemic of the hierarchical 'exclusives' was quite ineffective. John Steven, giving evidence to the Committee on Secondary Punishments in 1832, described a time when convicts had not been allowed to wear the long coat of a civilian. 'I have been present when the magistrates have ordered the long coat of a convict to be cut off.'[36] Lack of further evidence suggests that such overt attempts to regulate and define social status were unsuccessful and not frequent enough to warrant comment.

There was one significant attempt in 1814 to intervene in the appearance of a single category of convicts through the imposition of a uniform government dress. In this year Governor Macquarie introduced the humiliating parti-coloured dress for gaol gangs doing hard labour in New South Wales. It was in use in Van Diemen's Land soon after. The introduction of the uniform came at precisely the same time that officials were manifesting increasing signs of scrutinising the nature and amount of convict clothing being issued. For example, a major report into convict welfare, health and supplies was submitted in 1814 by Sydney's Assistant Surgeon, William Redfern.

In contrast to Phillip's request for uniforms, Macquarie's order was an intentional move to bring government clothing into line with penal experiments in Britain, where classification according to crime was being correlated with the issue of an appropriate dress. The government order laid down: 'In order to brand their ill conduct with a public mark of disgrace and to distinguish them from the better behaved they are to be clothed in a party coloured dress half black and half white, which they are to wear at all times during the time they are sentenced for.'[37]

The intention behind the introduction of parti-coloured dress was the belief, first formulated in the Penal Act of 1779, that clothing could be used as part of a progressive reform system. By the early nineteenth century clothing and character were believed

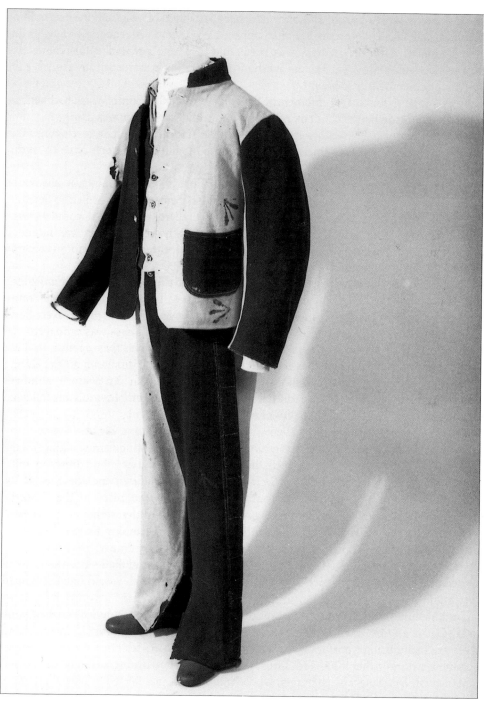

**5**  Yellow and black convict suit (Western Australian Museum).

to be in some senses linked, and reformers felt that any progress in moral reclamation should be signalled by the reward of an appropriate dress. In Macquarie's view, visible humiliation in the form of dress was preferable to severe corporal punishment, and was at the same time a convincing method of separating prisoners from the freer life of ordinary members of society.[38]

By this time the nature of commercial development in New South Wales had become more stable. Trade had expanded and dress within the settlement was somewhat more diverse than previously, with a definite stratum of fashionably dressed citizens. This kind of penal clothing was thus introduced in a situation where such obvious outfits would have a significant impact.

In Australia's open penal system, strict distinctions of dress could not always be rigorously maintained as they were in closed British penitentiaries or in the Separate Prison at Port Arthur. This was particularly so in regard to assigned convicts, who had a relatively free association with settlers. Although convict dress was intended to carry 'highly charged messages' of the wearer's penal status, this was not necessarily feasible in the unregulated colonial circumstances.[39]

Of all forms of distinctive penal clothing, parti-coloured dress was the most humiliating, as it was the descendant of the dress of the medieval fool. In nineteenth-century France the spectacle of prison chain gangs was linked with a long tradition of public executions, street theatre, saturnalia and festivals of fools.[40] Parti-coloured dress was probably used for the first time at the model Gloucester Reform Gaol, which was opened in 1791, and the uniform introduced there soon after bears a striking similarity to the design of the many surviving Australian suits of yellow and black felted cloth (Plate 5). Although certainly later in date than Macquarie's period, these existing examples probably followed the design of his half-black and half-white suits.[41]

Despite the introduction of parti-coloured suits, at the time of Bigge's *Reports* many convicts did not wear a uniform government dress or any distinguishing signs.[42] Bigge believed in the necessity for clear distinctions between convicts and other colonial inhabitants. He favoured uniforms for all convicts, but did not include this in his recommendations. The necessity for punishment took second place to the concerns he obviously had for the feelings and social rituals of wealthy settlers. It was hard enough to obtain reliable convict servants at all, let alone employ assigned servants in a distinctive convict dress. Thus convicts in private service continued to wear working-class slops or livery, theoretically paid for by the settler, as they had since the General Order of October 1800. In such slop clothing their penal status would have remained unremarked.

The difficulties implicit in the lack of differentiation between convict and free were exacerbated as the penal settlements of New South Wales and Van Diemen's Land were gradually being transformed into fully fledged colonial societies with more regular economies during the 1820s and 1830s. At the same time an increasingly militarised language of discipline was emerging, whose rigidity was manifested in official attempts to categorise some adult male convicts more visibly in uniforms and set them apart from free working men.

One of the changes to convict dress occurred when yellow and grey supplanted blue as the dominant colour for male dress by about 1820. Clothing of a coarse yellow cloth (probably kersey) had been sent to the eastern colonies by chance in 1817.[43] Yellow was traditionally the colour of disgrace in Europe and had been worn for purposes of punishment in eighteenth-century charity schools. Its use became synonymous with Australian convicts in the 1820s and 1830s. When yellow was joined to black or grey to make the parti-coloured suit worn by men doing hard labour, the visual signification of the so-called 'canary birds' became more dramatic.

By 1827 government gangs in Sydney were also wearing white frocks and trousers of locally made woollen Parramatta factory cloth, or grey, or yellow jackets daubed all over with labels. These consisted of conspicuously broad arrows, PB's and CB's, referring to the Prisoners' Barracks and the Carters' Barracks. Earle's caricature of a group of convicts in a chain gang shows some of these marks applied to their jackets and trousers (Plate 3). Crudely stamped or painted arrows are also found on many surviving articles of convict dress, from trousers and jackets to hats and shoes. The arrow mark signified government property and was not reserved particularly for convict issue.

When the Board of Ordnance took over supplies to the various penal settlements in the 1820s, it applied the BO stamp as well to all forms of issue. The stamp is found on a rare example of a man's blue striped cotton working shirt with bone buttons, now housed in the Hyde Park Barracks Museum. On the left side, clearly stamped in red, are both the broad arrow and BO marks (Plate 6). It is tempting to conclude that this important relic was convict issue, but its style and markings could well mean that it had once belonged to a soldier. The duties of the Ordnance were taken over by the War Department in 1855 and subsequently the BO mark was superseded by the WD mark. This change in authority is a useful key to dating some surviving articles of convict dress. However, neither BO nor WD were marks reserved for convict issue alone.

In Britain the use of a distinguishing label on convict dress derives from the Penal Act of 1779 and the humiliating badges and numbers on charity clothes. It is not clear when marks of this kind were first introduced into Australia, but some form of regulation stamp is likely to have been used on penal garments from the early years of settlement. There is no official mention of labelling until the time of Bigge's report. Major Druitt, in his evidence of 1819, stated that all convict dress was marked and numbered and bore broad arrows in several places.[44] Information here is conflicting, and it may be that the marks were small and located on the inside of garments. Larger numbers were applied to convict dress by the 1820s, as uniforms generally became more conspicuous.

Uniforms were increasingly issued to adult convicts in New South Wales and Van Diemen's Land from the mid-1820s. Changes to official policy in this regard, by governors like Arthur and Darling, were part of stricter bureaucratic controls instituted to deal with large numbers of transportees in the settlements. Yet these garments were not standardised. They were altered from year to year and were subject to variations based on criminal classification and location, but chiefly subject to available supplies.[45] This contributed even further to the sense of disorder in settlement dressing.

In Van Diemen's Land, Governor Arthur created seven classes of male prisoner in 1826.[46] Clothing was mostly grey or blue, but the lowest convict class was required to wear yellow garments branded with a black arrow. The Principal Superintendent

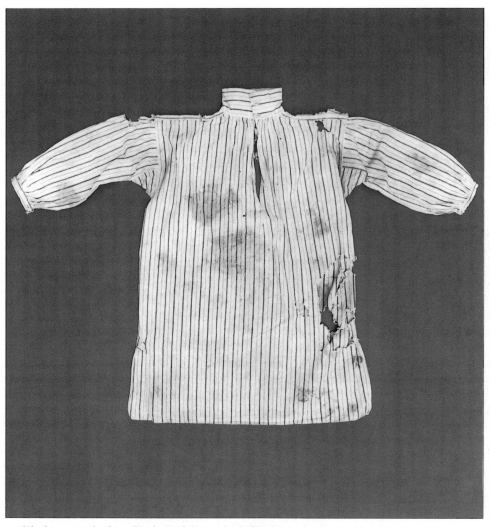

**6** Working man's shirt (Hyde Park Barracks, NSW Historic Houses Trust).

of Convicts in Hobart also recommended to the Colonial Secretary in 1826 that prisoners in barracks wear yellow trousers and jackets, and that gaol prisoners wear yellow and black parti-coloured dress.[47] Early in the next decade black and yellow parti-coloured suits were reported as being worn by Van Diemen's Land chain gangs as well.[48]

On the mainland, Governor Darling was responsible for introducing more stringent discipline and administrative procedures in convict management. In 1830, determined upon tighter control, he ordered Sydney's Hyde Park Barracks convicts to wear frocks and trousers of broad black and white stripes, two and a half inches wide.[49] Other reports suggest that chain gangs were wearing grey and yellow parti-coloured dress, with plain grey for men out of irons. In the 1830s parti-coloured woollen clothing was worn in winter and branded linen clothing in summer. The apparent lack of any consistency in the issue of these types of garment suggests that at no time were systematic penal classifications regularly sustained. Beyond the early 1830s (with the exception of chain gangs) regulation clothing was not in consistent use in New South Wales.

## The Dress of Convict Women

The stricter controls over management of male convict dress introduced in the 1820s had their parallel in similar categorisation and management of the dress of convict women. This was in line with tougher attitudes toward convict discipline following the British government's consideration of the Bigge report, the influx of convicts on an increasingly large scale, and the appointment of highly disciplinarian governors like Darling and Arthur. Official attempts to enforce uniform dressing were infused with concerns to reclaim the morality of women, rather than merely to police their criminality. Unlike the many examples of parti-coloured male penal dress that exist in museums, no known dress of convict women has survived. Perhaps this was because these garments were comparatively drab and therefore seemed less worthy of preservation. There are also practically no known illustrations of women convicts.

Women transportees were not required to wear any form of uniform until the 1820s. Up till then both women and girls were issued with government clothing that was similar to working-class dress, consisting of jackets, skirts, shifts and caps or hats. In 1812 they were issued with brown serge jackets and petticoats (skirts) for use after arrival, and this varied little over the following years.[50] Such was also the clothing of free working women.

Byrne has suggested that convict women engaged as domestic servants had a different relationship with authority to male convicts. She maintains that they moved about freely during the day, unlike the men, who were in collective work situations.[51] Her argument that women were not visibly delineated in the same way as men can be supported by the evidence offered by their appearance. In 1828 the Principal Super-intendent's Office in Hobart recommended that the dress of female convicts in private service consist of a cotton gown, bedgowns or jackets, chemises, calico caps, neck handkerchiefs and aprons.[52] These were virtually the same types of garment as had been recommended for women on the First Fleet, and were probably indistinguishable from normal working-class dress.

When women convicts began to be confined more closely at the Parramatta Female Factory in 1821, it became feasible to impose a uniform dress. Macquarie divided the women at the Factory into three sections defined as aged, married and young. Children were not specified. Within each group the women could rise to a merit class or fall to a crime class. He decided that the women would be supplied with a uniform dress suited to their station, consisting of a gown of blue or brown serge or stuff. They would also receive a straw bonnet and white apron for Sundays and a jacket and a coarse apron for weekdays. To distinguish the crime or lower class, a badge had to be worn on their dress at all times.[53]

A more rigorous dress classification was established during Brisbane's administration in 1824, when the classes of women were more visibly defined. This stricter form of categorisation was again part of the general increase in severity introduced into convict management during the 1820s. Women in the First Class, comprising those recently arrived and destitute women from whom assigned labour was drawn, were ordered to wear drab serge petticoats and jackets with a red calico jacket, blue gurrah petticoats and white caps frilled with muslin on Sundays. Second Class or probationary women, who could not be assigned, had to wear blue gurrah petticoats and jackets and a calico cap, while the Third Class, the lowest criminals, were most strikingly differentiated in striped linsey-woolsey jackets and petticoats.[54]

Officials also introduced an obvious dress distinction for convict women in Van Diemen's Land during the 1820s. Three classes of criminal were created at the new Female Factory, or House of Correction, Hobart, which began admitting inmates in 1828. The women were issued with coarse clothing consisting of petticoats, aprons, jackets, neckerchiefs, chemises, stockings, shoes, a bonnet and caps.[55] The Second Class and the Criminal Class of women were distinguished by a prominent yellow C used as a dress label. The Second Class had the C on the left sleeve and the Third Class had it on the centre back of the jacket, and on the sleeve and the back of the petticoat.[56]

Attempts to enforce the wearing of government clothing were part of a more general endeavour to instil a sense of humility and decency in convict women. The colonial classification of women into two categories, one respectable and one immoral, extended to the belief that immoral women could be reclaimed through philanthropic works, dispensation of charity, and moral example. This notion was echoed in some of Bigge's pronouncements. He reported that 'all employments that have a tendency to encourage a passion for dress should be studiously avoided and the female convicts should be compelled to consider that the dress that is provided by the government is that which is most suitable to their condition'.[57] Clearly, he regarded preoccupation with personal adornment as potentially immoral, frivolous, and symptomatic of the frailty of women.

Some of the concern to enforce uniform dressing for women was undoubtedly due to the influence of the Quaker prison reformer Elizabeth Fry. In a letter to Undersecretary Horton in 1823, she urged the need for sufficient quantities of a strong, decent uniform dress for the women. She saw this as an important way of establishing order, especially while convicts were waiting for departure and on the voyage to Australia. She specified that it should not be parti-coloured but gave no reason, and women were never subjected to the indignity of a parti-coloured dress.[58] Fry recommended in 1827 that a regular prison dress was important and that it should be perfectly plain, with some variety to distinguish each class.[59] Earrings, curled hair and all kinds of finery were forbidden.

Evidently for Fry there was a clear correlation between dress and morality, and affectations such as earrings contained social messages that she deemed inappropriate for female detainees. As Sturma has shown, it was the sexual behaviour of convict women, undoubtedly marked out by the evidence of their clothing, that was the principal criterion used by contemporaries in evaluating their conduct.[60] There was also a subtext in attempts to prevent convict women from dressing too finely. The reason was that, despite certain official impediments, authorities wished to promote social stability and marriage amongst transportees. Hence the encouragement of a modest, domestic demeanour in women prisoners.

Although women in New South Wales and Van Diemen's Land, confined to the respective Female Factories, were required to wear a uniform, they were alleged to be even less likely to wear the issued clothing than the men. Women were said to be more difficult to control in this regard, and early in the century had been described as never appearing in their issue dress.[61] Records of the Female Factory indicate that uniforms were not regularly worn there either. The 'Report of the Board of the Female Factory' in 1826 described the women as generally carelessly dressed, and it appeared as if there had been no regularity in the issue of slops.[62] Thus attempts to conform to the standards of penal development in Britain were often unsustainable in the settlements, even when inmates were confined to Factories or Houses of Correction.

For officials, maintaining a distinction between convict and free amongst the women proved to be even more perplexing than amongst the men. According to evidence submitted to the Select Committee on Transportation in 1838, 'the women always found the means to dress better'.[63] On the other hand, an inquiry into female convict discipline in Hobart in 1841-3 stated that harsh treatment of some assigned female servants and lack of both food and clothes drove women to prostitution.[64] The inference in various official statements was that the women were prostituting themselves to be able to buy dress and fashionable trinkets. If such was the case, the differences between the appearance of convict women and free are likely to have been further reduced. Criticism of boldness in women's dress must also be considered in the context of male perceptions of sexuality. Soliciting custom was necessary for effective prostitution, and advertisement through dress can be regarded as an occupational necessity.

There is little doubt that it was convict women's morality, not their convictism, that was being policed and subjected to close scrutiny.[65] The government's apparent failure to control their dress was deemed to be the result of their moral, not criminal, laxity, caused largely by the alleged weakness the women had for fashion. What was seen as the excessive boldness of convict women made them harder to reclaim than the men. Dress is one of the most significant indicators of normality or abnormality, and morality or immorality. Derogatory labelling of convict women by various commentators, as being overly fine in their dress, must be viewed as a judgement passed on that which lacked conformity with the variables of a perceived status quo. Implicit within this was the continuing desire to sustain a distinction between convict and free.

The recalcitrance shown by women towards government dress was one of the few ways in which they could visibly rebel. Convict women probably acted out of a sense of effrontery towards officials as much as anything else. For example in 1840, a group of women labelled 'The Flash Mob', at the Female Factory in Hobart, wore earrings and silk scarves as a deliberate protest against the Factory rules.[66] This demonstration by convict women is important, and indicates that dress can be a site of resistance to authority and an obvious signifier of nonconformity. Kay Daniels contends that, despite historians' denial of the agency of women convicts, they did act riotously. They also developed subtle strategies of resistance, including scandalising officials.[67] It is likely that exaggerated forms of dressing were regarded by these women as a tool of rebellion and were indeed one of the few positive methods by which they could register their protest.

The concerted attempts to introduce categories of convict uniform for both men and women in the 1820s were not sustained. By the late 1830s insufficient supplies of clothing and the freedom implicit in the assignment system caused intervention into the dress of convicts to diminish. By then the distinction between categories of transportee had virtually disappeared. Convict servants wore their master's livery and could not be distinguished from other workers.

As the transportation system was dismantled, the original problem that had confronted Phillip in maintaining a distinction between convicts and settlers was less pressing. By then the focus of concern about uniforms was directed rather at maintaining discipline amongst male convicts. The Chief Police Magistrate and Superintendent of Convicts in Hobart, replying to a despatch from the Secretary of State in 1839, outlined these difficulties. He suggested that unless regular and reliable supplies of uniforms in specific categories were made available, he could not guarantee that discipline of convicts would be effective.[68]

Lack of reliable dress supplies, the inability to control the appearance of convicts, and the presence of Aborigines in the penal settlements combined to produce considerable differences in meanings implicit in colonial codes of dress, in comparison to those existing in Britain. In New South Wales and Van Diemen's Land clothing assumed a character that was quite specific to local conditions. The government's failure to introduce strict categories of uniform and the irregular nature of incoming supplies created a situation where society was split into the 'respectable' and the 'non-respectable'. The wealthy elite set themselves apart categorically by their stylish dress, but there was much confusion about the status of the majority of inhabitants consisting of convicts and working people.

# 2

# FRAYING AT THE EDGES: CLOTHING SUPPLIES AND MANUFACTURING

Throughout the transportation period in Australia, the British government was responsible for feeding and clothing the majority of convicts and their guards, as well as some civilians and Aborigines. This paternalism had a double-edged effect. Not only did it fail to meet these basic needs on a regular and adequate basis; it also fostered an unhealthy reliance on official supplies. On the one hand bureaucrats theoretically determined and regulated the kind and quantity of garments that were issued. Yet the perception that the government was an overall provider also created a dependent attitude across a wide social spectrum, thus discouraging local enterprise, which was struggling in any case from a lack of capital and labour difficulties, at a time when it really needed official encouragement. The inept nature of the supply system locked the early inhabitants into an invidious position whereby their dress needs were not met, while their own manufacturing initiatives, which should have helped to alleviate both the government's and the population's difficulties, were given little assistance.

From the 1790s a limited range of civilian clothing for men, women and children was speculatively imported into the settlements. This consisted of readymade clothing and shoes for men and women as well as fabric, leather and sewing accessories. Most supply ships came from Britain, but there was also a vigorous trade with India. The amount of private commerce increased rapidly over the years, augmenting goverment supplies of garments. This was of little use to convicts, whose misery and discomfort remains, for all intents and purposes, unrecorded.

For its part the government did not initiate or administer a reliable policy or orderly system for replacement clothing. Nor were officials able or willing to encourage the development of a viable local clothing or textile industry to sustain the population's needs. This caused drastic shortages of garments and footwear. Although the settlement was self-sufficient in basic European types of food by 1805, this never extended to clothing.[1] Successful garment and particularly footwear factories were established in Australia later in the century, but the early problems of labour and capital in the clothing trades continued to cause concern. These difficulties remain largely unresolved in the 1990s.

## Administration of Convict Supplies

The problems associated with clothing the convicts in the penal settlements have never been closely assessed. For the entire transportation period, the major difficulty faced by the government was the sheer quantity of transportees needing supplies, let alone requirements of other individuals. Estimates of well over 80,000 male and female convicts sent to New South Wales between 1788 and 1840 give some idea of the size of the task. Much of this huge influx occurred after the end of the Napoleonic Wars. The size of the penal establishment varied widely, particularly when convicts were moved incessantly in and out of assignment. A letter sent by Governor Darling to Viscount Goderich, Chancellor of the Exchequer, in 1827 highlights the difficulties in clothing variable numbers of assigned convicts: 'The trouble, which is occasioned by their being dispersed over the Colony is inconceivable. The fluctuation is incessant, men being assigned and returned from assignment almost daily. These are frequently sent in nearly naked and the references to ascertain their claims are in fact endless.'[2]

Clothing was supplied to the colonies by procedures which were lengthy and often inefficient. Provisioning was organised by a complex hierarchy of government departments. The Navy Board was responsible for the dress of convicts on the First and Second Fleets, but increasing references are found after 1825 to the involvement of the Board of Ordnance in clothing supplies. It also supplied settlers with clothing and haberdashery.[3] Its protracted estimating and supply systems inevitably affected the way clothing was administered and ultimately issued in the colonies. Two or more years could elapse between the placement of orders and their final arrival. The ordnance records bulge with details of contracts not met—fabrics of the wrong colour, size or weight, out-of-date patterns, delays, damage from moths and damp in transit—the list is endless.

These supply procedures caused particular difficulties for settlers when they were assigned ill-clothed convicts. In 1826 a hostile Hawkesbury settler wrote angrily to the *Monitor* about his newly assigned men who had arrived barefoot, one with old trousers that had no knees and a rimless straw hat. Others were like 'Sir John Falstaff's set of raggamuffin recruits'.[4] Problems with clothing caused scandalous rumours to circulate. Frederick Goulburn, Colonial Secretary of New South Wales, allegedly auctioned convicts' jackets, trousers and shoes for funds, and forced them to wear remnants of blankets like 'the Highland petticoat'.[5]

The problems experienced by the convicts are more difficult to ascertain. The Tasmanian archives have a poignant list of complaints made by newly arrived convicts, some of whom were given no shirts for eighteen months after arrival. Convict Smith's difficulty, recorded in 1829, reads as a cryptic note penned by a Lumber Yard official. 'Received no shirt since his arrival, applied several times, informed there was none in the stores, the shirt he landed with exchanged at the Penitentiary for an old one.'[6] For the disempowered, there was little recourse. Convicts clearly suffered considerable frustration and physical hardship from lack of clothing and footwear.

## The First and Second Fleets

From the time of first settlement, dress supplies were parsimonious. Determining clothing needs for the First Fleet was initially the responsibility of the Home Office, which had little experience in the matter. Private contractors rather than the government had earlier provisioned the convicts sent to America. There was little known of the local climatic conditions in Australia, and bureaucrats were anxious to save costs. Apart from any private possessions they had, convicts were to be entirely dependent on government provisioning until further supplies arrived. In the new colonies they would, in effect, have to exist entirely outside their familiar patterns of clothes marketing. In Britain this had included access to a complex provisioning network of cast-off or stolen dress, slop shops selling readymade garments, and secondhand and pawnshop clothes brokers.[7]

It was the Navy Board that was finally charged with supplying the male and female convicts with dress, using marine suppliers for all the garments. Although nineteen children accompanied their convict parents to Botany Bay, existing British records fail to mention their supply. The Navy Board normally dealt with slop merchants and was quite able to supply readymade garments to order on a very large scale. Most of the convict women's dress, including shifts, white, grey and check jackets and woollen and canvas petticoats, was supplied by the naval contractor James Wadham, linen draper of Borough.[8] The dress of the Marines was handled as a separate matter.

Although the contracts for the dress of the First Fleet have not survived, the system followed standard Admiralty procedures of a written pattern specification for each type of garment. Details included the type of fabric, buttons, quality of sewing and size of each section of garment. More information is available about contracts for the Second Fleet. For instance on 27 August 1789, George Whitlock of Crutched Friars was contracted to supply convict dress for the Second Fleet 'agreeable to a pattern sealed and kept at the Navy Office'.[9]

First Fleet contractors substantially undercut the original official estimates and the government seems to have made quite large savings on the costs of convict dress (see Appendix I). This was fairly standard practice at the time. Contractors continued to undercut the price of convict clothing throughout the transportation period, leading to the issue of small sizes or poor-quality ill-fitting garments and footwear. As a result of this, transportees inevitably suffered considerable hardship. The coarse nature of these issued slops is clearly delineated in Delessert's woodcut of hard labour convicts in 1844–7 (Plate 7).

Controversy still exists as to the motives behind settlement of Australia and whether or not the First Fleet was provisioned adequately. Some observers at the time considered that the First Fleet was fitted out quite sufficiently and the transportees well catered

7   M. E. Delassert, *Hard Labour Convicts*, 1844–7, illustration from *Voyages Dans les Deux Oceans.*

for.[10] Yet the government was clearly trying to do things on the cheap. According to David Mackay, the settlement in New South Wales was crisis orientated.[11] In his view, despatch of the Fleet was a reckless act: it was poorly organised and there was no preliminary feasibility survey. What he infers about the general provisioning for either a strategic base or a commercial settlement is certainly borne out by the ill-considered dress issue.

Adult convicts were issued with readymade clothing intended to last only for two years.[12] No thought appears to have been given to the issue of back-up supplies, although the question of replacement dress was raised privately by Phillip before the fleet sailed.[13] Despite the inclusion of one hundred scissors and ninety-six pounds of sewing twine, no extra fabric for new clothing or repairs was issued.

Difficulties with convict clothing commenced almost immediately after departure. Some of the women's dress was worn out by the time the fleet arrived at Rio de Janeiro. Phillip noted in his despatch that, 'with respect to the women's cloathing, it was made of very slight material most too small, and in general came to pieces in a few weeks'.[14] To solve the problem, he proposed to cut up sacks of strong Russia (canvas) that had contained casada, to clothe those who he maintained were nearly naked. It is exceedingly curious that he did not supply the women with some of the large stock of new clothes that were issued to them just prior to landing at Port Jackson. The surgeon on the *Lady Penrhyn* noted that an issue of slops was given to convict women and children just before landing, and added with some surprise that certain of the women could even be described as well dressed.[15]

Compared to the First Fleet, the unsystematic issue of clothing to convicts on the Second Fleet was chaotic. According to one account, some male convicts had no trousers, some no shirts or jackets, and many arrived completely naked.[16] The problems of disorder that were engendered and the associated emotive terminology in despatches became a constant feature of the penal settlement. Supplies continued to be hampered by many factors: irregular shipments; the consistent undercutting of garment sizes by contractors (Appendix I indicates this was more prevalent for women's dress than men's); the poor quality of items; and the damage of goods in transit. All these problems contributed to a situation in early Australia where regulating dress was impossible and conventional dress codes of the time were somewhat randomly sustained.

Nevertheless, clothing did reach the settlement. Supplies held in the New South Wales Commissariat between 1790 and 1792 included shoes and hats for men, women and children. There were also trousers, waistcoats and frocks (loose-fitting, readymade jackets) for men, and shifts, stays and jackets for women.[17] Yet the quantities of garments received into the Sydney and Parramatta stores were small (only eight pairs of stays and two striped jackets in 1790). They were never sufficient for the needs of the free or convict population.

Additional clothes were obtained by other means. By the end of the 1790s free and ex-convict settlers became the colony's first traders, middlemen and small shopkeepers, whose commercial activities increased the availability of goods and small luxuries. Sydney was a flourishing small township by 1792 and officers of the New South Wales Corps began to make highly profitable trading initiatives, using the financial privileges of their official position.[18] It was they who speculated by purchasing and reselling consignments of readymade clothing from India and cargoes of calicoes, gurrah shirts, muslins, shoes and hats, often at hugely inflated prices.[19]

Despite the speculative trading, petulant requests for clothes by governors from Hunter onward punctuated despatch after despatch. In 1802 King injected a note of well-informed irony into what was by then a familiar lament. 'Of slops we shall have few or none after the next serving in July. At Norfolk Island they now have none. I, therefore, hope a proportion will be sent as soon as possible, otherwise we shall not only be *sans culottes* but *sans chemises*.'[20] Lack of clothing may have been exaggerated in reports such as this in order to speed up procedures but little was achieved to place garment supplies on a systematic basis.

If clothing was not forthcoming or if estimates were inaccurate, convicts either went without or the Governor had to purchase where he could from ships or merchants, often at hugely inflated prices. Macquarie had to justify one such unusually large expenditure in 1812 to the Earl of Liverpool, when he obtained garments from English and Indian trading ships. He maintained that the circumstances were unusual, but that government and assigned convicts had been destitute and without regular supplies for the entire eighteen months after his arrival.[21] A similar situation occurred in 1820 with convicts 'in a deplorable state of rags'.[22] The purchase of whatever supplies were available at the time inevitably meant that penal clothing could not be regulated, that convict dress was often indistinguishable from the slops worn by settlers, and that convicts were constantly reported in a state of complete or semi-nudity.

Convict behaviour compounded the government's difficulties in the administration of dress supplies. Transportees lacked conventional respect for clothing and did not maintain the dress issued to them. Controls on dress were ineffectual, particularly in the case of assigned convicts. From the Government Order of 31 October 1800, settlers were expected to clothe their own assigned convicts. They did not always comply with regulations, and even in 1831 the government was still demanding that settlers pay for their servants' clothing.[23] As a result of their laxity, and government ineptitude, convicts received clothing quite unsystematically and this meant further difficulties in the demarcation of penal status.

The problems experienced by officials in maintaining clothing supplies were exacerbated by the fact that garments were regarded as a valuable commodity. In a colony that had no proper currency until 1813, cloth and clothes were frequently used as a form of exchange. Whilst this was not unusual in preindustrial communities, it did compound official supply difficulties. Even the government used clothing as a payment system. Prisoners eligible for wages in 1819 were given clothing first, and only if they had sufficient garments could they demand money.[24] This was an indeterminate form of payment and reinforced patriarchal dependence on the government as a kind of family head.

Although a weekly inspection of convict clothing was instigated in 1803, there was little that could be done to prevent convicts from bartering clothes (especially for liquor), and gambling them away.[25] In his *Report* of 1822, Bigge, who commented quite fully on convict clothing, advised that they should be issued with their clothing only as required and not on arrival. The reason was that garments were sold and the money used immediately to buy spirits.

Due to the extreme scarcity of clothing in the early years, even settlers were eager to purchase convict dress, albeit illegally. As a result, the government totally prohibited all buying or selling of government slops in 1801.[26] Obviously this did not halt the problem, and as late as 1828 the New South Wales Parliament was still seeking to legislate against persons obtaining clothes from convicts.[27] The special circumstances prevailing in the colony combined to make clothes scarce. This envalued clothes as commodities for barter, diminishing their role as signifiers of class and occupation, and working against any sense of stability in terms of social demarcation.

## Local Cloth Manufacturing

One evident solution to the clothing problems was the encouragement of local manufacturing. If the cloth and clothing industries had been given some impetus, dress could have been issued more regularly, resulting in clearer definitions of social position. This did not occur. The government did show some concern to establish a local cloth industry from the time of first settlement. The interest fluctuated with prevailing circumstances and little success was recorded.

References to growing flax appeared first in the Heads of a Plan, prepared by Lord Sydney in 1786, but there were few specific details in Phillip's final instructions. Indeed the degree of importance which officials attached to flax cultivation, specifically in relation to marine supplies, has been the subject of vigorous debate.[28] Mackay suggests that the whole thing was a smokescreen to disguise the main purpose of the venture— the transport of convicts.[29]

In his instructions of 1787, Phillip was directed to occupy Norfolk Island where New Zealand flax was known to grow abundantly. Here he was to set up manufacturing on a modest scale.[30] Aside from its possible marine uses, Phillip was required to commence flax cultivation for the purpose of providing garments for the settlement, since much common clothing of the period was made of a type of coarse linen. He was required to attend to flax, 'not only as a means of acquiring clothing for the convicts and other persons who may become settlers, but from its superior excellence for a variety of maritime purposes'.[31]

Despite the clear instructions given to Phillip regarding flax cultivation for clothes, both Alan Frost and Geoffrey Blainey believe that Phillip and his officers were primarily intent upon setting up a source of naval supplies.[32] In fact much historiographical debate concentrates on the strategic importance of flax at the expense of the more significant consideration of the textile needs of the colony. This omission indicates historians' blindness to clothing needs as a factor in the manoeuvrings of historical protagonists. Surely a likely reason for the development of any form of flax industry in an undeveloped and remote colony would be the importance of cheap replacement clothing, arguably as immediate a concern as the possibility of a naval resource.

Authorities provided Phillip with only a single canvas loom and one flax-dressing machine, which hardly indicates strong encouragement for any flax enterprise. Only two free persons with some knowledge of working flax, and two convict flax dressers accompanied the First Fleet. Gillen contends that they were not chosen specifically for their skill with flax culture or manufacture.[33] These sparse resources were obviously insufficient to set up what was a complex industry, especially as there was a stated need for textiles to supply convict clothing. The development of a cloth-manufacturing industry of even a modest size proved far more problematic than had been envisaged by any remote decision-makers in Britain.

Experiments with flax cultivation began soon after arrival. In February 1788, Lieutenant Governor Philip Gidley King was despatched to Norfolk Island, taking with him a small party including a so-called flax dresser. The latter was unable to prepare flax: he had a loom but no dressing oil and no tools.[34] Eventually, after numerous production difficulties, King reported in 1796 that the island was suitable for manufacturing clothing linen and canvas in large quantities.[35] Yet no attempt was made to set up a viable manufactory, despite almost intolerable shortages of dress on the mainland. Although officials continued to encourage the development of a flax industry for supplying dress, and the significance of flax was frequently mentioned in official correspondence, the interest was never wholehearted.

For instance in 1798 the Duke of Portland, who envisaged a largely self-funding penal colony, was optimistic that total self-sufficiency in linen manufacture for clothing could be achieved; he suggested that 'sailors' frocks such as are made of Russia duck, and which is a dress best adapted for the climate of this settlement, may very soon be provided on the spot by these means without the necessity of sending them from hence'.[36] The year before an assortment of articles 'proper for weaving coarse cloth' was ordered for despatch, but amongst the equipment there was only one loom.[37] In fact, Portland's prophecy of self-sufficiency in flax manufacture never eventuated. The settlements in Australia did go on to develop a small cloth-manufacturing industry in the 1830s but it was confined to wool; linen fabric was never produced on a commercial scale. Even in the 1990s Australian mills do not produce competitively priced or high-quality woollen textiles.

Cloth manufacturing in the settlement was beset by numerous problems, including the fact that officials believed convicts required only crude fabrics for their dress.[38] The establishment of a viable textile industry also hinged on the question of experienced labour. Although by the late eighteenth century home production of cloth and clothing was common for the working poor in the north of England, more than half the New South Wales convicts came from British towns where readymade clothes or secondhand items were readily available and home manufacture of clothing was not the norm. Many women convicts may have been unused to anything other than minor sewing tasks and few of them were likely to have been able to weave, since weaving was traditionally a male occupation. In this context the government attempted to set up a weaving establishment at Parramatta.

Sometime during the construction of a new stone gaol there (certainly before April 1803), it was decided to set aside space for a permanent wool and linen manufactory.[39] The factory experienced problems with labour from the outset, since the convicts were allegedly unskilled, unmotivated and under-supervised.[40] Although production had increased sufficiently by 1803 for the Governor to foreshadow that demands for clothing would diminish by the following year, this was clearly wishful thinking.[41] The poor-quality, raw colonial wool and flax produced such rough fabric that it could not be used even for slops. Officials continued to argue that the penal nature of the settlement precluded any need to manufacture finer varieties of fabric, and there was no attempt to mechanise or seriously improve the quality of the products. Parramatta Factory fabric was still so coarse in 1819 that it could be used only for watchcoats or crude slops, and the colony remained largely dependent on imports for penal dress.[42]

The Female Factory which opened at Parramatta in 1821, accommodating three hundred women, should have given impetus to local cloth production by increasing available labour. Yet in 1826 the Female Factory Board reported considerable dissatisfaction with the entire process of cloth production.[43] In this year the weaving establishment was put in control of the Civil Engineer and moved to the Lumber Yard. Spinning was left to the women in the Factory. The weaving establishment, thus reconstituted, increased its output, making 30,000 yards of cloth annually by 1828.[44] This level of productivity suggests the equivalent of a small factory; it seems that by the end of the 1820s a reasonably viable government industry was in place.

It is likely that the women did little or no weaving at the Female Factory for most of its period of operations, despite Annette Salt's assumption that women at the Factory were weaving on a regular basis.[45] It was only in 1829 that the Factory Board of Management noted the establishment of a new Weaving Shop where, apparently for the first time, women were being taught to weave.[46] Even at this point the primary intention was not the production of cloth, but rather an attempt to encourage women to acquire skills that would gain them employment on settlers' estates and relieve the overcrowded accommodation. Despite these new initiatives, government weaving was unable to compete either with imports or with local manufacturing. By the 1830s its technology was obsolete and records of government cloth-weaving cease.

From the early years of the colony, settlers were encouraged to augment cloth supplies by spinning and weaving in their own homes. In 1802 the government offered prizes for the manufacture of the most linen.[47] The extent of the local cottage industry, although likely to have been fairly substantial, is little documented. Atkinson in his *Account* of 1826 suggests that spinning wheels and looms were manufactured in the colony. He claimed that cloth was made by settlers especially for clothing their servants, and that the coarse woollen fabric was much esteemed as clothing by the labouring class.[48]

Some local products found their way onto the general market but local homespun fabric lacked variety and could not satisfy the increasingly diverse requirements of urban dwellers, nor demands from new settlers used to British merchandise. Neither could it match the wide range of imported fabrics that were for sale by the 1820s, especially Indian cottons.[49] Although coarse woollens and homespuns were still being made in New South Wales pastoral areas in the late 1830s, the practice is not recorded later than this date and the skill seems to have died out in all regions.[50] Hugh Watson, who emigrated to South Australia in 1839, observed that there was plenty of wool in the colony but no spinning wheels.[51]

Private firms manufacturing cloth were negligible in the settlements until the 1830s. The enterprise of Simeon Lord was one exception. He began producing fabric in his Macquarie Street manufactory in 1813, and the following year built a factory and fulling mill at a more suitable site at Botany Bay. It opened in 1815, advertising the production of coarse cloths, flannels and blankets.[52] Yet his cloth was expensive, a problem which would plague locally made Australian fabrics, garments and footwear throughout the nineteenth century. His best fabric retailed at 15s. a yard compared to about 2s. 6d. a yard for Parramatta Factory cloth, which was loosely spun and not milled.[53] Only the prosperous could afford Simeon Lord's cloth.

Gradually more private cloth mills were to open. There were eleven such establishments operating in New South Wales during the 1830s.[54] The severe depression of the early 1840s stifled expansion, and the number of mills declined. The relatively stagnant cloth-manufacturing industry in New South Wales stood in marked contrast to both Britain and America, where there was an outpouring of good-quality textiles in the nineteenth century.

When the depression began to bite in 1842, there was a drive to encourage people to buy local fabric. A promotional article in the *Australian* pointed out, 'cloth of quality good enough for every common purpose is now largely manufactured, and the people...ought to show the value which they entertain for such establishments, by using it as much as possible in articles of their dress'.[55] In the same year the Hunter River Society was formed at East Maitland. Its aim was to establish a sensible system of land cultivation, to promote prosperity, and to foster a warm, patriotic attachment to the members' adopted country.[56] An annual dinner was proposed where members were 'expected to appear dressed in Colonial cloth; and that no fruit, wines or viands of any kind be used, but such as have been produced in the colony'.[57]

To what degree clothing of this kind was actually worn at society events is a matter of surmise. The intention, though, was a patriotic one. It attempted to foster local manufacturing of cloth as part of a more general attempt to influence Australia's economy and stimulate the purchase of Australian products, as does the comparable campaign being waged in the 1990s. A similar promotion was organised by the Canadian elite in the 1830s, suggesting the wearing of indigenous homespun cloth (not commercially produced fabric) as well as the consumption of traditional food and drinks, in the hope that domestic manufactures could replace imports.[58] In the Australian colonies the ideas of the Hunter Society were shortlived, and the wearing of 'Australian' clothing of this kind did not become common. The attempt to encourage local textile manufacturing was equally ephemeral, and woollen cloth production was never sustained as a successful industry.

## Local Clothing Manufacture

Making clothes, including footwear, in the penal settlements would clearly have been advantageous to both the government and local inhabitants. Fabric, garments and shoes often arrived on supply vessels in a waterlogged condition, or items were the wrong size or poorly constructed. No female clothing at all was sent by contractor Alexander Davison in 1791, while the hats despatched were too small and the linen cloth was flimsy.[59] Bales of clothing were received in 1792 which, 'though not rotten, have been so much injured from the damp that they have scarcely borne washing a second time'.[60] Locally made clothes and shoes could at least have been made to fit.

Convict tailors and shoemakers, as well as unskilled workers of both sexes, made some clothing from the first years of settlement. The Marines were also quite accustomed to altering and mending their own clothes. Major Ross indicated in 1788 that his men were cutting up issue trousers that were found to be unsuitably small and turning them into larger sizes.[61] The amount of government clothes made during the early years varied considerably, according to prevailing circumstances and the extent to which workers of both sexes could be made available for these tasks. All in all, local garment output remained low until the 1820s.

The making of clothes in the eighteenth and early nineteenth centuries comprised tasks divided between men and women according to traditional guild practices. It was by no means a predominantly female occupation. Throughout the transportation period, female convicts who made clothes did not necessarily possess trade skills. They were required to sew partly for occupation and partly to save the cost of importing garments. The encouragement of trade skills and production of good-quality local products was of little interest to officials. Although clothing was a primary need, its manufacture seems to have taken second place to the utilisation of labour for other tasks. If the overwhelming concern of early governors was for self-sufficiency, as argued by Hirst, it is curious that this did not seem to apply to clothing.[62]

In 1812 Macquarie alleged that female convicts at the Parramatta Factory who were not assigned were 'burthensome' and 'difficult of appropriation'. He suggested that in order to keep them busy and to save costs they should be used to make Parramatta cloth into convict dress.[63] The Management Board of the Factory continued to consider that sewing tasks were a suitable occupation for the inmates, and it was primarily for this reason that it continued to encourage needlework.[64] By the mid-1820s the women were engaged in making adult and children's slop clothing, shifts and linen caps, and knitting socks.[65] The *Sydney Gazette* carried an advertisement detailing the civilian garments available from the Factory in 1829. These included nightdresses, chemises, pelerines, baby linen, and gentlemen's shirts and trousers.[66]

It is likely that the women were given little incentive to sew and may have had poor tools. This was reflected in the poor quality of work produced and the small output. Gipps was still complaining in 1840 that manufacture of articles of needlework for sale at the Factory was unsatisfactory and also that it was unprofitable. Nevertheless, Factory women continued to make some slop clothing and gaol clothes, as well as garments to sell privately to settlers, until the end of the transportation period.[67]

All in all, convict tradespeople could not keep up with local penal dress requirements. This contributed to the debate, one that continued throughout the transportation period, as to whether clothes should be made in the settlements or imported. Bigge, who examined the question of quality and supply of convict dress in some detail, found the clothing made by convict tailors in the Lumber Yard insufficient for the settlement's needs.[68]

Convicts' attitudes toward work continued to lie at the centre of officials' problems with clothing manufacture. In 1826 a Board of Enquiry re-examined the entire matter of making government dress. The board recommended that two new workshops for men's clothing be established at the Hyde Park Barracks, one for shoemakers and one for tailors. It was proposed that all men's frocks and winter trousers, and possibly the shirts as well, be made in the colony. Yet a report tabled the following year describing the changes noted that the establishments were not working to full capacity.[69] The reason given was that some of the men employed were considered incapable of the amount of work usually performed by tradesmen, and that there were problems in maintaining supplies of materials. These were much the same difficulties that had been encountered regularly since the early settlement years.

Alford, in her discussion of the 1830s, suggests that all the penal clothing for the settlement was made by women in the Female Factory.[70] This assertion cannot be sustained. Even in 1828 the 'Estimate for the Colonial Convict Establishment' noted that government tailors were making all the 10,000 woollen convict frocks and 5000 pairs of trousers required that year out of local cloth.[71] Moreover, contracts and letters throughout the 1830s in the files of the Board of Ordnance suggest that large quantities of clothing for convicts in New South Wales and Van Diemen's Land were still being sent out readymade.

## Footwear

The problems that beset the manufacture of clothes in the penal settlement extended equally to footwear. Boots and shoes wore out especially quickly in the rough conditions; this difficulty is recorded by Marines from the time of first settlement. Soon after arrival at Sydney Cove in 1788 Newton Fowell, midshipman on the *Sirius*, described himself well off for clothes yet in desperate need of shoes.[72]

From the 1790s convict shoemakers made large quantities of footwear for local use out of imported leather. For instance, in 1798 materials to make 5000 pairs of shoes were sent to New South Wales at a cost of 3s. 5d. each.[73] Experiments with tanning began in 1794 and a Government tanyard was established at Parramatta by 1801.[74] Despite the quantity of shoes being made, there were continuing shortages and problems with manufacture. Although attempts were made to tan kangaroo skins for upper leathers in 1805, sole leather was to prove more difficult to supply locally, as the Bengal cattle skins were not strong enough for soles.[75]

In his *Report*, Bigge found that convict shoemakers could not keep up with demands and that the quality of locally tanned leather was quite poor.[76] In the 'Return of Labour' of 1800 only five convict shoemakers were recorded at Sydney and three at Parramatta.[77] Some of their work was for the civil establishment as well as convict use. Shoemakers at Parramatta were documented in the 'Return' as undertaking a 'vast quantity of work' for the wealthy Reverend Marsden and his family, indicating a blurring of task definition between penal and civil activities. This applied to convict tailors as well. The use of convict labour for the civil establishment is likely to have continued and was possibly one of the reasons why a scarcity of shoes was recorded by Bigge.

Maintaining supplies of footwear with insufficient tradespeople was to be a continuing problem in Australia. This was particularly so in outback environments, where boots and shoes wore out extremely rapidly. At the time of the New South Wales *Census* in 1828, Sydney had only one shoemaker or bootmaker (including bootclosers and shoebinders) for every 236 inhabitants. The lack of local tradesmen meant that a large proportion of shoes must have been imported, or made by workers not designated as tradesmen. The Macarthurs, for instance, placed orders annually for their family's shoes in England and continued to do so in the 1830s.[78] The lack of choice and paucity of local goods, particularly quality items, fostered a dependence on imported boots and shoes that continued throughout the nineteenth century. Yet hard-wearing footwear became the most successful of all Australia's comparable garment trades by the 1840s, and local boot and shoe manufacturers continued to provide Australians with basic requirements throughout the period and into the twentieth century.

## Private Garment Manufacturing

Although government manufacture of garments and shoes was limited during the penal period, some small-scale private clothing businesses in New South Wales had commenced by the 1820s. The industry developed slowly and was far behind its counterparts in Europe and North America. Early in the decade Sydney had an embryonic ready-to-wear industry for men, although it appears that there was practically no local readymade clothing for women and children until the 1880s. The industry in the 1820s was in the hands of Simeon Lord who, as well as being the colony's largest private cloth producer, was selling readymade shirts, stockings, hats, trousers and shoes, and exporting to Port Dalrymple.[79] Bigge reported that Lord operated two hat manufactories and that he produced coarse hats, not as durable as English ones, but far cheaper.

The situation of an entrepreneur like Lord is a good example of the kind of difficulties that would become persistent for later manufacturers trying to compete with English products. His advertisements in the 1820s seek to compare his wares favourably with imports.[80] The competition with imported readymade clothing continued to inhibit growth in the manufacturing industry even during the economic prosperity of the 1830s. In 1834 journeymen tailors in Hobart were reported to be out of work because local garments were outpriced by quantities of cheap, imported clothes.[81] Such complaints continued to plague the garment industry in Australia throughout the nineteenth century, and their lamentable echo remains in the pleadings of garment manufacturers even in the 1990s.

Lord's activities marked a period of transition: the government ceased to be the leading producer or supplier of goods, and private enterprise and commerce rapidly gained ground. In Lord's case there was a relationship with government production that continued into the early 1830s, since his firm used government so-called 'Parramatta cloth' to make readymade garments.[82] This kind of continuing dependence on government supplies fostered a lack of local manufacturing initiative. It also contributed to a clothing and supply market which was entirely different from that in Britain.

## Imported Clothing

Until the 1820s the supply of imported clothing into New South Wales was sporadic and unreliable. Difficulties were exacerbated by the fact that New South Wales, like other colonial markets including the Cape Colony, was a haven for speculators. The economy was constantly subject to scarcity, or conversely oversupply, such as the flood of Indian goods that entered the market in 1811-12.[83] Prices could alter in spectacular manner. For instance there was the change from low prices in 1800-3, to the 'price truly astonishing' of clothing recorded by Mrs Macarthur in 1807.[84] The trade was also subject to the European financial tribulations of 1810-12. Sydney suffered a continuous and serious depression from 1810 through to 1815-16. After about 1816 commercial swings became less dramatic. Small-scale speculation declined in favour of more routine trading in which the importation of consumer goods of wide variety increased rapidly.

Readymade clothing was brought in chiefly on speculative consignment or retailed through the government store whose establishment had been initiated in 1800. In addition to consignment clothing, free settlers and emancipists could occasionally obtain replacement dress from resale of damaged and secondhand goods, or from deceased estates, although there was nothing like the complex trading networks available to British consumers in the early industrial period. Records, including advertisements, indicate that there was less imported readymade clothing available for women and children than for men, yet by 1814 women and children made up about half of the population.

The chief retailing method in Sydney was by public auction, although the public store and an ever-increasing number of private shops sold clothing. Auctioning remained the chief method of retailing cheap slop clothing and finer-quality garments well into the 1840s and later in some cases.[85] Goods were sold off when shipments arrived, and costs were linked to prices that consumers were prepared to pay at the time. This speculative form of exchange contributed to a degree of irregularity in patterns of consumption until it was superseded much later by fixed price selling.

Mixed cargoes, brought into the country by professional merchants, were bought up, or auctioned off in parts. The consignment by Captain Parkes of the vessel *Cato* in 1803 included food and jewellery, as well as many readymade goods chiefly for male customers.[86] The items on offer reflected the diverse nature of the Sydney clothing market in the early years of the century, a diversity that matched the general growth of economic complexity. There were men's frilled, white linen shirts, worsted pantaloons and breeches, leather breeches (quite commonly readymade at this time), canvas trousers, greatcoats, felt plated and fine hats, beaver gloves for men and also Norwich shawls.

Sales were sometimes conducted on board trading vessels. Durant in pieces, lace on cards, leather and thread for shoes and men's readymade clothes were advertised to be sold on board the *Bridgewater* in 1803.[87] In New South Wales and Van Diemen's Land customers could pay for clothes in wheat, skins or other produce if they preferred, a choice due partly to the unstable currency.[88] This was a common practice in other countries, like America, at a time of transition from home production of commodities to a full industrial economy. In Australia it continued as a custom in rural communities well into the twentieth century.

The irregularities in local clothing supplies had important implications for the meaning of dress in the penal settlements. Until the 1820s, commercial instability inevitably affected the goods available for purchase and therefore the choice available to consumers. What was frequently a limited selection tended to diffuse social distinctions, since settlers were obliged to dress in whatever they could obtain. The wealthy elite were somewhat insulated from these commercial activities, since they were less dependent on local purchases and could order large amounts of clothing directly from Britain.

The lack of adequate provision for a continuing supply of basic clothing needs was compounded by bureaucratic ineptitude and produced an Australian experience of dress in the early days of settlement quite distinct from that of Britain. Apart from Aborigines, the dress of the lower social group categorised them as a homogeneous class, one that included tradespeople, convicts, farmers and poor settlers. The lack of a distinction between convict and free within this social grouping lent an aura of egalitarianism to Australian dress, later promulgated as a more general characteristic of the colony.

# 3

# A Cut Above: Fashion, Class and Power

Until the consumer revolution of the eighteenth century, fashionable dressing in Europe was almost exclusively a sign of the upper classes and their power. By the beginning of the nineteenth century, fashionable dress was becoming far more widely accessible to a range of social groups. The public were fascinated with stylish dress, and apparel was a key element of popular consumerism.[1] Yet fashion's role as a signifier of power and prestige remained. In the small outposts of the early settlement years in New South Wales, Van Diemen's Land and in Western Australia, stylish dressing was a conspicuous symbol for the small elite group—made up of military officers, government officials and some wealthy free settlers—and increasingly for emancipists. An overt display of fashion and elaborate social mores clearly signalled a moral and aesthetic legitimation of the 'civilising' presence of Europeans in an alien and savage environment, where convict dressing was unregulated and many inhabitants still lived practically naked.

Fashion does not represent a unified message about style. Rather it generates a profusion of meanings. These complex messages are variously decoded according to the class and gender of those that perceive them. More than this, fashion is constituted partly through the effects of language and through the circulation of discourses. At any one time these discourses may include those addressing morality, sexuality, beauty, class, location, and economics. Power relations of class, race and sex are negotiated constantly through dress of this kind. Thus in the early settlement years the pastoral gentry, the mercantile capitalists, and the emancipists, each in their own ways, regarded fashion as a significant element in attempts to pinpoint and reinforce their own precise level of status. In the latter case this was of particular importance as Australia's settlements slowly progressed from being penal establishments, with the presence of convicts a defining feature, to free though still colonial societies. But more generally, stylish dress was a highly visible, almost contemptuous means of separating the appearance of the ruling elite from what was the generally homogeneous clothed appearance of the majority of inhabitants, made up of tradespeople, convicts, farmers and poor settlers.

A close examination of the genre of travellers' accounts of life in the colonies during the early decades of the nineteenth century reveals that comments on local fashion habits and manners are amongst the most common.[2] Passages on dress are at times repetitive, and it seems to have been generally agreed that undue preoccupation with demeanour and extravagant dressing was especially characteristic of women in the settlements. Descriptions, admittedly more often than not compiled by men, registered amazement at the zealous attention to dress and the ways in which they kept up with European styles. In 1811 Daniel Mann mentions in *The Present Picture of New South Wales* that apparel and ornament were greedily purchased and with no regard for expense.[3] Years later Robert Burford, picking up Mann's words in some detail in his *Description of a View of the Town of Sydney*, noted that 'articles of female apparel and ornament are purchased with avidity; costliness of dress is considered indispensible, and the ladies spare neither pains nor expense in decorating their persons'.[4] Such passages show the way commentators follow the confines of a patriarchal convention that regarded women as vain and decorative objects, competing for the attention and pleasure of the male viewer.

Descriptive comments on dress and social life were undoubtedly coloured by relief that the colonies were not as uncouth as had been imagined. Alan Frost has argued that travellers came to New South Wales expecting to find themselves at the periphery of the European world and were surprised to find a centre.[5] Frost's suggestion can equally be applied to other colonies. In 1831 George Fletcher Moore, Advocate-General and first judge of the Civil Court, was agreeably surprised at the gaiety of dress he found in Perth and delighted he could still wear his slight shoes, silk stockings and kid gloves.[6]

For those accepted into the ranks of the socially elite, including some emancipists, there was a gay round of balls, dinner parties, levees, races and weddings. Increasingly these public events, initially sponsored by the Governor, were supplanted by private parties and professionally hosted balls.

By the second decade of the century there was substantial architectural development in New South Wales; the dominance of the pastoral elite was demonstrated by their extravagant building programmes and cultivated estate lifestyle.[7] By this time Sydney boasted finely appointed mansions and charming cottages. The streets were busy with London carriages, much commercial activity and elegant shopping facilities. The vibrant social life of the stylish Pipers, who lived at Henrietta Villa on Point Piper, was typical of this exclusive milieu. Guests at picnics and parties were wafted in decorated boats from Farm Cove to the Point by liveried boatmen, who doubled as musicians; they wore white suits and white top hats, adorned with badges and coloured scarves.[8]

Increasingly there are other dimensions to texts describing dress beyond satisfaction at finding a foreign place made English. Ladies were said to have eagerly followed every ephemeral detail of English fashions and mannerisms, but by the 1830s this was alleged to be at the expense of both finesse and more cerebral and cultural pursuits.

Louisa Meredith remarked a little darkly that 'all are dressed in the latest known fashion but not always with that tasteful attention to the accordance or contrast of colour which an elegant English woman would observe'.[9] There are hints in her remarks of a censoriousness and of undisclosed antagonisms. Peter Cunningham, Louisa Meredith and others maintained there was too much preoccupation with stylish dress and affected behaviour, but beneath both the approbation and the critique of fashion lie subtexts. These point to problematic nuances of class definition that continued to plague social relations in Australia. Even at the end of the 1850s Clara Aspinall, the sister of a Melbourne barrister, claimed that it took longer there for a stranger to be initiated into 'who's who' than anywhere in the world because of the difficulty of telling by appearance who was important.[10]

In order to obtain some picture of what constituted stylish dress at this time, the definition of fashion needs clarification. Such dressing is a means of shaping and reshaping the body by a continually changing succession of appearances. Fashion creates the illusion of an autonomous independent force, but its commodities are locked into structures of both production and consumption. Like all kinds of dress, fashion constitutes a meaningful sign system. Encoded in the varying forms of fashion are gendered messages concerning social class, morality and sexual ideals. According to the economist Thorstein Veblen, wearing conspicuously expensive fashions is one of the primary ways in which the elite classes can show their position as leisured and not physically productive.[11] Thus it can be argued that stylish clothing is a powerful tool used by the socially and financially dominant to signal their identity and position.

More significantly, fashion is essentially a competitive medium. According to Georg Simmel it represents the antagonism between a desire for individual differentiation and change and that of social equalisation.[12] Fashion is in fact located at the core of struggles between classes, and marks negotiations from one to another. By the early nineteenth century access to fashionable clothing was no longer the prerogative of the rich. The commercialisation of fashion on a large scale in the later eighteenth century had meant almost all ranks had access to some form of stylish dress. The aspiration to fashionable dressing and the novelty of new styles had been well and truly kindled by this period. As goods became more readily available, the time lag for fashion changes diminished. Not only were new needs and desires created, but all classes were encouraged to participate in the contest of acquisition. With some provisos this situation had more or less translated into the commercial life of the colonies by the 1820s.

In the period between 1820 and 1840 Connell and Irving have postulated two polarised and somewhat incompatible structures of colonial society. One centred on assignment relation in the pastoral industry, and the other on mercantile capital and small production in the towns.[13] The pastoral gentry, defined from the structure of the first, was the most self-conscious of all the colonies' social groups, which stemmed from the status-consciousness of officials and officers in the early settlement years. There were close links between the pastoralists and wealthy merchants who, with their wives and children, were of a more or less equal status, even though trade was increasingly identified in the 1820s as an interest quite separate from the pastoral. In addition, there were public and assigned convicts, Aborigines, working free settlers and emancipists. Records show that convicts, who had in 1810 constituted 59 per cent of the population, had dwindled to 43 per cent by 1828, and by 1841 to only 22 per cent.

Macquarie's recognition of emancipists enabled some of them to participate in the activities of upper social circles if they met certain criteria, but the availability of suitable dress commodities and the wealth to purchase exterior trappings did not automatically translate into social position. The 'exclusives', for instance, were extremely self-conscious in their attempts to clarify their status in the hierarchy. A degree of upward mobility for ex-convicts caused acute problems; out of these developed a theory of 'moral ascendancy', whereby true virtue was held to reside in wealthy settler families with no links to convictism.[14] Thus from the early 1820s, amongst the socially dominant, there were emancipists on one hand seeking equality, and 'exclusives' on the other obsessed with visibly demonstrating hereditary status. This is not to suggest that the appearance of these two groups was necessarily clearly differentiated; neither can individual preferences be discounted. Being dressed in an 'acceptable' manner was a matter of subtle degree.

Elaborate clothing was sometimes deemed unnecessary by the prosperous in more secluded areas, such as the districts inhabited by the Macarthur family. They had all their clothes despatched from England in half-yearly shipments. In a letter dated 1824 to her son John, then in London, Elizabeth Macarthur described her needs: 'It is of consequence that what we have for our personal use should be appropriate and of superior quality. We wear things out, and therefore wear them long. We have no opportunity of changing often . . . At this distance from the Mother Country mere articles of show are ridiculous.'[15] She indicated that the good quality of clothing she requested was not only for practical reasons but that this form of clothing was 'clearly more respectable', suggesting that subtle distinctions of class still operated even if the style of garment was plain.

Unquestionably the dress and behaviour of the elite were partly premised on the formalised system of organising social and domestic life emerging in Britain in the 1820s, defined by the term 'Society'.[16] Made up of the aristocracy and, increasingly, the new middle classes, English Society sought to regulate the newcomers. In so doing, it reinterpreted itself through increased control of social interaction, elaborate etiquette and greater exclusivity. Translated into the context of New South Wales society, the features of this aristocratic inheritance of manners seemed, if anything, to be even more cherished than they were in Britain. Attention to behaviour, manners and dress was excessive. For instance Judge Advocate Ellis Bent, in his comments about Governor Bligh's daughter, noted that in public everything about her conduct was studied, 'her walk—her talking—everything—and you have but to observe her mode of sitting down'.[17] Somewhat later in the 1820s the naval surgeon Peter Cunningham still claimed, rather extravagantly, that 'the pride and dignified *hauteur* of some of our *ultra* aristocracy far eclipse the nobility of England'.[18]

Colonial observers were clear that these social conventions—with their emphasis on dress styles, jewellery, accessories and manners—were regulated, as they were in Britain, by women. Cunningham was adamant that it was colonial women who were preoccupied with the trivialities of dress, although the interest in elaborate social rituals was a quite general feature of colonial life.[19] The charge of being preoccupied with little else beyond their children and the latest style of dress was levelled equally at women in other colonial outposts like India. In New South Wales it can be directly related to the move toward a more public, male-dominated arena for politics that superseded Macquarie's paternalistic rule. This in turn had ramifications affecting all classes of colonial women.[20] For privileged women it meant a narrowing of interests and a resulting redirection of their energies toward organising charitable activities and social events. Their roles were so restricted that clothing and etiquette were likely to have been among the few means they had of exerting social or political influence.

## Fashionable Dress Supplies

A degree of fashionable dressing existed in New South Wales as early as the 1790s, when trafficking in consumer goods commenced. In fact Ravenet's wash drawing of 1793, *Man and Woman of New Holland* (Plate 8), shows a woman of the settlement wearing an extremely stylish gown and undergown, with fine linen fichu or buffon and the very high crowned hat fashionable in Britain in the 1790s. Generally speaking, the lack of shopping facilities and irregular supplies of fashionable goods at this early period meant that, whenever possible, the small civil and military establishment privately commissioned high-quality clothing from Britain. Other fashionable dress was sent out by friends or relatives, and occasionally with general shipments. For example, a stock of the latest London fashions was advertised in 1810 by the 'tailor, habit and staymaker' W. Barnfield, for a select clientele of ladies and gentlemen.[21]

In the early years, imported stylish garments, like all clothes, were received sporadically. The vagaries of shipments caused variable time lags in the reception of dress from Europe, resulting in disruptions of supply to consumers. Frequently, fashionable garments were received with surprise. Responding to a bonnet sent out to the colony in 1799, Elizabeth Marsden, wife of the Reverend Marsden, remarked in a postscript to a letter to Mrs Stokes, 'ps. We are surprised to see the alteration in the fashion. The Bonnet with white satin ribbons is much admired.'[22]

To judge from newspaper advertisements, readymade clothing, including the more fashionable styles for women and children readily available in Britain, was less often offered for sale in the settlements. Imports for women early in the century were more commonly shoes, fabrics, accessories or fashionable millinery, such as the 'Ladies Bonnets and fashionable Turbans' for sale at the house of John Driver, Chapel Row.[23] It seems that speculative traders were not eager to deal in female clothes for resale in such a predominantly male society as New South Wales. It is also likely that women, more than men, relied on family and friends to send them articles of fashionable dress. Mary Putland, daughter of William Bligh, thanked her mother in 1807 for the gift of such a gown. She noted it was 'altogether different and superior to anything of the kind that had been seen in this country'.[24]

Some fashionable dress was also being made locally during the first years of the century. The question arises as to who was actually sewing and tailoring fashionable garments and what their quality may have been. For example, there are relatively few

**8**   Juan Ravenet, *Man and Woman of New Holland*, 1793, wash drawing (Dixson Galleries, State Library of NSW).

references in the New South Wales Musters to the tailoring and dressmaking trades. Garments are likely to have been made by those who did not qualify for an official trade designation. Between 1806 and 1822, none of the free women emigrants entering the colony, and only a small percentage of ex-convict women, are officially listed as possessing needlework or seamstress skills.[25] Only one free mantua-maker and two ticket-of-leave needlewomen were recorded at the Muster of 1814, for a total female population (mainland New South Wales) of 2681.[26] Many women would have undertaken casual sewing work, despite the fact that they had no official trade, so these figures may well be inaccurate. They are likely to reflect the nature of data collection rather than present an accurate picture of contemporary trade skills.

Despite the paucity of designated tradeswomen, fashionable dress, or allegedly stylish clothing, was certainly being made in Sydney in the first years of the century. M. Hayes, milliner, advertised in 1803 that she could execute orders in 'a style of fashionable taste and neatness with the utmost punctuality'.[27] Five years later Catherine Mellon, a freed woman working from Back-Row East, advertised her skills as a mantua-maker and milliner, capable of executing orders 'either in a plain or fashionable mode'.[28] Mantua-maker was a title for a dressmaker, but the fact that Mellon offered services for two types of customer or two types of clothing is indicative of the existence of some form of hierarchy of dress. For the socially elite, whose fashion aspirations were directed towards Europe, a certain stigma seemed to be attached to the colonial article. Yet the advertisement does indicates that a differentiation in social dressing did exist and that fashionable dress, or allegedly stylish clothing, could be Australian-made even though based on English patterns.

With a recorded colonial mainland population of 29,783 by the time of the 1821 Muster (excluding the military and their families), commercial opportunities expanded considerably, and a fairly wide range of female dressmaking skills was recorded. An increasing number of dressmakers and needlewomen were working in the colony, expanding the potential for fashionable garments and millinery to be locally made. In 1821 in a total of 1623 ex-convict women, there were ten mantua-makers, three staymakers, seven straw bonnet makers, eight needlewomen, two lace workers, four milliners and one shoe binder.[29] At the time of the 1828 Census, the concentration of dressmaking skills was in Sydney, with twenty-five of the thirty women dressmakers listed living there. This represented one dressmaker for 136 women, convict and free, including girls below the age of twelve. The collection of data was uncertain, and it is likely that married women were excluded from a trade designation, so these figures are only a guide. At this point just over 4 per cent of the adult female labour force was engaged in the clothing trades.[30]

There was a similar lack of qualified tailors in the early years of settlement. The Muster of 1814 registered nineteen tailors, including three government men, which is the equivalent of only one tailor for 273 men (including the military, but excluding convicts). Generally speaking, there were few apprenticeships available early in the century, so there were few opportunities for those wishing to gain tailoring skills.[31] The number of tailors had increased by 1828. Sydney had 109 tailors, including government employees, representing one tradesman to about sixty-eight men. The reason for this increase is not clear, but it is probably a reflection of the expanded market for quality clothing.

Sydney had at least one working hatter by 1804. He was William Simmonds of Chapel Row, who trimmed headwear as well as cleaned and scoured beaver hats.[32] During the first decade of the century professional female bonnet and hat makers are also recorded in Sydney. In 1811 Simeon Lord, the highly motivated emancipist, was also operating a small hat manufactory with Rueben Uther in Macquarie Street, using convict labour. He produced ready-to-wear items as well as hats made-to-measure for fashionable occasions, describing his customers as being both 'ladies' and 'gentlemen'.[33]

Despite the small number of civil tradespeople, local tailoring and dressmaking had sufficiently improved in reputation by the mid-1820s to be accepted by elite members of society, including the military and those within the privileged Government House set. For example, at the King's Birthday Ball given by Governor Darling in April 1826, the *Sydney Gazette* noted that two hundred guests at Government House, representing 'the beauty and fashion and the loyalty of Australia', were largely dressed by colonial tradespeople. 'Tailors and tailoresses, shoemakers and shopmen, were in great requisition up to the auspicious moment. The dollars and dumps were circulating in every direction— shopping here—shopping there—shopping everywhere.'[34]

Stylish dress as a symbol of social dominance altered and became more complex in the eastern colonies in the 1820s, with the pronounced influx of emancipists into society and with the more expansive consumerism of the decade. Fashions were marginally out of date compared to Europe, yet citizens of the higher social stratum attempted to sustain the notion that their dress was its equal. Richard Read Senior's portrait of *Miss Julia Johnston*, daughter of Lieutenant Colonel George Johnston, was painted in 1824—probably at Annandale, the family property (Plate 9). It shows her pert coiled hairstyle and a tasteful cashmere shawl worn with a slender walking gown trimmed with blue and white. Compared to imported fashion prints of the same date, she is only slightly behind the styles for women in Britain. Represented pictorially as a decorative object, she is finely adorned and on display for the viewer. Her appearance is carefully constructed through her garments, hairdressing and gestures, demonstrating according to current codes the constituents of sexual propriety and feminine charm. At the same time her dress carries signifiers of social dominance. The fact that her mother was a convict on the First Fleet apparently caused no problems within the prosperous 'exclusive' circles in which she moved, and her clothing represents an effective statement of her elite, though still slightly precarious, position.

## Shopping

By the 1820s travellers were astounded at the tasteful and civilised nature of Sydney. The town was a centre with a noticeably expanded market for consumer items, and its inhabitants came from many nations. Some, like Lady Forbes, the wife of the Chief Justice, were disparaging about Sydney's shopping facilities. Having brought all her clothes from England, she maintained that she seldom went into the town as the shops were not tempting. She noted, 'I remember one of the best shops was constructed merely of slabs, on wheels, so that it could be moved from one part of the town to another, if business became slack.'[35]

**9**  Richard Read the Elder, *Miss Julia Johnston*, 1824, oil (Private Collection).

There were many who disagreed with her opinion. Christiana Brooks, wife of a former captain of a convict transport Captain Richard Brooks, described the town toward the end of the decade as crowded and bustling, with well-supplied shops and numberless well-dressed people. It was expensive too. She describes, 'price of leghorn bonnets very high. Nothing wearable less than 6gns.'[36] By this time specialist shops and 'showrooms', sometimes called repositories, were becoming more common. Peter Cunningham suggested that public auction rooms handling mixed business were more popular than retail stores at this period, but that a change to specialised shops was slowly occurring.[37]

A small-scale ready-to-wear industry for men's clothing had started up in Sydney, and customers could place orders by mail. The facility offered in 1827 by A.J. Russell, wholesale and retail manufacturer and cap maker, catered to the country trade, making it possible for urban fashions to extend out into rural areas.[38] Detailed self-measuring guides were published by outfitters in the 1830s, in accordance with British prototypes, allowing customers to mail their orders. In 1834 the letterhead of J.G. Maelzer, tailor and habit maker of George Street (provisioner for the Macarthurs), included a proportional diagram and measuring directives for customers: 'Please be particular by taking the measure round the chest and waist over a waistcoat only and likewise mention the height of person or peculiarity of figure.'[39]

Women more frequently established small clothing and haberdashery businesses from the 1820s, although the goods were mostly items for ladies and children.[40] By this period the *Sydney Gazette*'s fashion advertisements emphasised goods that catered to seasonal differences and were of the newest styles.[41] The proportion of women to men had not increased significantly since first settlement (3.5 men to every woman in 1788 and 3.1 in 1828) but many of these advertisements reflect a wider market for varied, and report-edly elegant, fabrics and items of clothing for women customers. More than 15 per cent of the population were children, and advertisements catered for their requirements as well. For women there were silk and satin dresses; embossed china crepe; chenilled and sewn Jaconet flounced robes; Italian net dresses; coloured bordered dresses; fashionable trimmed and untrimmed Leghorn and straw bonnets; Edinburgh shawls; foundation muslin drawers; and night and morning gowns.[42] For children, lace caps and cap crowns, shoes, beaver hats, print fabrics and straw bonnets were on sale.[43]

Undoubtedly, British fashion exerted a crucial influence on dress in the settlement. Indeed, one of the strategies of the upper ranks of society in maintaining exclusivity in dress was assiduously to follow the lead of Britain. This meant that the style of garment, as well as the fabric from which it was made, bore social messages of elitism. According to Cunningham, the moment a lady 'blooming fresh from England' was to be seen in Sydney, the smallest detail of her dress was copied—'the cut of her gown, the figure of her bonnet, and the pattern and colour of the scarf or shawl she displays'.[44] In what was still essentially a penal settlement, this particular deference to English style was a way of defining and demarcating social boundaries; but equally it was one of the colonisers' most highly visible tokens of presence.

Historians have seemingly given priority to Australia's links with Britain. In fact, the important influence of French taste and styles emerged in the 1820s and would continue to play a significant role in Australia's dress history throughout the nineteenth and early twentieth centuries. The close emulation of seductive French fashions was partly an affectation, as was the judicious use of French vocabulary, but it was also a way in which the ruling class could reinforce its sense of exclusivity. French fabrics, jewellery and accessories were readily available in Hobart and Sydney at this period, and Parisian milliners ran successful businesses.[45]

This predilection for Parisian modes may have reflected the general opening up of trade between Britain and France after the end of the Napoleonic Wars. Cunningham inferred that considerable rivalry existed amongst women in Sydney between London and French styles, suggesting that 'party feeling on the important subject of gowns and bonnets is consequently in a state of high excitement'. He maintained that Madame Rens, *Marchande de Modes* from Paris in Sydney, had set herself up in opposition to other businesses, seducing young women with her 'flaring announcements'.[46] One of her advertisements appeared in the *Australian* of 1827.[47] For ladies, there was a choice selection of evening dresses, cashmere and ball dresses, as well as Brussels and French lace dresses; for men, there were waistcoats and gloves.

Besides French imports, some fashionable fabrics, accessories and garments were also brought from India. In 1820 Mrs Plomer, mantua-maker of Upper Pitt Street, advertised that she had in her possession 'the latest fashions from India', implying that some imported dress from India was designated as stylish.[48] A great variety of cottons of Indian origin, like cossah, tannah, sannah, emerties, baftahs and izarees, is described in the *Sydney Gazette* and in clothing accounts and trade lists. Mrs John Macarthur noted the purchase of Missapore print, Bandah, Lucknow chintz, Patna chintz, white Baftan and white Juliapore.[49] Some of these fabrics would certainly have been suitable for the fashionable, high-waisted gowns of the period.

The influence of India on fashion is illustrated by the wedding of Anna Blaxland in 1823. She came from a highly respectable family and married Thomas Walker, the Assistant Commissary General, in an early-morning ceremony at St John's Church, Parramatta. She decided that everything must be in Indian style. The bride and bridesmaids were attired in low-necked, high-waisted gowns: the bride was in cream striped silk with trimmings, and the bridesmaids were in muslin which had been especially brought from India.[50] Anna's delicate gown (thought to be Australian-made), trimmed with corded tabs and military-style cord lacing, still survives, along with her silk wedding shoes of unusual style, stockings, and kid gloves.[51]

Anna was extremely enterprising, and reared silkworms for a hobby at the family home at Newington. A cream scarf was spun, woven and embroidered in China entirely from her own silk and embroidered with a floral meander border pattern and basket motif, with carnations and pineapples at each end. It was part of the wedding ensemble and is still extant, but the Indian bridesmaids' dresses have been lost.[52] The family had strong links with India. Anna's grandmother, the daughter of a Calcutta merchant, bequeathed to her one of her crimson embroidered cashmere shawls, allegedly given to her by Warren Hastings, and it may be this treasured Indian wrap with its floral borders that is worn in a portrait of Anna painted in 1840 by Maurice Felton (Mitchell Library, Sydney).

There seems, however, to have been a specifically colonial prejudice against the use of some Indian fabrics for stylish dress. In the late 1820s, Peter Cunningham suggested that Sydney 'belles' did not yearn for China crepes and India muslins like English beauties, because the products of the Eastern loom were too common, too cheap and too durable (therefore not suited for the changeable nature of fashionable wear).[53] Perhaps they resembled too closely the coarse Indian fabrics, like the blue cotton gurrah from the Bengal and Orissa areas which was worn by convicts and working-class 'dungaree' settlers.[54]

## Fashion and Its Meanings

There is little comment on fashion in the early years of settlement, although European fashion magazines were available and some reporting of overseas fashion or extracts from British magazines appeared in Sydney and Hobart newspapers. Such reports were addressed chiefly to women readers. The news appeared irregularly and was often only a brief comment. Occasionally descriptions were sufficiently detailed to allow dressmakers to make up the garments. This form of reportage allowed fashionable ladies closely to follow the lead of Europe, although there were no fashion illustrations. One of these reports in the *Monitor* of 1826 described a fawn-coloured *gros de Naples* 'Dinner Dress' and 'Ball Dress'. The latter gown, of fine tulle, had a skirt 'ornamented with two rows of festoons, edged with three narrow pipings of cherry-coloured satin, the centre of the upper festoon being attached to the points of the lower by a full blown Provence rose, suspended by a narrow white satin corkscrew trimming'.[55]

There are few references to fashion in the *Sydney Gazette*, which commenced weekly publication in 1803, and which was the only Sydney newspaper for some years. One isolated, censorious passage about fashion change was published in 1804. Couched in almost the exact terms of an English fashion magazine, the paper complained that:

> To such a pitch of extravagance do our female *noblesse* extend their improvements on the lap'ear'd bonnet, as to be literally hoodwkin's [sic], they have consequently *lost sight* of the once matchless *turbot* [sic] and since their faces have been retired from the world who knows but upon the next flippant change they may be induced to take the veil.[56]

The text is significant in that it suggests that a turnover of style existed in the colony and that sufficient consumer items were available to make such changes possible.

Comments on fashion grow more frequent from the 1820s onward and many focus quite critically on what was claimed to be the overly stylish dressing of colonial ladies. By the 1830s the criticisms had become a veritable literary cliché and directed at the dress of all classes of women, although for differing reasons. To understand the nature of these criticisms when directed at the middle classes, we need to be aware of the significance of fashion to this class of woman. For instance, comments regarding their excessively elaborate dress must be seen in context with commonplace nineteenth-century views regarding the appearance of bourgeois women and their receptivity to the vagaries of fashion.

As has been argued on a number of occasions, fashion is an important contributing factor to the social construction of femininity within the patriarchal social order.[57]

The role of women in the nineteenth century was defined largely on the basis of their appearance, and not on intellectual or occupational grounds. The very idea of women's beauty was associated with their femininity. Failure to appear properly dressed, according to bourgeois prescriptive guidelines, was more problematic in the case of women than in the case of men. A fine line existed between fashionable dress representing moral decorum and social status, and fashion perceived to be inappropriate or lacking conformity with the status quo. Thus any critique of early colonial women who were regarded as overdressed must be located within the more general criticisms of women as vain and preoccupied with material triviality, rather than with more desirable feminine qualities of modesty and cleanliness of attire.[58]

In New South Wales it is likely that for women there were vested interests in maintaining elaborate modes and etiquette practices. Fashion was considered by the elite to be a regulatory mechanism with regard to the lower classes, but there were other issues at stake. For instance, stylish dress and adornment were an ideal medium for formulating self-images that demonstrated allegiance to British mores, but which also effectively masked social fears and moral anxieties in a predominantly male, penal environment. For both emancipist and 'exclusive' women, this form of dress was a sign of clear differentiation from the darker side of colonial life, which included not only convicts but Aborigines, who sometimes still went naked or semi-naked on Sydney streets.

Thus for women, conspicuously fashionable and expensive styles and copious jewellery, as well as contrived forms of etiquette, were crucial indicators of social difference. This is well demonstrated in two contemporary portraits, one painted by Lemprière about 1838, showing a stylish Mrs O'Hara Booth, wife of Charles Booth, Commandant of Port Arthur; she is dressed in a low-necked formal gown which has pleated sleeves and is trimmed with bows. She wears fine gold miniatures on chains, pendant earrings and has a cluster of blooms in her hair (Plate 10). The other portrait painted in 1840 by Maurice Felton shows the newly married Mrs Alexander Sparke, a woman of some substance, although not quite of the highest echelon of society. Dressed in a sparkling white, lace-trimmed evening gown, she is weighed down with a veritable storehouse of jewellery as a symbol of her husband's social position (Plate 11). As Joan Kerr has suggested, one of the tasks of colonial painters was to transmit selected forms of information and transform the negative aspects of colonial society by images of disguise, omission or substitution.[59] Portraits of fashionably dressed citizens like Mrs Booth and Mrs Sparke thus ensured a double transformation.

By the 1820s bourgeois women in New South Wales had been largely excluded from business and commercial activities. Their sphere of influence was predominantly home-based, and they were relegated to the tasks of organising social events and philanthropic endeavours.[60] For these women, fashionable dress became a highly visible sign of status. Indeed, it meant more than status. Fashion was something which conveyed moral overtones and could be used positively and effectively to sustain notions of their superior moral worth. Stylish dress signified to the lower classes the benefits that accrued from propriety and diligence. For instance at Sydney's Female School of Industry, founded in 1826, a formidable group of women philanthropists consciously paraded their wealth and social standing by wearing fashionable dress to the organisation's meetings.[61] These

**10**  Thomas Lemprière, *Mrs Charles O'Hara Booth*, mid–late 1830s, oil painting (Tasmanian Museum and Art Gallery).

women, who were intent upon moulding the morals and manners of Sydney society via the dispensation of their philanthropy, clearly used dress at times to impress on the lower classes their subservient status and to remind them of the generosity and condescension of those offering charitable services.

**11**   Maurice Felton, *Mrs Alexander Sparke*, 1840, oil painting (Art Gallery of New South Wales).

In the new settlements, sustaining the appearance of respectability was a crucial part of the social cohesion of the gentry in contradistinction to the 'non-respectable' classes.[62] The stakes regarding fine dressing were thus extremely high, and for the elite the demarcation between acceptable and inappropriate was a delicate matter. As well, for women living in a penal colony, excessively fashionable dress posed sexual problems. In 1834 Ellen Viveash confessed that she had never seen anything like the extravagant dress in Hobart. One lady, walking in the morning, even wore black satin shoes. Moreover, she observed that 'the ladies many of them, wear low dresses and only a net Pilerine [sic] over to walk in the streets amongst a convict population and where females are in small proportion'.[63] Although her comments are about Hobart, they show that significant sexual as well as class tensions attended any form of fashionable dressing for bourgeois women within a penal settlement where men were in the majority. It also cogently indicates the somewhat ill-defined line between fashion used as a tool of social dominance and dress perceived to be overly stylish, inappropriate or disreputable.

For those women intent on social climbing, the motives behind decorative dressing are likely to have been quite similar to those of the elite. In their case it was more important to keep up appearances to achieve their goals than it was for men, as their positions were more socially precarious. Louisa Meredith indicated that women emancipists paid more attention to their attire than their husbands did to theirs. She noted that the wives and daughters of men with immense property (emancipists) often dressed in the extreme of finery. Conversely, the husband could be as dirty and slovenly in his apparel as a common mechanic. She found in one case the son glistening with rings and other gems but wearing shoes plus spurs with no socks or stockings, leaving 'a debatable ground between them and his trowsers'—an unpardonable breach of etiquette.[64]

From the 1820s, the critique of fashion also extended more broadly into a moral debate about the dress and etiquette of working and convict women. The concern with dress manifested itself in Bigge's reports; it can be linked specifically to policies supporting colonial marriages put forward by governors from Macquarie onward, including both moral and material inducements.[65] It was a bourgeois prescription that women's specialised role was to attend to a decorous, though not necessarily decorative, personal appearance in order to attract and maintain the interests of a husband.[66] Thus dress had an important role to play in the formulation of an appropriate and exemplary kind of femininity. Christiana Brooks entered this moral debate about marriage and the importance of dress when she noted that the School of Industry in Sydney would be instrumental in changing the dress habits of the lower class in Sydney by teaching young women useful skills. Her remarks had a subtext of moral censoriousness and the fear that over-fine or inappropriate dress was a disadvantage and might bar young women from the goal of marriage. She considered that in time their offspring would become 'a superior race to those who lounge over the shop doors in Sydney: a *half* dressed or *over* dressed generation—who seem born for no other purpose but to gossip with their male acquaintances'.[67]

The question of convict women and their clothing was an especially contentious one and in the 1820s and 1830s warnings about the moral dangers of elaborate dressing were frequently sounded. As Sturma has shown, it was the sexual behaviour of convict women that was the principal criterion used by contemporaries in evaluating their conduct.[68] This concern to judge the women on grounds of sexual behaviour extended to moral pronouncements on their dress. Elizabeth Fry deplored the use of earrings, curled hair, and all forms of 'finery and superfluity of dress'.[69] James Mudie strongly disapproved of the dazzling appearance of newly arriving 'lady' convicts in their rich silk bonnets, long pendant earrings, kid gloves, parasols, 'dispensing sweet odours from their profusely perfumed forms'.[70]

Underlying such criticisms was the firm belief that any form of decorative dress was not compatible with convict status, and that neat and becoming clothing would help in the reform process for women transportees and smooth their paths toward marriage. The labelling of the dress of convict women as 'vulgar' and inappropriately fine had the effect of regulating the dress of all women, thereby officially encouraging what was considered to be a respectable appearance. It is also possible that convict women wearing fine dress and accessories might have appeared uncomfortably similar to the upper classes.

Convict women were reportedly more difficult to control than convict men and allegedly could always find a way to flout clothing regulations and dress more fashionably. According to evidence submitted by a Police Magistrate to the House of Commons Select Committee on Transportation in 1838, convict women always found ways to dress more elaborately than in their government issue.[71] Officials explained the laxity in women's attitudes toward government dress as a sign of their moral weakness for fashion rather than their criminality. Bigge was adamant that all employments that had a tendency to encourage 'a passion for dress' amongst women convicts should be avoided.[72] For convict women who sought masculine favours, the wearing of noticeably bright fashions and trinkets was a form of self-advertisement and is likely to have been regarded as an economic and occupational necessity.

Although generally speaking the fashions of women are most commonly discussed in colonial literature, there is evidence to suggest that the colony also had its 'spruce dandies', self-consciously concerned to demonstrate social status through their dress.[73] Tropical white cotton jackets and trousers were generally worn with straw hats by men of fashion in Sydney by the 1820s, and blue jackets were used for riding and in cooler weather. These outfits were quite different from the ill-fitting drab slops of free working men and convicts. In a letter from Thomas Gates Darton in 1838, bourgeois men in Sydney are described as 'quite in Indian style in silk trousers etc'.[74]

The critique of men's dress derived from a quite different principle from that of women. The 'exclusives' criticised the dress of gentlemen convicts on the grounds of transgressing class boundaries, not for their moral turpitude. Marsden, in his evidence to Bigge, complained bitterly about the convict who lived like a man of fashion. Such a man, in his fine boots, coat and chaise, 'loses no opportunity to push himself forward into that Rank of Society, or even into a higher one than the one from which he had sunk by the Sentence of the Law'.[75]

It was the heartfelt desire on the part of 'exclusives' that dress be retained as an absolute mark of social definition. This did not always happen by any means in the unregulated conditions of the colony. John Jamison recorded that the fashionable styles of dress of many convicts caused great confusion for strangers and lower classes and gave them a false sense of social position.[76] Marsden said that imperious gentlemen convicts should wear common clothing because 'there is not a convict in the colony who would have the assurance to rank himself by your side if he had a coat as long and of the same colour as that you wear'.[77] This form of critique marks an important difference in attitudes toward male and female convicts. Anxiety was engendered by the class transgressions of the men but by the supposed moral laxity of the women. Dress thus entered the contemporary rhetoric articulating the penal, sexual double standard of morality.

During the 1820s and 1830s, fashionable styles in New South Wales were essentially motivated by cultural imperialism, although the meanings of stylish attire varied across gender and class boundaries. The pastoral gentry, as well as the wealthy mercantile capitalists and emancipists, each had their own differing interests in fashion as signifiers of their own precise level of social position. For the elite, defending their status and distinction by devising controls of social admission became a priority. Fashionable and expensive styles, deferential to European models, copious jewellery and contrived forms of etiquette were suitably conspicuous indicators.

The wearing of ultra-stylish dress in the European mode was a triumphant sign of the colonisers' ability to transcend the stain of convict association. Reports of reassuringly 'civilised' behaviour and mannerisms could thus be conveyed back to Britain, erasing other less salubrious issues. Fashion became a social and moral exemplar which could be effectively used by those in political control to demonstrate their power over the lower classes. But beneath the fashionable appearances lay subtexts and anxieties about class, particularly with regard to the dress of women. These anxieties would alter somewhat as bourgeois habits gradually came to dominate, but they remained essentially unresolved throughout the nineteenth century.

# 4

# ON THE FRINGE: CLOTHING AND ABORIGINAL–COLONIAL RELATIONS

Studies of early colonial race and gender relations show that complex, confused social reactions and interactions between Aborigines and whites commenced at the time of first contact. These interactions were subject to many variables, and considerable changes occurred even during the first year of settlement.[1] Whilst Aborigines were not a homogeneous unified racial group as the term implies, clearly imperialism created new sites for gender struggles and cultural confrontations between the two races.[2] Many of these interchanges centred on differing attitudes toward sexuality as denoted by ornamentation and clothing.

As early as the second decade of the nineteenth century the traditional attire of those Aborigines in proximity to Europeans began to be dramatically affected by this contact. Whilst the naked appearance of blacks was initially a matter of sexual or cultural curiosity to whites, it came to be regarded as a sign of their inherent inferiority. Lack of clothing was seen as morally incompatible with the 'superior' European way of life. The presence of Aborigines and the changing nature of racial interactions relating to their respective appearances demonstrate some of the ways in which codes of dress were uniquely sustained in the Australian colonies.

British officials played a key role in clothing responsibilities when transportation ceased, but government involvement with clothing Aborigines remained a separate matter. Indeed the British government, and later colonial officials, through various agencies and committees, played an increasingly interventionist role with regard to dispensing clothes and blankets to certain groups of Aborigines. As well, the evangelical desire to convert blacks to Christianity extended to attempts to force European clothing habits upon them. The supply of blankets and clothing continued throughout the colonial period. In 1882 the New South Wales Department of the Protector of Aborigines was still issuing such items to blacks.[3]

Aboriginal men and women were under continual pressure to assume white clothing. As the men were increasingly accepted as stockmen and stationhands and the women domesticated, they were required to dress in ways that conformed with white working-class habits. In some cases this was advantageous to them but frequently it meant that older skills were lost and former customs abandoned. Thus the adoption of European dress is likely to have aided in the destruction of the Aboriginal culture through the undermining of self-esteem and erosion of health. More than this, the traditional meanings of black codes of bodily decoration and covering were altered, contributing significantly to changes in the nature of Aboriginal social practices.

## First Encounters

The blacks encountered by the first European inhabitants at Port Jackson were people about whom virtually nothing was known and who were thought to be without political authority, social organisation or religious beliefs.[4] Aboriginal society with its diverse peoples and plurality of languages and customs was regarded as one single group. The major differences between Aborigines and other racial groups were initially more apparent than the less obvious differences from one another. The customs which marked Aborigines out as strikingly different from Europeans were thus most readily documented by whites, sometimes in realistic detail and at other times with contempt or indifference.

In late eighteenth-century Europe, clothing was regarded as a key marker of rank and an essential sign of the civilised, harmonious ordering of society. Not surprisingly then, observers at the time of first settlement at Port Jackson found the scant attire of the Aborigines, the sticks or bones in their noses and their disfiguring scarification or clay markings both curious and uncivilised. Phillip, who himself wore a wig on formal occasions, probably made from another's hair, was affected by the strangeness of black men who 'hang in their hair the teeth of dogs and other animals, lobsters' claws and several small bones, which they secure by gum'.[5] In the same year, 1788, Hunter was disturbed by the wood or bones through the noses of some of the Aborigines whom he encountered and their greasy skins; he gave precise details of the marks and streaks of white and red clay and ochre on their black bodies and faces. He claimed these conspicuous paint marks were intended to strike terror in onlookers and he himself found them 'most shocking'. He said that he had the impression that the blacks 'were like so many moving skeletons'.[6]

Aborigines responded to European clothes in a variety of ways. Many of the men seemed puzzled at the lack of facial hair and the way European clothing disguised gender. Consequently they sought visual reassurance on the matter. Others appeared to admire the appearance of the Europeans and appreciate their gifts of clothing. Some eagerly accepted baubles and allowed sailors to dress them with coloured papers and foolscaps.[7] Flinders, making contact with Aborigines at King George Sound in 1801, described the local people screaming, supposedly with delight, at the sight of Marines in red and white uniforms and bright muskets.[8] Aboriginal women too seemed pleased to have trinkets placed ornamentally on their bodies and to cherish the attention.

Yet there were frequent disquieting demonstrations by blacks showing what whites considered a lack of respect for European dress. Even at the Endeavour River in 1773, Parkinson, Banks' artist, had found the natives neither asked for clothes nor made any use of the shirt which was offered. They simply tore it into shreds.[9] At other times blacks, who seemed initially to admire the appearance of European clothes, soon gave the impression of finding these articles a disappointment and either disfigured them or threw them away. A number of Aborigines who had never before seen Europeans were encountered by an exploratory party near the Vasse River in Western Australia in 1827. They were encouraged to board the ship and were dressed in mariner's clothing. But once back on land, 'the jackets were torn to pieces and each man who was so fortunate as to obtain a piece tied it around his neck'.[10] In this case it was as if the material goods were of interest but not the habit of wearing them. Thus the initial interest turned shortly to what looked like unseemly disrespect for the very nature of 'civilisation' itself.

## Aboriginal Clothing

Aboriginal men and women traditionally wore little clothing although customs among the various groups included the wearing of cloaks, some foot protection, and ornamental belts, headbands and fringes. Apart from the lack of clothing, Europeans often found the most significant aspect of the appearance of Aborigines was their customary skin decorations, including body colouring and scarification. The garments closest to the experience of whites were Aboriginal cloaks. Depending on the locality, cloaks made from skins of opossum, brush-tailed opossum and also kangaroo were used by both men and women as a form of protection.[11]

The native opossum cloaks characteristically worn in south-eastern Australia were made from forty to sixty stretched skins of animals, dyed and then stitched together with a thread made of the stringy-bark tree or emu or kangaroo sinew.[12] In his Field Book of 1828–30 T. L. Mitchell described these garments as looking like Roman togas with two corners fastened across the breast. The skins were rubbed or shaved to make them more supple and then designs were added with mussel shells, according to tribal custom, in figurative, geometric or abstract patterns.[13]

The way cloaks were worn varied according to the type of skins, the season, the place, and the age and sex of the wearer. Some reached almost to the ground and were fastened at the neck with a bone clasp. Others were shorter and draped like a poncho to knee level. Cloaks could be worn bare side exposed (with fur inside) on cold mornings and with the fur outside when it was wet. Cloaks in the south of Western Australia were normally worn thrown over the back and left shoulder and pinned so that the right arm and shoulder were left unconfined.[14] In Victoria the kangaroo cloaks worn in winter looked more like mantles. Women in some tribes tied their cloaks with a string so as to form a pouch at the back in which to carry a child. The Tasmanians had cloaks made from a single kangaroo only or occasionally an opossum skin. The skin covered the shoulders and back and was held in place by tying strips from the animal's legs across the chest and sometimes the abdomen.[15]

Europeans admired the practicality of opossum cloaks and rugs, and acquired them directly from Aborigines. Eugene Von Guerard's painting *Barter* of 1854 (Geelong Art Gallery) represents a group of Aborigines selling one of these articles to two white men. Alternatively, Europeans made opossum skin rugs or cloaks into garments to wear in cold areas. Mrs Louisa Meredith described her male companion on a snowy journey over the Blue Mountains in about 1840, as having 'retired into a grotesque cloak-hood and coat sort of garment, made of thick furry opossum skins of the Colony, and looked like an exaggerated Esquimaux, as we caught a glimpse of his portly figure'.[16]

Opossum cloaks were practically the only item of Aboriginal attire which whites coveted to the extent of appropriating them for their own wear. On the other hand, the interventionist practices of Europeans fostered amongst blacks a progressive dependency on European clothing. This was to have a devastating effect on their traditional skills and engendered a radical transformation of their own customary methods of dress.

## *Nudity*

Despite the variation in styles of dress and bodily adornment of different groups of Aborigines, the fact that blacks went about naked or semi-naked featured most prominently in European accounts of Aboriginal life and customs. This practice occurred even in major Australian towns in the 1860s, and well beyond this time in remoter inland areas. Since dress was perceived to be fundamental to the 'civilised' European way of life, Aboriginal nudity was regarded as one of the most important defining characteristics of these peoples. It was also a powerful factor in reinforcing white prejudices about the need for racial exclusion. At times, romantic responses about nudity did tend toward an aesthetic appreciation of a 'noble savage', living a life of unspoiled virtue. More frequently, white stereotypes condemned Aboriginals as culturally degraded or grotesque comics. The perceived morality and rational order of the European way of life was reinforced and legitimised through relegating Aborigines to such stereotyped categories of difference.

Aboriginal nudity provoked whites to disguise their supposed shame by supplying them with European clothing. Even in the case of early colonial artists like Lycett, Aboriginal custom was ignored and painted loincloths were judiciously used to cover the bodies of male Aborigines, while the torsos of women were overlaid with drapery.[17]

Sometimes it was merely the covering of naked Aboriginal bodies with slops or blankets that was important to whites, not the differentiation of gender. In the first year of settlement, Phillip advised Nepean that only long frocks and jackets (items of men's dress) were required for gifts to Aborigines, for these would do for men and women alike.[18] Ann McGrath has discussed how Aboriginal society in the Port Jackson area had an internal emphasis on gender as a social, economic and political demarcation. The whites' disregard for the importance of differentiating the sex of Aboriginal peoples through dress showed total lack of respect for the fundamental basis of their culture. Degrading gestures of this kind continued in various forms throughout the colonial period.

Aboriginal nudity was even more questionable because in the early years of settlement male convicts also went naked at times, thus blurring boundaries of racial difference.[19]

One account of 1809 described how convicts 'staked their clothes upon their backs, standing in the midst of their associates naked and as indifferent about it as the unconscious natives of the country'.[20] Convicts who gambled away their dress or worked naked in the fields were unacceptably close to the local male Aboriginal population in appearance, doubly transgressing accepted lines of racial and sexual order.

The nakedness of both convicts and Aborigines began quite early to elicit official outrage. On the one hand reports of convicts who were naked like 'savages' were used by governors to stress problems of a moral nature, to force the British government into activating supplies to the settlement. On the other hand, anxiety and hostility about Aboriginal nakedness was easily deployed to augment populist racial prejudices, reinforced by respectable 'authorities', that black people were amongst the most rudimentary in the chain of human life.[21]

For government agencies and later missionaries, nudity became the site of a major cultural struggle to bring Aborigines within the sphere of Christian influence.[22] As white settlement progressed, the habit of Aboriginal people to be without clothes was increasingly regarded as barbarous. Whites were outraged at the allegedly 'disgusting' spectacle of absolutely nude and 'offensive' black bodies.[23] Yet Aboriginal people were deemed to be expendable in the context of a natural flow of white progress. Thus at times of confrontation, acts of violent aggression against naked 'uncivilised' black people may well have been more straightforward for Europeans than if they had encountered clothed opponents. Generally speaking, fear and the inability to come to terms with the reality of Aboriginal customs and culture lay at the heart of the whites' confused reactions to the physical appearance of these people.

Some of the conflicting problems experienced by whites encountering Aboriginal nudity are illustrated in an incident in 1829 when George Robinson, Aboriginal Conciliator in Van Diemen's Land, went on board the vessel *Prince Regent*, with two naked black women in his charge. He claimed that at first sight the ladies on the ship mistook the Aboriginal women for beautiful young boys.[24] One cannot assume that middle-class women were as ignorant about the facts of the human body as this anecdote would imply. What it does suggest is that clothes and hairstyles define gender; if these signs are not recognisable, the information received can be misinterpreted.

A major point of interest is that, according to Robinson, once the identity of the women was discovered, the ladies felt the urge to dress up the naked Tasmanian Aborigines like charming toys, not just to cover their nakedness.

> As if apprehensive that pollution might follow this development of unsophisticated nature or beauty unadorned, they flew to their wardrobe and equipped their visitors in a style not plain but gaudy, not as a country maid but in silks and satins, after the manner of a drawing-room belle at the west end of the metropolis.[25]

Robinson thought that the women had been unwise in their actions, and immediately exerted his authority by arranging for the Aborigines to be dressed in more appropriate clothes made at a convict settlement. The incident highlights the patriarchal, patronising attitude of white men but also the relegation of Aboriginal women to a role of complete passivity by white women.

Something of this patronising 'making-over' of Aboriginal women is evident in the 1838 painting of 'Gunbal' by James Wilson (Australian National Gallery). Painted at Braidwood and probably given to Lady Franklyn as a gift, the portrait shows a disempowered Aboriginal girl, from whom practically all traces of a traditional appearance have been erased. Rather than being portrayed naked, she is shown 'dressed up' as a black courtesan, with make-up and jewellery as well as an exotic wrapped headdress and ermine cape—the latter traditionally regarded as a sign of prestige in British portraiture.

Emerging as a particular issue in the 1820s and 1830s was the conflict posed by the appearance of naked Aborigines in colonial settlement areas. Aborigines without clothing were seen to reflect poorly on the bustling respectability of colonial towns. Although Cunningham noted that 'colonial climatised' women were less embarrassed by naked blacks than newcomers, the issue was still contentious.[26] In 1837 at Holdfast Bay, South Australia, the Governor ordered blacks to be issued with slops to prevent embarrassment to settlers.[27] Some years later in 1845, Penelope Selby, writing to England from Port Fairy, complained about the 'disgusting' natives and the lack of delicacy of feeling in colonial society, which she claimed was due to all the classes constantly coming into contact with naked black men and women: 'I must say I have felt my own cheeks burn when I have seen ladies in company with gentlemen talking and laughing with savages in that state . . . I hope my boys will not get contaminated.'[28]

For the middle classes the intermingling of naked Aborigines with whites (especially men and women in groups, or women alone) was morally and sexually contentious. It was one of the primary reasons that various official agencies and private groups were constrained to intervene so overtly in attempting to 're-educate' blacks in their clothing habits.

It was deemed especially inappropriate for white women to observe black men walking about in their 'natural costume', for there were clearly unwelcome 'educational' effects of such encounters. Accounts by middle-class women, from the mid-1820s onward, suggest that they themselves found direct contact with naked Aborigines especially distasteful. Whilst male commentators like Cunningham offered exaggerated descriptions of naked Aboriginals, labelling them 'exquisites' or 'dingy dandies', middle-class women registered emotions of a more moralistic nature. For these women, discussing the body and sexuality in other than euphemistic terms was normally inconceivable. Thus someone like Christiana, the wife of Captain Richard Brooks, considered it was 'disgraceful to a town such as Sydney to meet the Natives of both sexes entirely naked'.[29]

In 1825, according to Christiana Brooks, the Superintendent of Police in Sydney began to order constables to impound Aborigines not decently clothed. She intimated that forcing Aborigines to be adequately clothed in town was a way to make them 'carefully treasure the bounty of the charitable' for, as she implied, Aborigines appeared to show puzzlingly little gratitude toward their European benefactors.[30] But more importantly there was a significant link between civic pride and distaste for Aboriginal nudity. In Perth for instance, with the town growing and becoming more settled by 1838, justification was found to exclude Aborigines on the grounds of their unclothed appearance and violent behaviour.[31] There was clearly no place for naked blacks in white cities.

## Aborigines, Dress and European Intervention

Offence to white sensibilities, belief in the contamination of whites, and the continuance of heathen practices were arguments deployed in order to coerce Aborigines into wearing European clothes. With obdurate persistence, government agencies, settlers and later missionaries tried to reshape the lives of Aborigines by imposing on them supposedly orderly European standards of cleanliness and clothing. The process was facilitated by official government policies whereby clothing and blankets were issued to blacks, but the underlying intentions were obscured by claims of philanthropy. At first this occurred directly through the agency of the governors and later through various Protectorates, commencing with the Port Phillip Protectorate established in 1838.

The initial indication of an official, interventionist programme to bring Aborigines into line with the European working classes occurred during Macquarie's governorship. He was responsible for the first attempt to incorporate Aborigines into colonial society, both by regularising their way of life and by imposing upon them European clothing habits. He had general hopes that they would become useful as labourers or a lower kind of mechanic, living a village-like existence.[32] Macquarie urged sixteen families of Aborigines from the Broken Bay group to take up residence in huts at George's Head, Port Jackson, in 1815. As part of the reward he gave each adult rations and workers' slop clothing.[33] The establishment of schools for Aborigines and the Native Institution at Parramatta (set up in 1814) involved the government in the further supply of rations and European slop clothing. These regular issues of clothing marked the first steps toward fostering a dependence on European dress, which set in train the homogenising of the appearance of Aborigines with that of a certain class of white inhabitants.

As a gesture of goodwill, Macquarie instituted a feast for all New South Wales Aborigines at Parramatta in 1816. It became a popular annual event at which pipes, tobacco, blankets and slops were distributed. The warm blankets were useful to the Aborigines, as indigenous animals like opossums and kangaroos evacuated areas where Europeans settled. For instance there were few kangaroos in the Sydney area that could be used for skins; the local people did not make opossum cloaks, sometimes substituting teatree bark, or else obtaining kangaroo skins from other parts of the colony. Giving Aborigines gifts such as slops and blankets was a direct intervention into their traditional customs and skills, with resulting long-term cultural effects. Increasingly, without traditional sources for making their own cloaks, Aborigines became dependent on blankets for clothing. Blankets therefore took on special significance in the relationship between whites and blacks.

Although Aborigines liked the blankets issued, they frequently bartered them or other gifts of clothing for food or liquor.[34] As a result of the perceived misuse of dress, Governor Bourke abolished the feast in 1835 and ceased to allow blankets to be distributed in the customary manner.[35] Instead he ordered that they be issued annually, just prior to the winter months, at local stations and police offices. In such local distribution of blankets, Bourke sought to control the movements of Aborigines and keep them away from the towns.

Aborigines in the Sydney and Port Phillip areas preferred gifts of blankets to other forms of covering because they permitted mobility and most resembled their traditional opossum cloaks.[36] European clothing was not an advantage when hunting because trousers impeded movement. Although Aborigines often appeared indifferent to European material goods and clothing, blankets were generally an exception; if clothes were issued, the Aborigines would sometimes register such discontent that the clothes would be replaced with blankets.[37]

In attempting to economise and prevent indiscriminate issue of blankets to 'indolent' Aborigines, Gipps decided in 1838 that preference should be given to those who had rendered particular services, or had earned money by labouring. Working Aborigines would be rewarded with blankets but troublesome ones would be denied them.[38] When, for financial reasons, blankets were discontinued for a time in 1844, the Aborigines became discontented, and the aged and infirm suffered great hardship. Many perished in the cold since they no longer had the traditional skills of making coverings such as opossum cloaks.

The committee investigating the condition of the Aborigines in 1845 found that the question of blanket issue was of far greater significance than morality or clothing. Blankets had become official symbols of government or missionary recognition of Aborigines. From the European point of view these garments were also important items by which control could be exercised and were a major element in regulating, and ultimately rendering dependent, the Aboriginal people. A prime example of the degrading nature of these practices occurred with missionaries in the Moreton Bay area who distributed blankets on behalf of the government. They gave blankets only to those who rendered the 'best' service. Children who attended school were given pieces of blanket according to their age. Some had one-quarter and others half blankets.[39]

From the late 1820s the effect of missionaries on traditional Aboriginal clothing habits can be detected. The Reverend Threlkeld, appointed to work among Aborigines at Lake Macquarie, recorded in 1828 that he gave food and slops to the black labourers he employed.[40] The practice continued in varying ways and with varying degrees of intrusion at other settlements over the years. Much later, in the 1850s, a portrait by John Crossland of Samuel Kandwillan, a pupil of the Natives' Training Institution at Poonindie, South Australia (National Library of Australia), shows him dressed up, not in slops, but in fine European garments as a form of missionary propaganda. He is represented in white status symbols of European frockcoat and waistcoat and with stylish hairdressing, holding a bible as if to conduct a religious service.[41] As with the Aborigines of Coranderrk near Melbourne in 1867, who posed for the photographer Charles Walter in fashionable clothing, the intention was to promote blacks as having been tamed and regularised by European ways.[42] Their dress was a crucial emblem of their acculturation.

One of the most patronising instances of white intrusion in Aboriginal affairs was the distribution of brass 'King Plates' to specially designated or favoured blacks. The custom was begun by Governor Macquarie and later taken over by mainland settlers. Aboriginal culture was extremely elusive to white society, who did not appreciate that Aborigines had no concept of hereditary chiefs. The distribution of King Plates was really an attempt to impose a Europeanised sense of hierarchy onto the black community.

King Plates were crescents of brass that resembled the silver gorget or neckplate worn by military officers.[43] Gorgets of base metal had been used in the late eighteenth century to cement relations between the British and the American Indians, and it is possible Macquarie based his gesture on this precedent.[44] In 1815 he appointed the native Bungaree as 'chief' of the Broken Bay people and presented him with both clothes and a King Plate inscribed to this effect.[45] Macquarie presented a further number of brass plates to the leaders of peoples who gathered at the first Parramatta feast in the following year. Badges of distinction were given to the leaders and badges of merit rewarded other individuals.

The plates were believed to be looked upon with some pride by Aborigines, and by the early 1840s settlers commonly gave them to faithful servants.[46] The custom remained throughout the century. Aborigines who rounded up escaped convicts were designated bush constables and given similar tokens, together with muskets.[47] Aboriginal trackers and police were also rewarded in this way. Numerous illustrations, and later photographs, can be found of Aborigines wearing King Plates, either with tribal dress or with European clothing (Plate 12). These illustrations suggest that the custom of giving and wearing the plates continued well into the twentieth century.

## Tasmanian Aborigines

The so-called progress towards the dubious goal of a fully Europeanised dress is recorded in the attempts to subjugate the Tasmanian Aborigines and abolish their traditional clothing habits. Aborigines living on Bruny Island were first issued with blankets at the ration station in 1828.[48] Subsequently the station was turned into a mission and George Robinson was appointed as Aboriginal Conciliator in 1829. As part of his conciliatory task he was required to give religious instruction, institute a form of peasant or village life, and encourage the use of European dress.[49] This was clearly a desire on the part of the policy-makers that Aborigines conform to some ideal vision of the 'lower orders', rather than to the actualities of European working-class life.

Robinson was later involved in the programme to round up the remainder of the Tasmanian Aboriginal people and settle them on Flinders Island. When the Quaker James Backhouse visited the Flinders settlement in 1832, he was pleased to find many blacks at least partially clothed. He commented that the men had signified their willingness to cease from wearing red ochre and grease in their hair if they could have some form of cap. He carefully recorded that there was an understanding of the messages conveyed by European dress as well. When given scotch caps, the Aborigines, believing them to be similar to those of the military, 'immediately arranged themselves in a rank'.[50] On his next visit the following year he described what he considered to be marked progress in clothing habits. The men were wearing typical European working-class dress of duck frocks and trousers. The women wore stuff (woollen cloth) undergarments, check bedgowns and handkerchiefs on their heads and about their shoulders.[51]

Yet the experiment on Flinders Island ultimately failed. Dress began to be discarded, worn clothing remained unmended, and traditional tribal practices were carried on in secret. At Oyster Cove Aboriginal station, where the remnants of the Flinders Island people were eventually housed, the inhabitants lived in filthy conditions. Attempts

**12**   Oscar Fristrom, *King Sandy*, 1887, oil (Private Collection).

**13**   J. W. Beattie, *Aborigines at Oyster Cove*, 1860, photograph (Beatties Studio, Hobart).

had been made to induce the men and women to wear a kind of north European regional peasant dress. J. W. Beattie's photograph *Aborigines at Oyster Cove*, taken in 1860 (Plate 13) shows 'Truganini' and 'Flora' wearing folksy hand-knitted polka jackets with decorative trims, whilst 'King Billy' has a tam o'shanter cap and braces.

James Bonwick found in 1859 that most of this government-issue clothing of loose blue garments and red caps had been sold or exchanged for liquor, and the polka jackets were worn only on festive occasions.[52] The attempt to induce Tasmanian Aborigines to take up a European cottage lifestyle and to blend this with an alien culture proved to be fruitless.

**14**   Augustus Earle, *Natives of New South Wales*, 1830, lithograph (Mitchell Library, State Library of NSW).

## Appropriation of European Dress

The decline in numbers of Aborigines over the course of the nineteenth century is well documented. Few of the original Port Jackson people were left by the 1830s; many other groups in the south and east of Australia were on the point of extinction by about 1850.[53] Those remaining on stations, in towns and urban fringes increasingly assumed European dress, blankets, cast-offs and rags. Earle's lithograph of *Natives of New South Wales* 1830 (Plate 14) conforms to the stereotype of the Aborigines as derelicts; it shows a mixture of semi-nakedness, cast-off uniform and ragged clothing as well as the nudity of their infants. The artist has quite deliberately portrayed a foreground of almost grotesque black squatters in stark contrast to the fringe of well-dressed, 'respectable' European men and women behind.

Apart from being deliberately coerced into wearing European clothing, blacks were allegedly eager to assume certain items of dress when coming into towns or when they were in direct contact with settlers. The reasons may be put down to expedience, the desire to please, or merely to imitation. Trousers or petticoats were reportedly adopted, and even blankets were wrapped more circumspectly around the body when they entered the urban environment.[54] From the late 1830s Aborigines, who were beginning to be employed as station hands, stockmen and domestic servants, were encouraged by whites to adopt practical articles of slop clothing. Some stock workers and drovers appeared to take a more calculated interest in European dress, hairstyles and even cheap jewellery, and seemed proud of their ability to move more easily in the white man's world.[55]

As a way of reinforcing their prejudices, whites recorded that Aborigines took off their clothes when they left urban or homestead areas, and appeared to place little consistent value on European clothes other than blankets. William Thomas, Assistant Protector of the Yarra and Western Port tribes, giving evidence to the Select Committee on the Condition of the Aborigines in 1845, recounted that he had seen Aborigines burn their good clothes when leaving Melbourne. Shirts, he said, were generally torn up but blankets were mended and patched to the last.[56] Aboriginal servants who were attached to settlers' households and outfitted by them were said to return to their own customs and relinquish their clothes if their services were terminated. Sometimes just entering their own living quarters was reportedly enough to cause them to discard their European trappings.[57]

In other words the assumption of European dress by Aborigines cannot be construed as a form of urban alternative to black attire. Whites recorded this habit in a deprecating way and alleged it was a form of deference to themselves in rural and in urban areas. Aborigines continued to remain nude or wear traditional items of dress when living in areas away from Europeans. In fact, as La Trobe wrote in 1848, 'both by male and female, it is thrown aside without ceremony, as soon as circumstances tempt or permit'.[58]

Aborigines, it seems, did not take readily to any specific form of European clothing. They had their own particular preferences and dislikes and had especially strong objections to wearing anything that looked like convict dress.[59] Those Aborigines who did use European clothes frequently wore a shirt and possibly a jacket but not trousers. Male Aborigines appeared to dislike European slop trousers intensely, perhaps because their traditional attire included no leg coverings. Women as well would often wear nothing more than a man's shirt.[60] This practice of wearing only a shirt or jumper tied at the waist was still being recorded in the 1880s as is seen in a photograph of *Bloomfield River District Aborigines* in 1885-6 (John Oxley Library, Brisbane).

Uncovered legs offended the sensibilities of a culture for whom leg display had serious moral and sexual implications. In fact, what was held to be Aboriginal progress toward acceptability seemed partly to lie in the readiness to accept European 'nether' garments. In 1837, George Robinson, by then controller of the Tasmanian Aborigines on Flinders Island, reporting progress amongst his charges, says: 'they are not now satisfied as here to fore with one garment, i.e. a frock coat, but require trousers also, and their raiment is in general kept in clean and proper order . . . the females . . . likewise wear undergarments which they keep clean and in good order'.[61]

Once Aborigines were more commonly seen dressed like Europeans in the 1840s and 1850s, white colonists converted moral indignation about nudity into a different form of patronising criticism. As if seeking futher justification for their contempt, they reformulated their ideas by means of a new form of vilification. This was manifested in ruthless caricatures of what they regarded as the Aborigines' misappropriation of European clothing. Dress was a sign of 'civilisation', and its supposed misuse provided clear indication of what was believed to be the blacks' degraded nature.

Those who dressed differently from white people, or wore hardly anything at all, or who used European dress in an unconventional way, became the butt of endless jokes and anecdotes. These reinforced existing bourgeois prejudices, and helped to promote the idea of the Aborigine as a clownish figure, whilst at the same time legitimising white superiority and colonial domination. Mrs Meredith, for example, relished the blacks' comic use of portions of European clothing: 'one Wellington boot was sometimes worn, unaccompanied by any other article of apparel, and great was the pride and grandeur of him who could button his upper man in a dress-coat, that alone being considered an ample costume'.[62]

Literary texts such as these are often supported by visual quips and cartoons. For instance, a number of stereotypical images were produced of Aboriginal women wearing crinolines, accompanied by men in top hats, as in the caricature *Native Dignity* by S. T. Gill (Plate 15).[63] The crinoline was an ideal garment with which to compare the supposedly primitive habits of the native people to the cultivated artfulness of the well-dressed lady about town. In a Melbourne *Punch* cartoon of 1860 entitled 'Nature and Art', the situation is reversed but to the same effect. The European woman wears the crinoline and the image hammers home the cliché of 'art' (or civilisation) versus untamed 'nature'.[64] The crinoline was also used to promote the image of Aborigines as eccentric. A 'semi-civilized' Aboriginal woman with pipe in mouth, presented to C. H. Allen in the 1870s, was described as 'stalking in great pride through one of the towns of Queensland, with an enormous crinoline and a pink gown, or some other castaway dress of her white sisters hanging over it, and this she lifts up in a remarkable manner whenever she crosses a street'.[65]

Increased commercialism and urban development during the nineteenth century had profound effects on Aboriginal people, whose traditional customs of dress were regarded as inappropriate within such Europeanised environments. Official controls were imposed on their appearance in towns, as well as in country areas; the insidious effects of contact with whites meant that traditional clothing habits were gradually replaced by European dress. Intervention into the appearance of Aborigines was substantial, affecting traditional skills and radically altering black customs. Aborigines, except to some extent in the case of the Tasmanian people, were unable to resist official and cultural pressures and rapidly absorbed many European dress practices.

The physicality of the unclothed appearance of male and female Aborigines was extremely contentious for whites. Thus officials, settlers and missionaries sought to coerce them into wearing European garments. Aborigines were perceived to wear such clothing only in proximity to whites, and their assumption of European ways was regarded as sporadic and idiosyncratic. At the same time, Aborigines of either sex who adopted some degree of European dress were ridiculed by the dominant race. This was partly on moral grounds, but also because of the whites' anxiety to preserve their own racial superiority.

The presence of Aborigines in Australia meant that there were further distinctive dress practices that set the colonies apart from Europe. As well, the blacks' assumption of the whites' clothing was by no means thoroughgoing. In many instances articles of dress were worn in a manner that challenged the European norm. All these factors added a particular dimension of difference to colonial attire and behaviour.

**15**  S. T. Gill, *Native Dignity*, watercolour (Dixson Galleries, State Library of New South Wales).

# PART II

# Colonial Dress, 1840–1901

# 5

# DRESSING THE PART:
# URBAN CODES—CLASS AND GENDER

Following the report of the Molesworth Transportation Committee of 1837-8 and the abolition of transportation to the eastern colonies, Australia entered a complex phase of social and cultural development. Populations in urban areas in Australia began to rise markedly, together with increasing prosperity for the middle classes. Sydney and Hobart were already flourishing towns in the 1830s and Melbourne, settled in 1836, grew with phenomenal rapidity. Adelaide was surveyed in 1837. Despite financial dislocation and unemployment during the depression of the early 1840s, immigration policies and the newfound wealth of the gold rushes further expanded colonial urban areas. Australia had as well a huge migrant inflow in the first half of the century. It is recorded at the remarkable rate of 9 per cent per annum until 1860.[1]

The effective doubling of the population every eight years had a significant effect on social patterns in the colonies and this was reflected in clothing. A dichotomy of appearance had been evident in the early years between the elite on one level and the 'non-respectable' workers and convicts on the other; this changed into a society whose dress was much more diverse. Immigrants of many different nationalities were attracted to the colonies and they brought with them their own local habits. The resulting cosmopolitan nature of dress gave towns like Adelaide a colourful appearance. Here in 1845 Irish, Scotch, German, Chinese and French were amongst the ethnic dress differences that were recorded.[2] William Howitt described the streets of Melbourne in 1853 as filled with the people of numerous nations who appeared in their typical attire, including Americans, Persians and Chinese.[3] He also noted Turks, Lascars, Negroes and many other races in 'strange' clothing.

Yet the rapid growth of colonial towns and related industrialisation in major urban areas caused much of the cultural diversity of mid-century clothing to diminish. Whilst some ethnic groups like the Chinese continued to wear their own styles of dress in many parts of Australia, this was not generally the case in urban areas.[4] Here by the 1860s the dress of other cultures, common in the previous two decades, had virtually disappeared. Urban attire ostensibly moved closer to that of Britain and for the most part a more homogeneous form of clothing was to be found. Even so, travellers continued to notice ways in which a distinctive 'colonial' appearance manifested itself and how out of place they felt in their clothes of the 'mother country'.

As the European population of Australia rapidly expanded until about 1860, that of the Aborigines is estimated to have suffered a catastrophic decline. Controversial new estimates suggest that the pre-contact Aboriginal population was much larger than previously believed and that the extensive growth of the white population was in fact a displacement of the large number of original inhabitants, not a net increase in the total population of the continent.[5] The appearance of those Aborigines who did remain in cities and towns lent an 'exotic' and characteristic dimension to Australian life. According to one commentator, the 'painted feather ornamented natives' in their strange costumes, with savagely wild gestures, gave Melbourne a most singular aspect in 1845.[6] The town continued to be so regarded in the late 1850s, partly because of blacks in metropolitan areas who were still to be seen with their hair matted and wearing opossum cloaks or blankets.

A significant feature of Australia by the mid-nineteenth century was its high degree of urbanisation and the dominating nature of its capital cities. One-quarter of Australia's population lived in these cities by 1861 and total metropolitan growth outstripped that of the rest of the population in the two decades after 1871.[7] The population of Melbourne (and surrounding suburban municipalities) increased substantially in the 1850s and 1860s. Between 1871 and 1881 the area grew by 37 per cent compared with only 18 per cent in the whole of Victoria.[8] This emphasis on urban living had important implications for dress practices across all classes and social groups.

## Urban Dress

It is generally agreed that the environment of nineteenth-century European cities, and the crowding of urban life, had a major impact on social relationships and on public appearances. Cities brought large numbers of people into close daily contact, whilst the increased pace of urban life and associated constraints shaped the clothing worn by all classes. At the same time city life with its attendant complexities produced increased anxiety about the need to observe and interpret dress signals.

There is a number of generally accepted theories which relate to the development and meanings of clothing within the context of life in European and American cities. Some of these are summarised by Elizabeth Wilson in *Adorned in Dreams: Fashion and Modernity*.[9] These theories centre on the dress of the bourgeoisie, who allegedly developed discreet forms of street clothing in order to protect and distance themselves from the inquisitive gaze of the urban crowds. This refinement of attire was not merely an assumed disguise. It has been proposed that urban clothing was in fact redolent with subtle and expressive clues that subverted its apparent anonymity. Indeed, social differentiation was in part the ability to understand and decode the nuanced languages of manners and dress. To some degree these hypotheses can be applied to Australian cities since the traditions of Europe, and Britain in particular, were transposed to the colonies. Yet it is less the similarities than the many differences that need to be examined in order to understand the nature of colonial urban dress.

Indeed, serious problems arise when applying existing theoretical models of urban life to the Australian situation. For example, Sennett in *The Fall of Public Man* uses historical changes in behaviour, speech and dress, especially those that took place between the eighteenth and nineteenth centuries, in order to present a theory of bourgeois expression in society.[10] His argument deals primarily with the public life of urban dwellers, especially those in London and Paris, but he contends that his hypothesis applies to other Western capitals. Unfortunately his premise implies that all cities are formed on a northern-hemisphere pattern, thus excluding any possible differences that might exist in other places, like Australia. In fact each colonial city had its own class structures and formulations, demographies, patterns of economic growth, climate and social behaviours, and had variations from European cities as well.

In the Australian colonies, despite the high degree of urbanisation, the capital cities were significantly less densely populated than, for instance, American cities of a similar size. Melbourne's population was considerably smaller than that of London, Paris or Chicago, and there was a marked preference for suburban rather than inner-city living; this was encouraged by the development of railways, which began in the 1850s. Although there was a huge boost to the total metropolitan numbers in the 1880s, the population of the central district of Melbourne declined markedly compared to the outer metropolitan areas.[11] Similarly in Sydney the suburbs were preferred as places of residence to the inner city by the late 1870s. These less intense material conditions were distinct from major European and American cities, which generally had denser central populations.[12] This inevitably inflected colonial behaviour and had repercussions on social interaction and the interpretation of clothing signals.

In addition to this, rural dress (a vestige of the working-class dress of the early settlement years) was worn alongside urban clothing in colonial towns in the 1830s and 1840s, for the strong demarcation between country and urban clothing that would emerge in the 1850s was still under negotiation. The actual relationship between town and country life was frequently close, bringing all categories of workers, squatters and overlanders into contact in various ways. S. T. Gill's 1845 painting, *Rundle Street, Adelaide* (Plate 16), represents a range of classes and occupations in the town's main thoroughfare. It includes a number of country people who have come into town, such as (on the left side) wagoneers in rural dress bringing produce to market. By contrast, other male citizens are in urban dress: top hats with well-fitting jackets and pantaloons.

That bush clothing was not unusual in towns had much to do with the seasonal mobility of labour. Draymen, bushmen and stockmen in country dress were in fact recorded in Sydney, Melbourne and Brisbane throughout the nineteenth century.[13] In Sydney, even late in the century, the population varied with the seasons, swelling in

**16**   S. T. Gill, *Rundle Street, Adelaide*, 1845, watercolour (Art Gallery of South Australia).

winter when rural workers sought employment in town. The cost of city clothes was beyond the means of such men and these workers continued to wear in town the garments they already owned. The links with rural life remained strong, especially in smaller towns. Even in the late twentieth century the dress of the farmer or primary producer in Akubra hat and moleskins can still be seen in Australia's larger towns and cities, but until recently it has signified the conservative but prosperous values of country landowners.

Generally speaking, most colonial urban dress was closely modelled on European styles, fabrics and behavioural rituals. Much fashionable dress was imported or made up in accordance with overseas patterns. Nevertheless the specific demographic, economic and class patterns in the colonies, and the disproportionate ratio of men to women still evident after mid-century, in the emerging suburbs and fringes of metropolitan areas, shaped the overall social practices of Australian clothing in distinctive ways. In particular, there were openly acknowledged regional differences between Australia's cities. For instance the British journalist Twopeny, in his informative though personalised account of *Town Life in Australia* of 1883, interpreted the varied nature of social life in Australian towns and provided a register of comparative urban differences for use by potential immigrants. He claimed that the quasi-metropolis of Melbourne was the most fashionable of the colonial cities, and disparaged Sydney for being essentially provincial. He suggested that in the latter town, 'nobody seems to care much how they dress, and without being exactly countrified in their apparel, the Sydneyites succeed in looking pre-eminently dowdy'.[14]

The whole question of regional differences in Australian dress is somewhat problematic. Style and taste varied from one colonial city to another and to an extent these differences still prevail. Even today, Brisbane men and women are considered to be more casual in their dress than Melbourne dwellers. Although some of the variations had more to do with climatic differences, trade preferences and industrial progress than with local styles, perceptions of these distinctions clearly existed in the nineteenth century.

Before the specific characteristics of colonial dress can be discussed, it is important to have some clear understanding of the general development of middle-class clothing in Britain. Here a move toward homogeneously dark clothing for men's urban daywear had become generally accepted by the mid-1840s, although it was far less uniform than scholars like de Marly believe.[15] In contrast to the practicality of male attire, the dress for women of this class became correspondingly more colourful; waists were tightly laced and the full skirts were cumbersome to manage.

Australia followed this model to a degree, as the merchant classes adapted themselves to sedentary and entrepreneurial kinds of work. Portraits of the middle classes of mid-century show the men wearing dark-coloured or black outfits consisting of frockcoats, trousers and waistcoats, often offset with a fashionably tall top hat. Such sombre business uniforms for men, and even their somewhat richer evening attire, marked out their lives and social practices distinctly from those of their wives. The latter were shaped into the form of an hourglass by their firm corsetry and wore bright, decoratively trimmed gowns made of flimsier fabrics and elaborate millinery. This dichotomy was sustained until the later 1880s and 1890s when, for a number of reasons, streetwear and some leisurewear for women grew closer to that of men and became increasingly practical in colour, fabric and in style.

As in Britain, the dress of young bourgeois girls was distinct from the dress of adolescent boys; their clothing differed slightly from women's, chiefly in the shorter skirt and apron or pinafore. Boys were dressed like girls until the age of about six and then put into sailor suits, breeches or pantaloons until they reached early puberty. Some fine examples of these feminised dresses and small suits of young boys are now in the collection of the Western Australian Historical Society, Perth. Subsequently they dressed in a manner similar to men, and by about the age of fifteen the clothes of the son were virtually identical to his father's.[16]

Information about how the separate roles of urban working-class colonial men, women and children were defined by their clothes is not substantial and emanates chiefly from middle-class sources. It seems that the contrast between the everyday dress of men and women of the working classes was somewhat less marked than for the bourgeoisie, although there were some occupational and subcultural exceptions like prostitutes and larrikins. Unfortunately very little working-class dress survives, and photographic, painted and engraved images of working people were shaped by the prejudices of their production. Contemporary official documents which describe the clothes of working people show that the outer garments for men, like those of the bourgeoisie, were made from much heavier fabrics than those for women.[17] The styles of dress were sexually differentiated in that men wore readymade moleskin trousers and jackets, shirts and strong boots, and the women print or stuff gowns, aprons, bonnets and shawls; but

**17**    *Stanley Street, South Brisbane*, 1890, photograph (John Oxley Library, Brisbane).

the use of coarse fabrics was common to both. As well, the daily occupational dress of many urban working women was probably less constrained by tight corsetry than that of the bourgeoisie and was much the same as clothing for this class in rural areas. Working-class children, like the lads photographed during a flood in Brisbane in 1890 (Plate 17), wore either cast-off adult clothes or smaller versions of the dress of their parents.

## Men's Dress

Although urban dress for men in Australia was ostensibly a version of that worn in Europe, there were subtle but important features that differentiated colonial dress from that of Europeans. The Eurocentric model of middle-class men becoming uniformly drab in their dress does not match with the colonial experience. Some commentators were unable to find anything 'peculiar' about the appearance of Sydney or Melbourne inhabitants, but other writers in the 1860s and 1870s testified to considerable variances. David Kennedy alleged that fashion was as important for men in Melbourne as in any capital of Europe, but by comparison he was surprised by the great variety of hats he saw in the street which were high, low, straw, felt, white, black, beaver, broad-brimmed and narrow-brimmed.[18] In 1886 George Sutherland considered that Australia, unlike Britain, was the 'land of liberty' in dress and that 'every man seems to wear what he pleases'.[19] It seems then that urban clothing for middle-class colonial men was extremely varied, probably more so than in England and France. Part of this was due to the particular nature of its evolution over time, climatic factors and the links to rural lifestyles but also the manner in which it differed from town to town.

In the early years of urban settlement, one of the primary distinguishing features of dress for entrepreneurs and professional men was the use of cool, lightweight tropical gear. In a letter written by Thomas Gates Darton in 1838, men in Sydney were described as being quite 'Indian' in their style of dress.[20] Tropical or 'Indian' clothing consisted of white coat, trousers and waistcoat of silk or thin wool, accompanied by a broad-brimmed straw hat. Although seldom illustrated, the most noticeable feature of men's dress in Adelaide as well as Sydney during the 1840s continued to be white suits or trousers (without waistcoats in summer), Indian silk blouses and broad straw hats.[21]

In each of the major colonial cities, this tropical clothing was replaced by dark suits and top hats at different times, with men in Queensland responding more slowly to European urban dress conventions than in southern cities. This was partly due to the hot climate and slower pace of life, but also because of smaller populations and the later emergence of industrial development. The replacement of tropical dress varied from town to town, occurring first in major centres of commerce in New South Wales and Victoria. The wearing of heavy, dark woollen trousers, black cloth or tweed jackets and 'chimney-pot' hats was recorded in Sydney in the early 1850s.[22] It occurred fractionally later in Melbourne where, at the end of the 1850s, working men seemed more practical in their dress compared to the dark, hot clothing of the affluent classes. In fact, variable rates of changeover to conventional city suits gave a specific character to each of the colonial capitals.

Smaller, more conservative towns like Brisbane were markedly slower to adopt the sombre fashion. It was hardly seen in the Queensland capital until the 1880s, and white or light-coloured jackets and trousers continued to be worn throughout the century. White tropical suits, silk coats, boaters and helmets could also be found in the smaller and less commercially active towns of Adelaide and Ballarat in the 1880s. These garments continued to be worn in New South Wales country towns too, but only in summer.[23] Elsewhere, except for Queensland, they rapidly disappeared as an urban fashion. Yet older residents continued to wear them, and appeared more sensibly clothed in their tropical garments of linen, silk or light wool coats and trousers compared to those in the 'old country costume'.[24]

Alison Lurie has suggested that the use of 'British Colonial White' was a 'portable sign of status, and symbolically transformed military occupation and commercial exploitation into justice and virtue'.[25] This is no doubt correct in part. White clothing was certainly difficult to clean and was a status symbol. Yet Lurie does not acknowledge its practicality in hot climates. Nor does she explain why only some of Australia's towns, like Melbourne and Sydney, readily abandoned tropical white. This was despite Britain's overwhelming and continuing commercial interests in all the colonies, including Queensland.

According to William Kelly, an Irish magistrate and businessman, Melbourne adopted European urban dress quite suddenly during the gold rush.[26] In the mid-1850s the city underwent a profound transformation. New buildings and commercial activities accelerated, accompanied by the appearance of elegant shops and tastefully displayed merchandise.[27] Melbourne seemed to have become 'civilised' almost overnight, and its newfound mercantilism extended easily to the appearance of the citizens. Melbourne crowds had presented to the eye of William Howitt, early in 1852, a set of carelessly dressed men looking like manual workers, in blue flannel shirts, boots and cabbage-tree hats. But by the following year, after an absence of only four months, his contemporary, Kelly, claimed to have observed a remarkable alteration in the way people were clothed. The change matched what he testified to be a miraculous event in Melbourne—something 'truly wonderful, not to be imagined or understood in the ordinary growth of Old World Cities'. The casual garments of the country had been equally miraculously transformed: 'Respectable men had mustered up moral courage to wear frock-coats, and merchants ventured to the Chamber of Commerce in the regular British "bell-topper", some of the nattier going the length of sporting kid gloves.'[28]

Henceforth, black frockcoats, trousers and bell-toppers (top hats) became typical dress for Melbourne businessmen and were worn throughout the 1860s and 1870s. Slightly more informal morning coats became prevalent by the 1880s, and adventurous dressers even wore lounge suits.[29] Occasionally light tropical clothing was still worn there in summer. Vernon Lee Walker, an ironmonger's clerk who arrived in 1876, was surprised at the prevalence of silk coats and Indian pith helmets, and he considered it hardly safe to wear a brown hat.[30] Yet in the 1870s in Collins Street, black top hats would have been almost ubiquitous for affluent men and increasingly for their clerks as well (Plate 18).

Commentators regarded the colonial habit of adopting British urban fashions as uncomfortable, and as sheer folly especially in hot weather.[31] The foolishness of these clothes made the casual and practical nature of rural clothing seem more 'Australian' and all the more attractive. As urban dress was seen to be quite unsuitable for the Australian summer, the question of 'reforming' colonial men's dress was raised from time to time in the popular press. But it was really not until the 1920s that male dress reform became a significant issue, as it did in Britain. In Australia calls for reform, although sporadic, were made specifically in response to prevailing medical theories of heat and the belief that hot climates had a detrimental effect on the physical development of white races.[32]

Despite the varied nature of city dress in Australia, commentators frequently described men's clothing as virtually free of class differences. Newcomers seemed uneasy at the apparent lack of social differentiation, and this made them all the more critical of the appearance of Australians. Most agreed that colonial men looked extremely shabby and unkempt. Presumably they were more used to the custom-tailored suits for which Britain was well known, rather than the readymade clothing commonly worn in the colonies. The prevailing opinion was that Australian men's dress looked quite different from that worn by men in London or Manchester.

**18**  *Afternoon Sketch in Collins Street, Australasian Sketcher,* Jun 1879.

## Women's Dress

As with men's clothing, urban living and its associated activities, pleasures and commitments had a significant impact on bourgeois women's self-image and outer appearance during the colonial period. Fashionable streetwear and private attire for assemblies and balls followed styles in Europe quite closely, although visitors claimed that women's dress in Australia still had an identifiable quality and some regional differences.

Gowns for special occasions, provocatively and tightly corseted, were either imported or made locally following the latest styles of Paris or London. A judicious mixture of imported and colonial-made garments was a feature of ladies' wardrobes throughout the period. That of Annie Bowman, who married the wealthy Adelaide pastoralist Edmund Bowman in 1884, was typical of her class.[33] Labels on her gowns and millinery, now in the Art Gallery of South Australia, show that she purchased from dressmakers in London, Adelaide and Melbourne.

From about the 1870s dressmakers' labels begin to be stitched inside colonial women's gowns, shoes and hats. Whilst these often name specific colonial dressmakers, or stores like Farmer and Co. in Sydney, they sometimes include the name of a European supplier as well. Quality garments often came from Europe via local outlets; this complexity of supply is typical of the Australian market. Alternatively, local labels can obscure the fact of foreign manufacture. There is an elegant pair of bronze kid shoes with Louis heels, c.1880–90, decorated with beads and lined with pale blue satin, in the National Gallery of Victoria; they bear the Melbourne label Moubray, Rowan and Hicks, but they were undoubtedly made in Europe.

It is important to note how closely Australian women paid homage to styles of dress in Paris (not London) from the 1820s onward. The dominating influence of French fashion has been acknowledged in respect of nineteenth-century American dress, but virtually ignored in Australian fashion history.[34] The admiration for French styles and the quality of their designs was partly an affectation, but also a way in which the bourgeoisie could maintain and reinforce their sense of social refinement. London was the central clearing house for European and American goods and thus quantities of so-called British exports may have appeared more numerous than they were in reality. In effect the strength of the Parisian influence remained undiminished in Australia. Even in the 1940s women's magazines like the *Women's Weekly* were given over to articles on the significance of French couture; in the immediate post-war period, clothes by French designers were shown in all the capital cities with an astonishing degree of success.

The authority of France as the fashion capital of the world suffused published accounts of colonial dress as well as ladies' diaries. It was equally evident in the discriminating use of French words in conversation, in the names of small stores and in retailers' advertising copy. In 1861 the urbane Mrs Ramsay-Laye, who came to Melbourne as a new bride, found to her surprise that her Paris trousseau would serve her well. In her Parisian clothes she maintained that she always had the satisfaction of being well dressed and in good taste.[35] Parisian fashions, not British, were sent to Melbourne for the Queen's Birthday celebrations in 1861, and according to one commentator, 'the influence of the Parisian milliner or tailor is as potent in Sydney or Melbourne as in the gay capital of France'.[36]

Australian women, particularly those of the middle classes, were preoccupied with fashion within the constraints of their individual means. Their mid-century gowns for special occasions, of whatever origin, were styled from brilliant-coloured plain silk or brocaded fabrics—blues, greens, pinks, yellows and lavenders. Bessie Riddell described these dresses in her family diary. One of them which she herself wore was like 'danger signals'—made of a green fabric with red blobs.[37] Unlike men's dress, many of these magnificent garments with their boned bodices, wide skirts and tightly corseted waists survive in Australia's costume collections, as well as the somewhat later gowns with their more slender shape, bustled skirts and quieter colours. An example is the rust-coloured corded silk gown, with jacket and fishtail bustle skirt, of c.1870, labelled 'Victoria House—Farmer and Co.', which is held in the Powerhouse Museum. Intricate in cut and trimmed with deft handwork, lace and ribbons, these gowns mark out the extremes of gender differentiation and demonstrate the passively decorative role expected of bourgeois women at this time.

In the 1870s and 1880s French fashions, novelties and accessories continued to exert a strong fascination. The thrust of fashion news in widely diverging papers like *Tabletalk*, the Brisbane *Courier* or the *Sydney Mail* was a mixture of information from both Paris and London. English and Parisian millinery was sold by large department stores who also stocked a great variety of quality French and British fabrics. All the large shops in Sydney, Melbourne and even Brisbane employed agents in Europe and Britain to conduct their import business. James Hunter, who had six 'Boot Palaces' in Brisbane, employed agents in Paris, Vienna and other Continental cities, 'whose sole duties are to catch the latest fashions and send out samples to me here'.[38] The *Queenslander* had a resident correspondent in France who sent regular information to Brisbane, and it offered a cut-paper pattern service to the home dressmaker.[39]

Despite these close links with European styles, Twopeny believed that 'the French *modistes* manufacture a certain style of attire for the Australian taste . . . a compound of the *cocotte* and the American'.[40] This would suggest that to his mind there was a subtle distinctiveness in Australian dress that was not merely an uncritical acceptance of European taste, but one that was generated by local women and unique to the colonies.

Besides European influences, the effect of American styles on colonial women's fashion needs to be acknowledged. This was especially prevalent in the high-quality shoes available in the 1890s. American shoes had supplanted British footwear in the colonial market by about 1894, partly because they were cheaper but really because of the finish and softness of their patent and other fancy leathers.[41] Sydney even had an American Shoe Company in George Street in the 1890s, selling modish forms of footwear to local ladies.

Despite the closeness to European fashion ideals there was also some regionalism in colonial women's fashions, constituted by a subtle mixture of local factors including choice of colours, fabrics and dress styles. Certainly the climate, particularly in the tropical north, determined the kind of lightweight fabrics which women chose for their gowns.[42] There were also minor regional differences in taste between urban centres. Twopeny undoubtedly regarded Melbourne styles as different from those of Sydney and other towns: 'gorgeous and flash dresses are very rare in the smaller cities', he claimed.[43]

Further evidence can be found. Lucinda Sharpe, the female pseudonym used by William Lane for a series of letters to an imaginary girlfriend in America, published in the *Queensland Figaro* in the 1880s, described the subtle but definitive quality of local Brisbane fashions: 'Dresses here are rather different to dresses in the States. Nationally, I say that we are ahead; but I wouldn't be a bit astonished, between you and me, if this out of the way colony didn't fly newer fashions than we did in Chicago.'[44]

Lucinda went into some detail about local styles. 'Walking and house skirts here are about the same except that they are a little longer, only just clearing the ground behind, and not leaving a good inch or so clear as yours do. The waists are very different, never being "basque", but ending just below the waist.' According to Lucinda, Brisbane clothing stores had their own character as well and the service was very slow. Prints and silks were twice as dear as Chicago, but gloves and hats were much the same price, and lace 'ever so much cheaper'.[45]

In the sunny climate of Australia women were more likely to wear bright colours than in Britain, but quieter colour schemes for formal daywear, including calling, shopping and walking, were advocated by local etiquette columns in the 1870s and 1880s. In 1883 Twopeny himself noted that the fantastic dresses for which Melbourne ladies had been notorious were fast disappearing, and that 'bright colours are still in vogue, but they are not necessarily loud or unpleasant beneath the austral sun'.[46] This change is reflected as well in actual garments held in costume collections, which tend to be of more subtle colours of blue-green, grey, rust and mole. Evening gowns could still be quite startling in colour contrast in the 1880s, like the magnificent, vivid black and cream satin gown, with alternating diagonal stripes, trimmed with lace, ribbons, artificial flowers and glass buttons, now held in the collection of the National Trust, Victoria. Despite continuing comments like that of Beatrice Webb in 1898, who considered the appearance of Australian women to be quite 'fresh and flashy', criticism of the brash dress of all social groups, other than prostitutes, was to diminish considerably by the later part of the century.[47]

Garments illustrated in fashion plates and surviving in costume collections show that intricacy of pattern and elaborate decoration were still keynotes of women's dress even in the late 1870s and 1880s. By this time the cumbersomely wide crinoline had been replaced by a fashionably slimmer, more sexualised silhouette dependent on skilful cut, and sometimes a small bustle or tournure. Images of dress worn for social occasions, including balls, the races, and the theatre, reveal that sleek and alluringly shaped garments were popular (Plate 19).

Some surviving formal garments—like the ivory taffeta, figured silk gown of 1877 labelled 'Doak & Beattie, Robes & Nouveautes, Sydney', held by the National Trust Victoria—show that these were still copiously ornamented and extremely tightly fitted at the waist and hips.[48] This tightness restricted walking, as the crinoline had done in the 1850s, sustaining the notion that bourgeois women were quite inactive and still heavily dependent on men. This clothing in fact masked changes occurring within the lives of women as they grappled with exhortations to become more sexually attractive to their partners rather than merely moral guardians of the home.[49]

Nevertheless, by the late 1880s there was unquestionably a change in taste toward much simpler styles of dress for urban wear. This was, of course, not unique to Australia but symptomatic of a more widespread stylistic change that was occurring in European women's fashionable dress.[50] The reduction in decoration of daywear was dramatic. 'Our Ladies' Corner' in the *Illustrated Sydney News* in 1890 commented on this change in women's fashionable style, away from decorative trimming to a greater emphasis on the cut and fit of gowns.[51] Fashion columns emphasised the new taste for drab colours, tailored skirts and suits. According to *The Woman* in 1892 this more sober dress, which was an 'integral portion of the wardrobe', included dark, serviceable prints, shirts, skirts, ties, jackets and so-called 'tailormades'.[52] Some of the new taste was due to the austerity of the depression, and some was a kind of flirtation with masculine dress codes due to the effects of the rational dress movement. All in all it was symptomatic of a larger cultural change to generally more masculinised female clothing which diminished to a certain degree the gender differentiation, so pronounced in the 1850s and 1860s.

*Australian Etiquette* in 1885 advised that dress for summer could be bright and cool

**19** *The Autumn Races at Flemington, Australasian Sketcher, Mar 1881.*

but that colours, echoing those of men's garments, should tend more to greys, browns, olives and black, especially for streetwear. It maintained that 'the light showily trimmed dresses which were formerly displayed in the streets and fashionable promenades are now only worn in carriages'.[53] *Cole's Conduct* suggested that would-be ladies should never be conspicuous or wear decided colours, large patterns or extraordinary shapes. *Cole's* etiquette book was published some time in the 1890s, and its advice for women to choose generally plainer colours and simpler styles was indicative of the general changes that were being advocated. The text suggests that 'it is a test of your style being really very good that only the fashionable should be fully able to appreciate it'.[54]

There were some pleas to abandon the corset, and slightly informal teagowns were sometimes worn; otherwise there is virtually no evidence to suggest that urban colonial women adopted dress reform clothing until the 1890s, except to wear popular 'aesthetic' colour schemes and 'art' fabrics.[55] For instance in 1888 Foster and Kelk in Brisbane had a 'Liberty Room' where ladies could have 'classical' or 'artistic' costumes made up from imported Liberty designs. As well as this, teagowns, with their looser fit, were commonly worn as a somewhat more casual alternative to the fully formal gown and were often made up in 'artistic' fabrics. A Brisbane fashion model, posed in Poulson's photographic Queen Street studio in 1889 (Plate 20), wears a heavy winter teagown from Finney Isles and Co., which has ample medieval-style sleeves and pseudo-classical drapes in the 'artistic' style. It provides an interesting comparison with the vivid red and yellow, open-robe teagown, recalling a medieval or renaissance garment, with sham hanging sleeves and lace jabot, now in the Powerhouse Museum. This was worn by a Sydney lady in the last decades of the century.

## Rational Dress

By the 1890s the issue of dress reform, or so-called rational dress, was being more widely discussed in the popular women's press. Only in these years do calls increase for a more sensible kind of dress for 'advanced thinking' women. This attire was to be light, warm, healthy and unrestrictive, as a way of gaining freedom from the tyranny of tight clothing, masculine dependency and high heels.[56] In 1894 the *Woman's Voice* ran a competition for the best rational dress suggestion, and quite a number of articles were published on the subject in other women's magazines.[57]

A good deal of this publicity about rational dress was simply polemical, although retailers certainly saw in it sound potential for profit.[58] In Australia overtly rational dress and bifurcated garments like divided skirts and knickerbockers were considered quite controversial, even for cycling, and in 1895 the Melbourne Cycling Tourists' Club banned 'lady' members from club rides in such attire.[59] In any case, functional styles of clothing were already prevalent for women's streetwear by this time. These were the female equivalent of the male suit, openly demonstrating the use of masculinised features such as ties, waistcoats and stiff collars, obviating somewhat the need for truly radical styles. It is likely bifurcated rational garments were not commonly worn in everyday life.

**20**   *Model in a Teagown, The Princess,* 1889 (John Oxley Library, Brisbane).

## Dress of the Underclasses

The history of colonial dress for the urban working classes is hard to determine. There are virtually no surviving garments and few documents help to form an accurate picture of their living conditions. Twopeny, for instance, showed little inclination to penetrate

**21**   Albert Fullwood, *Sturt Street, Ballarat*, c.1887, gouache (Collection: Ballarat Fine Art Gallery).

the facade of supposedly affluent Melbourne life. Unlike Freeman in his book *Lights and Shadows of Melbourne Life*, published in 1888, or Henry Varley's investigation into Melbourne's urban evils, he failed to describe the appearance of the town's 'low life' that included beggars, chimneysweeps, costermongers, itinerant musicians and match sellers, and that segment of the city's population that lived below the breadline.[60] Kennedy estimates this to have been as much as one-quarter to one-third of the whole population.[61] Freeman, on the other hand, had a penetrating eye for working-class city 'types' and their appearance. In drawing a comparison between the distinctive dress of costermongers in London and the 'indifferent' style of those in Melbourne, he carefully described their impoverished clothing, noting the dirty and patched moleskins, short jackets and blucher boots of this class of worker.[62]

In the same way that many written commentaries avoided the issue of colonial poverty, numerous visual images of city life were celebratory, aiming to show well-dressed citizens in their best light. Fullwood's gouache of *Sturt Street, Ballarat* c.1887 (Plate 21), representing the busy traffic, falls within this genre of urban celebration of the well-appointed bourgeoisie. There are men, women and children in orderly groups, some travelling in opulent carriages, showing no evidence of the real poverty that existed.

In keeping with the contemporary interest in the categorising of social 'types' was the classification of adolescent social rebels from inner urban areas as larrikins. The term was first used in Melbourne in the 1870s, although it appears in official police records only from 1880 onward.[63] Gane suggested that they were one of the few 'types' in Australia who could be determined by their dress, unlike the numerous 'types' in Britain, including mashers, swells, music-hall gents and men of *ton*.[64] The characteristic dress of larrikins was recognisable by the 1870s, although these youths were sometimes identified merely by being 'hang-dog in look and careless in attire'.[65] By the second half of the 1880s, larrikins were more commonly described as appearing villainous and even spectacular in their mode of dress. This was comparable to other subculture groups like the London 'loafers' and San Francisco 'corner-boys', who wore exaggerated forms of bourgeois dress as a form of anti-authoritarianism. These garments were curiously prophetic of the 'Edwardian' drapes adopted by British Teddy boys in the early 1950s. Larrikins flaunted exaggerated dark or black suits with tight waists and velvet collars which were almost Spanish in style. Their trousers were either bellbottomed or cut very tightly, like 'fleshings', as can be seen in Whitelocke's *The Larrikin* of 1885 (Plate 22). They wore black slouch hats or small round hats, high-heeled shoes with extremely pointed toes, and sometimes 'loud' silk ties and jaunty waistcoats.[66]

Young female associates of larrikins were often described as gaudily dressed, but this was fairly typical of young, urban working-class women. Those with money to spend on their appearance, particularly tailoresses and milliners' assistants, tended to be aware of dress and wear exaggerated versions of the latest modes. Such a shop-woman's daughter was described, with a certain amount of moral disdain, in the *Australian Journal* in 1868. She was wearing 'a short dress, and *Marie* fichu, and ephemeral bonnet and *Benoiton*, and a chignon as large as a moderate size pillow, and a pair of crystal earrings two inches and one line in length, and a colonial brooch of the magnitude of—well, say a small cheese plate'.[67]

Whitelocke's bold engraving of *Cafe Belles* (Plate 23) reinforces literary descriptions of these fashion-conscious working-class girls of the mid-1880s, showing them wearing garments with outrageous hip swathes and ostentatious accessories, and behaving boldly by smoking in public.

Many other writers drew attention to the excessive style of Melbourne working women. For instance, Freeman described barmaids with their black lustre dresses and exaggerated headdresses, or alternatively with their hair cropped close like a boy, hinting at some gender ambiguity within urban bar culture of the time.[68] Yet even his text is silent about other categories of working women, and he never discusses the dress of the truly poor and destitute.

Despite the common presence of larrikins and other working-class groups in urban areas, Twopeny regarded the lower classes as homogeneous and claimed, like many other authors at the time, that they were better dressed than the equivalent social group in Britain. Gane, for instance, found almost no beggars in Melbourne. He ascribed this to the generally high wages.[69] These views were echoed by Edmond Marin La Meslee, who claimed that the city had no one in rags, for everyone had the means to dress decently.[70]

Generalised descriptions such as these, that view the colonial working classes as a single entity and concentrate on their allegedly high standard of living, are suspect given the amount of poverty, the fluctuating labour market, low-paid occupations and the deprived life of the underclasses during this period. Whether some working people were better off and better clothed than their counterparts in Britain is much debated. Jackson considers that Australians were better fed and clothed, compared to the standards of the old world.[71] Shirley Fitzgerald, on the other hand, contends that there is room

22  Nelson Whitelocke, *The Larrikin*, illustration from *A Walk in Sydney Streets*, 1885.

**CAFÉ BELLES.**

23 Nelson Whitelocke, *Cafe Belles*, illustration from *A Walk in Sydney Streets*, 1885.

for debate on the subject of standards of living and that evaluation of a range of factors beyond wages and prices is required before conclusions can be drawn.[72] She suggests, in fact, that many material aspects of life in Sydney deteriorated after 1870. Similarly White, seeking to challenge the notion of a 'worker's paradise', considers that accounts of Australia's high standard of living were exaggerated. He contends that the supposed benefits of high wages were available only to a small minority of skilled white males.[73]

## The Problems of Class

Dress, behaviour and speech are gendered cultural practices and also key elements in the way class difference was constituted and understood in the nineteenth century. In Australia it was difficult to determine class through dress codes, and accounts of appearance and social behaviour are punctuated with mention of these difficulties throughout the colonial period. This is not to suggest that in Britain comparable anxieties about class were not generated by dress codes. Rather it was the degree of contentiousness about the issue in Australia which is under discussion here.

For instance Clara Aspinall, sister of a Melbourne barrister, considered that the difficulty of telling by appearance who was 'important' was more bothersome in Melbourne than anywhere else in the world. It led her to experience serious problems with mistaken identity. As she said, it was exceedingly troubling to see 'ordinary people in very glossy coats' who were actually socially significant and to see distinguished-looking men who were not 'gentlemen'.[74] Many accounts other than this one ascribed to colonial inhabitants a lack of orthodox signifiers of social distinction in dress. This was a very clear acknowledgement that public statements about class were difficult to read.

Yet the problems of recognising class, as described in so many contemporary texts, do not seem to match entirely with surviving garments or with visual images. S. T. Gill's image of *The Queen's Birthday Review* of 1856 (Mitchell Library); for instance, clearly shows the top hats and fine clothes of the elite watching the parade, with a group of less affluent pedlars in the foreground in ill-fitting working-class dress.

Some surviving garments are clumsily made, and lack the finesse and craftsmanship one sees in the dress of the upper classes, suggesting that class differences were quite apparent. The Swan and Guildford Historical Society own a curious three-piece blue striped silk wedding gown of the 1880s, with a somewhat crude fringed overskirt that is quite roughly constructed, and more than likely homemade. The National Trust of Victoria too has a poor-quality black cape of the 1890s with silver beading (labelled George and George Ltd), that is obviously a lower-class garment.

Despite material evidence of this kind, there were current perceptions and acknowledgements that it was not easy to identify class in Australia. In the early years of settlement, one set of responses to the difficulties came from the elite, who sought to confirm their status by dressing in an overly elaborate manner. With the newfound wealth of the 1850s gold rush, and an emerging and consolidating bourgeoisie, this form of ostentatious dressing became less reliable as a form of class indicator and other techniques were found both in dress and in etiquette.

The precise historical impact of the gold rushes on Australia is an issue still under debate, but the gold euphoria had profound implications for the colonies' dress history. It is assumed by some historians that the gold rushes had a major effect on the shaping of Australia's class structure and that a characteristic sense of identity along with a democratic spirit was forged amongst those who lived and worked on the goldfields. This is borne out by contemporary comments that indicate 'the diggings, like the grave, had a wonderful tendency towards levelling distinctions'.[75] On the other hand, scholars suggest that the extent of the democratic attitude in the late 1850s has been exaggerated.[76] Penny Russell and Beverley Kingston both question the existence of egalitarianism in Australian society. Russell postulates that it is a myth maintained by historians concerned only with what have traditionally been regarded by men as important realities, such as economics and politics.[77] She further suggests that an upper social stratum continued to exist in Australia after 1860 and that it was ladies who worked assiduously on behalf of their husbands to create and sustain this class and its social mores.

In general terms the gold rushes raised overall income and meant that on average the Australian consumer was relatively prosperous. Jackson has contended that, although the distribution of wealth was most uneven, Australia was better off in per capita income at the end of the period than any other country in the world.[78] For some, increased income changed the way they dressed. The presence of 'new money' helped foster the belief that Australians (particularly women) favoured clothes that were brash and ostentatious. Newly acquired and unexpected wealth meant that former distinctions of social class were challenged by a new kind of snobbery of money. All in all, the gold rushes contributed to the increasingly complex nature of class difference and its dress signifiers from mid-century onward.

The maintenance of an elite social group in Australia, as inferred by Russell and Kingston, was certainly a crucial factor, borne out in descriptions of class differences in colonial dressing. At the same time the middle classes experienced increasing anxiety at the intrusion of emancipists and newly rich into their social sphere. The result was a considerable degree of tension between the need to be fashionably dressed and the fear of overdressing. Negotiating social position through clothing was clearly a pertinent although time-consuming aspect of the fluctuating hierarchy.

The allegedly ostentatious dressing of the newly rich meant that one of the usual means of defining class became unreliable. Thorstein Veblen believed that conspicuous consumption was the specific mark of an elite, leisured class.[79] However, in a society where both the elite and the newly rich could afford elaborate clothing, but where there was no inherited aristocracy, the conspicuous display of wealth, in Veblen's terms, did not necessarily aid in the demarcation of class boundaries. The denotation of class could be better served by discreet behaviour and refined appearance. Conspicuous display could at times be wasted effort. The inefficacy of such display was confirmed by Twopeny during the 1880s. He suggested, in fact, that the life of wealthy ladies was a 'reign in hell'. These women, he claimed, could afford to wear notably expensive imported couturier gowns but there was no one to appreciate this degree of superiority, and ultimately their taste was dulled through want of the means of comparison.[80]

From mid-century the expanding circle of tradesmen, entrepreneurs and their wives tried to upgrade their social status by assuming the trappings of the elite. In response to this, the upper social classes tried to distance themselves even more from allegedly ostentatious and 'brash' dressing by their reserved manner and discreet appearance. Some reacted to 'vulgarity' by various strategies of social distancing, either by punctilious attention to etiquette, by cultivation of French mannerisms and dress, or else by withdrawing in some way from social contact. When social disruption was severe in Melbourne during the mid-1850s, William Kelly noted a rapid increase in the use of colonial livery for servants.[81] The bourgeois maintenance of the correct style of servant establishment (where such staff was available) was an important way of marking out their difference from the newly rich, whose 'extemporised' servants often appeared ridiculously dressed.

Aside from physically withdrawing from social contact, the upper bourgeoisie sought to distance themselves through discretion and restraint in dress styles. For instance, a 'lady' such as Mary Allport deliberately signified her position by 'dressing down'. In her diary entry for 1853, she noted that her preference for a refined form of fabric was determined by the necessity to preserve her social position. This was in contrast to a digger's wife who had purchased eighteen yards of bright yellow satin for a gown. 'I bought three dresses for myself, but two were only prints which ladies must be contented to wear now, if they would be distinguished from the "slumocracy".'[82]

The use of dress as a means of determining class was a continuing and constantly shifting aspect of colonial life. In the latter years of the century newcomers continued to be baffled by the difficulties of assessing the social place of urban men by their clothing. Pinpointing that of women became less difficult. Increased urbanisation and the marketing of fashion brought the dress styles of women closer to British models. Despite some regional differences in urban dress, it is clear that there was less that was characteristically Australian about women's clothing than about that of men, since it was more closely related to imported European styles. On the other hand, throughout the second half of the century, 'new chums' regarded Australian men of urban areas as quite distinctive in their manner of dressing.

# 6

# FROM A DIFFERENT CLOTH: ETIQUETTE AND SOCIAL PRACTICE

Clothing and etiquette were primary markers of gender in the nineteenth century. Notions of masculinity and femininity were fabricated as a result of particular sets of social practices that produced bodies which in gestures and appearance were recognisably masculine or feminine.[1] As well, class identification and social position were demonstrated via unwritten messages circulating through clothing, demeanour and, of course, speech. In the colonies, patriarchal power and its disciplinary practices, that flowed through to dress and appearance, functioned in quite specific ways. Factors governing relationships of class and economics, along with regional demographic patterns and the climate, affected local tastes and dress practices. At times conventional middle-class gender distinctions in clothing and associated behaviour were severely disordered. Indeed some circumstances of living in the colonies put such a severe strain on the norms of bourgeois social practice that many British notions of class differentiation were undermined.

## Private and Public Life

The colonial middle classes sought a separation distinguishing the private and public spheres of life by the 1850s, following similar social patterns in Britain.[2] By the late 1840s the gentry in Sydney had begun to detach themselves from the new stratum of tradespeople, merchants and speculators in town, and stayed out of public view in their harbourside mansions. Increasingly, barristers and financiers were building their villas on the north shore of Sydney Harbour, taking advantage of the spectacular views. The popularity of suburban living gathered momentum, and middle-class families as well showed an increasing tendency to reside in the suburbs. By the 1870s Sydney's suburban population had outstripped that of the city. Older areas like Woolloomooloo were becoming terraced developments, whilst outer suburbs like Chatswood, St Leonards and south-east through Alexandria to Botany were expanding rapidly. In Melbourne there was a substantial population growth in the 1850s and new suburban areas like Essendon, Carlton and St Kilda were laid out to meet the growing demands of this expansion.

The trend toward outer-city living was closely implicated in the development of bourgeois life in Australia as elsewhere. With spheres of life in town and suburb clearly differentiated by mid-century, gender distinctions in the colour, style and fit of male and female dress, although quite noticeable in the 1820s and 1830s, became increasingly evident. Businessmen wore dark and discreet clothing as a sign of their purposefulness within the industrial and commercial workplace; in stark contrast, their wives wore highly decorative and tightly waisted floor-length gowns for public occasions. From the 1870s this situation changed somewhat, chiefly due to the new types of dress for both sexes which were flooding the market, most noticeably specialised leisurewear and sports clothes. These retail developments followed similar dress patterns in Europe, but with definite colonial resonances.

The ornamental dress worn by colonial middle-class women in the 1850s and 1860s, as has been shown, was characterised by its striking ebullience and brilliancy of colours—deep greens, gold, crimson—and also its elaborate nature. Bourgeois observers frequently claimed that the tendency of Australian ladies to wear bright colours verged on being improprietous and gave 'no repose for the eye'.[3] A number of boldly designed garments held in collections like that of the National Trust of Victoria support this perception of women's dress. Complaints about the overly decorative nature of women's fashions began early in the century and resounded throughout the colonial period, even when streetwear was tempered by a change of taste in the 1880s and 1890s. The critique served the interests of the imperial colonisers for, like racial criticism, it represented the colonies as socially inferior. These complaints were generally couched in terms of moral judgement, and the subtext of many of them seems to have been an anxiety about the degree of class transgression in the colonies.

The reality was that ladies of the elite in Australia, many of whom seemed to make dress a fulltime hobby, were subject to a constant tension between the concern for maintaining a suitably stylish appearance and trying to avoid the shame of vulgarity. An extremely narrow line marked the difference between being finely dressed, thus achieving social visibility, and seeming to be overdressed. As Kingston has shown, in the colonies it was the simulation of good taste, exclusivity, and the money to indulge it that replaced aristocratic breeding as the criteria by which women were judged.[4] For this reason the stakes for being fashionably dressed were social status and the power that came with it. Observing the nuances of fashion became almost an obsession with bourgeois women.

Although commentators frequently described the brilliance of Australian women's clothes, etiquette columns in the 1870s and 1880s advocated quieter colour schemes for urban activities of the affluent, such as calling, shopping and walking. There was a particular emphasis on simplicity, refinement and discretion for the well-dressed urban lady in Australia. The exact character of the upper middle classes was somewhat precariously sustained at this time, and in the slightly dubious moral climate of Australia it was crucial that bourgeois women did not expose themselves too noticeably in public spaces. Particular insulation from the 'vulgarity' of the emancipist and the working classes was required. Formal etiquette demanded that 'the true lady walks the streets, wrapped in a mantle of proper reserve, so impenetrable that insult and coarse familiarity shrink from her'.[5]

Bourgeois women's clothing was considered to be essential to the formation of their role as genteel, unobtrusive and pleasing adjuncts to men. Repressed and moulded by clothing mores, they were disciplined into believing that their femininity was defined by fashion and etiquette. Maintaining a dependent, appropriately decorative, appearance was an important signifier of class and a way of attracting a suitable husband, although in Australia there was little shortage of marriage partners early in the century. With demographic changes later in the period, the nature of the competition changed. In Victoria during the 1880s, for instance, the numbers of young women becoming available as potential wives increased, and consequently changes occurred in the tenor of instruction manuals and etiquette books. These focused on subtle suggestions whereby the pressing problems of attracting and keeping the attention of men could be overcome.[6]

Fashions for women formulated their femininity and their sexuality, but equally they were a form of learned but unspoken language of decorum, conveying precise messages about age, status and availability. Women were persuaded to believe that attention to fashionable dressing which signalled their inactivity in the formal workplace was a social duty and a necessary part of the display of domestic consumption (Plate 24). As with behaviour and language, clothing was a vital indicator of the family's social class. On public occasions such as visiting, balls, entertainments and shopping, women of the bourgeoisie dressed in such a way as to demonstrate precisely the degree of affluence of their husbands. This link between clothes and wealth had particular significance in Australia, where the lack of an aristocratic class placed the social emphasis squarely on visible indicators of wealth. When in 1885 the *Australasian* drew attention to the fact that a wife must dress according to the position of her husband, the text held special meaning for colonial women: 'all wives who hold the position they ought to in the marital partnership will know exactly the sum adequate for their requirements'.[7]

Ladies displayed their elaborately cut and styled clothing, their fine gowns, furs and jewels in certain prescribed public spaces of the city.[8] Their dress had to be suitably visible but equally subtly managed and accessorised. Ceremonial display on the Block in Melbourne or Sydney's Domain was a social activity that marked a contrast with the informal private life and dress of suburb and home. According to one commentator in the 1880s, 'it is on the Block that people show off their new dresses, bow to their friends, cut their enemies and, chatter small talk'.[9] There ladies would shop and display their finest outfits in a bright but dignified parade, rarely moving beyond areas such as Collins Street into more 'unceremonious' and risky sections of the city where there was an 'American go-a-head spirit', unless on urgent business.[10] On sunny days their gay attire made the long street look like a 'restless rainbow'.[11]

These 'accepted' areas were thus quite distinct from the disordered and less salubrious parts of town, such as the Rocks in Sydney where working women were recorded with 'dirty clothes, slovenly manner and repulsive countenances'.[12] Respectable spaces

**24**    *Model in a Fashionable Winter Gown, The Princess*, 1889 (John Oxley Library, Brisbane).

were also quite unlike Bourke Street where there was a more threatening social environment, comprising a greater 'mixture' of classes. Here, for instance, women of the
'demi-monde' were seen to flaunt themselves and to wear more garish-coloured gowns
than their married middle-class counterparts.[13]

In contrast to their sumptuously decorative and later rich but tailored streetwear,
and of course brilliant evening dress, colonial ladies wore simple garments within the

informality of the home. By mid-century, advertisements show that morning robes and gowns were common, as well as informal wrappers and ottomans. Later in the century, when competition for partners became more intense, women's informal as well as formal dress came under increased scrutiny. Young housewives were given specific instruction in the ways that they might safeguard the affection of their husbands. The charm of a neat and tidy appearance at home was alleged to be the most powerful of attractions in this regard.[14]

For breakfast, young women were advised to wear a neat print working dress of cotton or stuff, high at the neck and with long, close sleeves.[15] When their husbands returned at night, housewives were told to be ready to greet them, lightly clad in 'cool-looking' stuff. An article in *Castner*'s magazine of 1875 described the importance attached to wearing neat, readymade or homemade 'wash and wear' morning gowns in the house, where showy outdoor dresses were not recommended.[16] Ladies performing household tasks were advised to appear in washable gowns of this kind, and later it was blouses and skirts of a sensible length. These could be purchased readymade, and some local ready-to-wear clothing was available for women through mail-order by the late 1880s. In 1890 the magazine *Dawn* was offering morning gowns readymade in pretty striped prints and assorted colours in four sizes, adjustable with cord and eyelet holes for varying waists.[17]

Urban men, whether in large towns or smaller provincial centres, also changed into informal clothing such as pyjamas or loose jackets on their return home from work. The home represented a refuge from the hurly-burly of commercial life, where men could engage in pleasurable and 'unbusinesslike' activities. The young wife was advised to prepare for her husband's return by laying out a home jacket, pantaloons in which 'to loll at his ease', and a shirt made roomy at the neck.[18] This private aspect of the life of urban bourgeois man is seldom represented or discussed in descriptive texts.

## Recreational Dress

A clear distinction was made between occupational and recreational clothing for working-class and middle-class men by the 1870s. In Australia this separation occurred at the same time as the working week was restructured and workers gained progressive and guaranteed rights to leisure time. For instance, all government employees in Melbourne had gained an eight-hour day by 1874 and in 1880 many had Saturday afternoons off as well. With additional time to spend on pastimes including sporting activities, men liked to relax in clothing that was different from occupational or formal wear, be it old clothes or specific recreational dress. James Inglis described men on a leisure outing to Botany in 1880. In a certain sense his description matches with the kinds of clothing worn even today by spectators at cricket or football matches. He writes of motheaten fur caps, slouching sombreros, dilapidated wideawakes, cricket caps, red night caps, jumpers, guernseys and tatterdemalion jackets, instead of the 'natty habiliments' and 'shining beavers' of city life.[19]

The later nineteenth century was a time of accelerated changes to the ways in which leisure time was consumed, and this trademarked 'empty' time was readily exploited by capitalist endeavour. As new consumer desires and needs were created and extended forms of activities developed for men, women and adolescents, new kinds of purpose-made clothing for recreation and sport came on the market. Although for women specialised leisurewear remained largely the prerogative of the bourgeoisie, the general implications from the development of practical garments for recreational purposes were far reaching. These new types of dress were particularly indicative of the ways in which women and girls were extending the range of pursuits deemed appropriate for them.

The new leisure market was a key aspect of the expanding commercialisation of fashion. This expansion was stimulated in part by the increasing categorisation and subdivision of bourgeois wardrobes into specialised garments for all kinds of pursuits, matching other aspects of middle-class lives that were simultaneously being structured and regulated. The times of the day and the scope of activities were so fractured that the former clear but general division into simply formal and informal activities disappeared. Manufacturers responded to the emergence of new entertainments, pleasures and leisure activities by creating a vast new range of garment types. For the upper and middle classes these included specialised nightwear, morning, dinner, tea and recreational clothes. There were further subdivisions of travel wear, swimming costumes, tennis clothing, regatta and boating costume and dress for team sports. These new types of garment, which in some cases were worn by all classes, were the forerunners of the mass leisurewear industry of the twentieth century, with all the cultural implications it imposes on our modern way of life.

With women and girls pursuing more active lifestyles in the 1870s and 1880s, suitable garments for sports such as calisthenics, gymnastics, swimming, cycling, tennis and fencing were developed. These were sometimes bifurcated for private activities, and masculinised exercise suits, worn without corsets, were used for women's physical culture classes, first introduced in Melbourne in 1879.[20]

Capacious woollen 'sea side' costumes were available readymade for women by the 1870s, while tennis dresses, tennis blouses and light 'sportwear' corsets, designed specifically for tennis and rowing, could be purchased in the 1880s.[21] *Australian Etiquette* advised women to use grey flannel for bathing costumes and to wear these with oilskin caps and merino socks.[22] In the mid-1890s the cycling craze allowed further challenges to prevailing notions of femininity and was yet another opportunity for manufacturers to introduce new, specialised garments for women. Clothes developed for cycling included riding skirts and blouses or bloused jackets, sometimes called costumes, worn with stiff collars, men's ties and straw boaters.

New forms of leisurewear for women were also designed for travel and holidays. Increasingly Australia's urban-based population of the 1880s and 1890s invested the countryside with idealised notions of peace and rural tranquillity. Visits to the country and picnics became popular summer outings as early as the 1870s. Specific yet still elegant clothing for such outings was advised by fashion writers, although for walking and picnics masculinised rational dress with tailored jackets and bloomers was acceptable. According to *Castner*'s magazine in 1876 the country used to be the place where anything was good enough to wear, but this was no longer the custom, and new formal 'countrywear' for women was devised.[23]

Toward the end of the century travel further afield, to destinations such as New Zealand, was regarded as an opportunity to purchase new clothing. In 1899 *Worth's Australian Fashion Journal* recommended a blue serge coat and skirt, a white skirt and coat and half a dozen blouses at least of pale-coloured batistes, cream-coloured lace or crepe de chine 'of a tender hue' for ladies intending to travel across the Tasman and to fashionable watering places.[24]

Changes within the wardrobes of men and women of the bourgeoisie to include specialised clothes for travel, sport and recreation had important meanings for both sexes, but especially for women. It was a particular sign that their roles were becoming less constrained. It was also an aspect of increasing consumerism which marked the beginning of our modern cultural practices of dress.

## Colonial Etiquette

For the bourgeoisie and the gentry in the nineteenth century, appearance and modes of dressing were essential factors of etiquette, defining and proscribing the differences in gender roles. More generally, etiquette and its unspoken rules subtly reinforced and affirmed social position within these groups, while at the same time expanding their circles to include tutored newcomers.[25] Etiquette was fundamental to procedures governing middle-class rites of passage, including weddings, funerals, and changes from childhood to adolescence. In Australia, as in Britain and America, these artful codes of behaviour were part of the essential working activities of the highest class and provided a powerful way for middle-class values to become accepted as dominant.

The manner in which bourgeois women were identified with the domestic and moral spheres of life allowed them the time to attend to the rules of etiquette, for which they were almost solely responsible. Within upper social groupings, attention to dress and etiquette was often punctilious to the point of being excessive. The minute details of everyday existence—dress, personal behaviour and language—became the criteria for women 'to judge and be judged'.[26] The importance attached to the minutiae of these activities meant that women of the higher classes had a powerful role to play in sustaining the trappings of their class.

The attention to mannered behaviour was present in the colonies from the time of early settlement. The elaborate rituals and conduct associated with dining, calling and introductions, assemblies, weddings and mourning were particularly important to those who regarded Government House as their ultimate ideal. For women, their cherished ambitions and preoccupation with social rules may well have been reinforced by the fact that 'real' ladies were rarely born in the colonies but could, with care, occasionally be made.[27]

Although women had the responsibility of ensuring the maintenance of 'correct' dress styles and behaviour, separate rules regarding appearance and etiquette were clearly defined for men and women. These rules were codified and marketed by means of etiquette books. Australia may have differed from America in the use of such books. For example conduct-of-life manuals were published in significant quantities in America from 1830 onward, but few were published locally in Australia.[28] Newspapers did,

**25**    Eugene Von Guerard, *A Melbourne Man and Woman*, 1854, drawing (Dixson Galleries, State Library of NSW).

however, carry lengthy articles on manners from the 1830s and undoubtedly imported texts were also in use.[29] The only known locally printed etiquette book before the 1850s is *Hints on Etiquette*, an English bestseller reprinted in Hobart in 1838.[30]

The moral tone dispensed by such etiquette instruction provided a foundation for later texts, many of which continued to be published in newspapers and magazines. These followed the same predictable patterns and exhortations, with their emphatic instruction regarding refined manners and 'good' taste. *Australian Etiquette*, as a late example, published in 1885, follows this path of a moral exemplar, admonishing women with the reminder that, 'a woman will remember that to dress consistently and tastefully is one of the duties she owes to society'.[31]

Despite the importance of bourgeois etiquette, at times the exigencies of life in Australia were in marked contrast to the bourgeois vision of women as charming, dainty and fashion-conscious. Circumstances, particularly in rural areas, placed great strain on women trying to follow orthodox codes of dress and etiquette. Ladies maintained prescribed dress standards as far as they were able, but hardships and isolation imposed considerable constraints on their clothing and social behaviour.

Visitors to colonial towns and rural areas frequently remarked on the lack of gentility and behavioural niceties they had observed. Some of this was due to sheer physical circumstances. Melbourne in the early 1850s suffered from shocking dust storms and torrential rains, with roads at times practically impassable for pedestrians. Von Guerard's satirical drawing of *A Melbourne Man and Woman* of 1854 (Plate 25) shows the lady, with her gown pulled up unceremoniously in contravention of discreet codes of bourgeois dressing, trying to negotiate the appallingly wet and muddy conditions of the street.

Although colonial women were deemed to fail in their efforts to match the standards of femininity displayed by their British counterparts, travellers found it hard to pinpoint the exact factors that made them look and behave so differently from their expectations. 'Australian ladies are very different to English' wrote Gertrude Gooch in 1862.[32] The implication behind such statements was that in the colonies the carefully constructed norms of bourgeois dress, and the defined roles for women, were being undermined. The unspoken subtext was that the formal British notions of sustaining class differences were not maintained in Australia.

Indeed, these codes of etiquette were frequently followed quite imprecisely. Mrs McConnel, writing in her memoirs about her first impressions of Queensland in 1849, found that 'no calling cards were ever used in Brisbane, but that it was as well to have a piece of chalk in my pocket so that I might write my name on the door if people were out'.[33] Card etiquette, designed for more compact areas like Mayfair, Kensington and Bath, was simply cumbersome when negotiating the sprawling suburbs of Melbourne or even Brisbane in the 1880s and 1890s.[34]

One of the problems for the colonial middle classes was that the growing preponderance of a stratum of entrepreneurs, and the new materialism of gold, caused an acceleration in social mobility without supportive education in etiquette and the accompanying ways of dressing. This put a great deal of strain on bourgeois ideals and ways in which femininity was prescribed. In Melbourne the power of women to form the manners of colonists was said to have been almost neutralised by the amount of vulgarity induced by newfound wealth.[35]

The nouveau riche, who mixed fairly commonly with the colonial elite, were alleged to demonstrate a complete lack of propriety in selection of garments, fabrics and styles. This caused a good deal of anxiety. For instance in the 1850s, William Kelly incredulously described the Governor in Melbourne receiving female 'hoi-polloi' in the morning, who were wearing entirely inappropriate low-cut evening gowns for the occasion.[36] Louisa Meredith found women in Melbourne attending a fete on the poop of the *Royal Charter* in the early 1860s, dancing in large hats, small bonnets and delicate gowns of satin, silk and muslin. She tells how as they gyrated they revealed to her view 'the occasional discrepancies of thick cloth boots and ebon hosen'.[37] This combination of evening dress with working boots and black stockings was an unmistakable sign of individuals whose behaviour and taste did not accord with her own middle-class mores.

The impropriety evident at a small-town colonial assembly is clearly lampooned in Abbold's drawing of *A Bendigo Ball*, 1851-4 (Plate 26). The lady is unchaperoned, and for a man to smoke and wear a country hat with his hands in his pockets in the presence of a lady in evening dress was highly indecorous. The contrast between male and female attire in this drawing is noteworthy, and reflects the disjunction between the casual nature of the man's clothing compared to the formality expected of the woman.

There were demographic problems in the colonies too. Not only did the classes often mix in a way that was alarming to the bourgeoisie, but Clara Aspinall claimed that there were no elderly dowagers at Australian balls, which would have been the way to give tone and richness to assemblies.[38] In other words there was often an unacceptable

**26**   Charles Abbold, *A Bendigo Ball*, 1851–4, ink drawing (Dixson Library, State Library of NSW).

age and social mix, as well as lack of decorum, at social events, which the upper-bourgeoisie found hard to accept.

Early marriages in the colonies, with the onset of the responsibilities of childbearing for many women, occasioned premature ageing, which affected conventional notions of feminine elegance.[39] The genteel world of French or British fashions, and the prescription that women's role and behaviour be refined, was often mitigated by the greater demands for housework. The bourgeois ideal of domestic gentility was dependent on the presentation of well-appointed homes, carefully orchestrated social events and well-regulated children. These practices in turn required an adequate number of reliable servants.[40] However, Australia had a more or less permanent 'servant difficulty', and there was a good deal of expense and trauma involved in obtaining these symbols of bourgeois status.[41]

This lack of servants was a major factor preventing the kind of genteel lifestyle and fashionable decorum possible in Britain, and other colonies such as India and Africa, and it meant that ladies had more daily household work and nursery chores.[42] Consequently they had less time to spend on their appearance. 'Some do dress shockingly. Ladies are so ill supplied with servants in the colonies, and have to do so much with their own hands, that it would be unreasonable to expect them to be handsomely dressed.'[43]

Problems with obtaining reliable servants were endemic to the colonies, and the gold rushes compounded the difficulties. In 1852 John Godley noted how discontented the New South Wales elite had become, because masters and servants had changed places. He stated that 'society so far as it is connected with entertainments . . . is at an end in Sydney'. His views were echoed by his wife Charlotte the following year. She described how many of the best families had been driven back to England by the gold rushes, hoping to return to Australia when ladies did not have to open their own street doors.[44]

Often homes did not have either nurseries or nannies, so that children spent more time with adults. Indeed, children were viewed as headstrong and ill-disciplined. According to one account, 'Australian children are just like the vegetation here for neither submit to much control.'[45] Preserving a sense of acceptable behaviour and fashionable style was difficult and at times it was very artificially maintained. Joseph Elliott, a newspaper proprietor in Adelaide who did not keep a servant, wrote an extremely detailed account of his home in 1860, describing how he and his wife and their three small children slept in the same bedroom.[46] The intimate lives of the whole family were so interrelated that it suggests that the prescribed and orthodox distinctions between public and private space were not well defined at all. Indeed families with this kind of association are unlikely to have been able to maintain conventional codes of masculine and feminine behaviour.

## Rural Life

Middle-class women were constrained into believing they were the arbiters of taste and the upholders of traditional social values, and that the power to transform men's behaviour lay in their hands. It was a middle-class perception that the increasing number of women who joined men in the bush from the 1840s onward added a 'civilising' dimension to the outback.[47] Although the imbalance between the sexes had nearly disappeared in towns and urban areas of New South Wales by 1851, the ratio of men to women in country areas remained high (60.8 per cent of country residents were men). By 1856 the percentage of women in rural New South Wales was little changed and was still well below the ratio in the city of Sydney, where there was an almost even balance of the sexes.[48] The ratio of men to women varied quite considerably from colony to colony and between rural and urban areas. In 1871 in Queensland for instance, 48 per cent of women still lived in rural areas, and throughout the whole of this colony the masculinity ratio remained higher than elsewhere, with 171 men to every 100 women even in 1900.

Women in rural areas felt a compulsion to keep up acceptable standards of dress and behaviour, although to some extent there was an understanding that urban dress was not necessarily appropriate for country wear. Women who lived on remote stations, like Rachel Henning in North Queensland, regarded certain styles of garment as 'too good' for the bush.[49] The rough conditions inevitably took their toll. Charles Forman's wife Jane for instance, living at Mount Egerton, found that thirteen months away from a shop window caused her to 'forget all about fashions' and wear only a cotton hood for a bonnet and a cotton frock.[50]

On the whole, bourgeois women attempted to give the impression that stylish dressing and social niceties were sustained in the country, regardless of circumstances. Katie Hume, wife of a government surveyor at Drayton, a small community near Toowoomba, described the preoccupation with fashion in 1867: 'I remember Charlie being much amused at my taking a "dinner dress" into the Bush, but I assure you people dress here almost more than at home.'[51]

The strength of bourgeois prescriptions about dress and femininity meant that women in country areas were subject to particular tensions in their endeavours to match ideals with social realities. They had to contend not only with inadequate communication with fashion centres, but also poor shopping facilities in remote bush and goldfields areas, and often limited dressmaking services. Penelope Selby, writing to her sister in 1847 from Farnham, Port Fairy, noted her need to 'furbish up' her silk gowns because she was living in a slightly more 'civilised place'. 'But I am rather at a non plus for I saw in the paper that the sleeves are worn full . . . Now mine are large with vengeance, I wish I had you or some fashionable [sic] to give me a shape.'[52]

Without adequate servants in the bush, these attempts to maintain some semblance of style were especially taxing. Louisa Meredith, describing social mores in Van Diemen's Land, noted the pretentious habit of hard-working country ladies, who had no female servants, receiving visitors in their finest clothes at any time of the day, pretending they had nothing else to do. Guests like herself had to wait endlessly for them to get dressed in order to present themselves in their finery for the formal reception.[53]

In the bush female fashion could well lag at least twelve months behind European styles, and in some places even more.[54] When bush and station dwellers like Penelope Selby and Rachel Henning journeyed into town, they experienced the pleasurable anticipation of new clothes to be acquired, but they also felt some trepidation at their shabbiness. Selby wrote of the way she herself had laughed at old-fashioned figures she saw in Melbourne after 'a few years rustication in the Bush'.[55] Henning also described her anxiety about travel to Sydney in 1865: 'we shall be taken for aborigines, I expect, when we present ourselves in the town'.[56] She was referring partly to her dilapidated clothes but more particularly to her skin, which had become deeply tanned as a result of the tropical sunshine. For a middle-class woman at this period, a pale, clear complexion conveyed notions of purity and was a sign of gentility. By comparison a coarse and tanned skin was associated with working people and manual labour.

For women busy with housework or daily station business, 'modernising' their clothes required a substantial input of time and effort unless they had the means to employ a dressmaker. Katie Hume expressed the great difficulty she had in this regard when fashions were changing radically in the 1860s. She complained wearily to her sister in 1868: 'I suppose all my things will want altering, & goring to suit the present fashion & it is a great trouble.'[57] Katie Hume, unlike many, was occasionally able to obtain the services of a dressmaker in Brisbane, and her knowledge of fashionable styles was consequently quite up to date.

All classes of women in rural areas wore stays and the cage crinoline made of hoops of whalebone, which was a particular norm of fashionable city dress in the 1850s. They continued to wear these restrictive garments throughout the 1860s, and even later, despite the fact that hooped petticoats, although helping to support the weight of several petticoats, were very wide and cumbersome. On an extremely uncomfortable journey north of Rockhampton in 1862, Rachel Henning wrote of the difficulty in cramming crinolines and dresses into a valise which her brother had to carry before him on his horse.[58] Charles Eden, in his autobiographical account of Queensland, published in 1872, marvelled at these understructures which were such an extremely fast-selling commodity in Queensland station stores, although they had ceased to be worn in fashionable circles the previous decade.[59]

As one would expect, the crinoline was adopted as a fashion in rural areas some time after it was taken up in town. Jane Forman, who lived in the Victorian countryside in the late 1850s, described the relativity of fashion at this time: 'quinalines of course are all in Donoly they dress like the west end of London but yer in the country they are colonial' (sic).[60] Once crinolines were established as a style, the insistent way in which rural women, regardless of class, maintained this constrictive form of dress reveals the strength exerted by fashionable norms and the manner in which these extended beyond the lives of the bourgeoisie. It also indicates that women's role in life was more circumscribed by clothing than that of men. Although crinolines were likely to have been reserved primarily for special occasions, photographs of women in rural areas often show them posed self-consciously in front of their slab huts wearing crinolines beneath their best gowns.

Not surprisingly, many middle-class descriptions of women's rural costume evade the harsh realities of life in remote outback areas. They are sanitised accounts which merely point to the virtues of women who sustained bourgeois styles of dress and who maintained a neat and clean appearance. There are only a few vague hints to suggest that middle-class codes of dress were ever transgressed because of climatic or environmental factors. One rare case is described by Penelope Selby at Yarra Yarra in 1841. She wrote of her dress at four o'clock in the afternoon when the temperature had reached 98 degrees: 'it consists of shoes, stockings, shift and cotton gown. Mrs Dawson leaves out the stockings but the flies bite my legs. Three hours from this time I shall be glad to put on all my petticoats and make a good fire.'[61]

The diaries and letters of outback women convey an extraordinary commitment to maintaining orthodox bourgeois standards of dress and behaviour. The likelihood is that middle-class women were reluctant to record those frequent occasions when they were not dressed according to the conventions. Perhaps men seldom saw women in casual clothing or else felt inhibited about recording it. Surprisingly, in 1857 *Sydney Punch* hinted at another side to colonial women's activities out-of-doors. It jokingly contrasted a young woman riding sidesaddle in public, wearing a finely tailored riding habit, and the same young lady in the bush astride her horse, forgetting the rules of ladylike behaviour, 'when she thinks nobody is looking'.[62]

A myth has developed about settler women, partly as a consequence of their own writings, that centres on their dedication to the virtues of homemaking and raising families. Yet in many instances the lives of these women were very different.[63] The myth has overlooked the numbers of women who did not conform to this particular stereotype. Women worked extremely hard in rural areas and were vital as producers within the family farming unit. They ploughed and sowed alongside men and were active in control of stock and in the dairy. In fact some women like Constance Ellis, who led an adventurous existence in Western Queensland far from the niceties of bourgeois life, blithely contravened accepted notions of appropriate feminine behaviour.[64]

Other women lived outside the family unit, about whom the records are virtually silent, such as those co-habiting with sawyers and cedar-getters, or on the goldfields. These women displayed impropriety both in behaviour and morality. Their dress was equally unorthodox. Photographs of the Lynch sisters, for instance, who were timber workers living near Kingaroy at the turn of the century, indicate that they did not wear corsetry or tight underclothing as many women did. These images, now in the Oxley Library, show the women dressed in skirts and roughly fitted blouses, with rolled sleeves and wide masculine-style brimmed hats to cover their unconventionally loose hair.

Victorian bourgeois morality precluded women from the use of trousers in public except in rare cases and for certain forms of exercise. It would have been sensible to wear trousers in rural areas and undoubtedly some women did. Yet there is only minimal evidence to show that men's clothing was worn by women in the outback.[65] Riding astride in divided skirts was certainly a common practice, although only in outback areas. The National Gallery of Victoria has a pair of open-legged underdrawers (1868–80) made of unbleached cotton and designed for riding, which could be used either under a sidesaddle skirt or for riding astride. When women did wear masculine attire, it was usually as a form of disguise. For instance there are accounts of women wearing men's clothing in order to travel unmolested, and some texts mention frightened women in homesteads dressing in their husband's clothes when they were alone in order to deceive Aborigines.[66]

Although they may have failed to record the actual clothes of rural women, bourgeois newcomers were certainly preoccupied with noting the deterioration in colonial manners. Katie Hume, who came out from Britain to marry her surveyor husband, tells in her diary how women's behaviour in Queensland differed from her expectations. In 1866 she travelled to Warwick where she met the Gores family of Lyndhurst, whose Queensland-style behaviour she found strange and very tiresome. Katie considered the mother, Mrs Gores, to be ladylike although she had 'roughed it' at times, and there was a certain amount of 'hugger mugger' perceptible in the household. The Miss Gores, the so-called Warwick Flashers, she deemed decidedly 'fast'; they were fond of riding and shooting, and one of them was an undignified five foot nine inches tall. 'The whole family bathe in the Condamine together! It was my first introduction to real colonial young ladies. They have never been out of the Colony & I must say I was reminded of "Gerty" (in Hillyars & Burtons) . . . They talked *almost* as much slang & their manners are very offhand.'[67]

Although bourgeois women living in Queensland, like Katie Hume, endeavoured to keep up the kind of social standards they had been used to in Britain, many ideals about women's lives were challenged and reshaped by colonial conditions. This was particularly so when white women came in contact with indigenous people. Middle-class women were discouraged from developing close relations with Aborigines for fear of contamination, and their feelings about them oscillated between condescension and fear. For instance Rachel Henning found Aborigines to be 'very queer' and their semi-nude appearance distasteful.[68]

In order to minimise their own distaste at the sight of nakedness, women settlers gave the Aborigines whatever old clothes they had available. Otherwise they supplied garments that they had made themselves. 'I am trying to manufacture a dress for Biddy, the black gin, out of two stout blue linen shirts which I got out of the store. I think it will make her a very strong garment', wrote Rachel Henning in one of her letters.[69] In order that the bourgeois order would not be transgressed, white women like Henning satisfied their morality and charitable impulses by imposing their dress habits on the Aborigines with whom they were in close contact. Conversely, Aboriginal women seemed disinclined to resist white imperatives and apparently responded to clothing initiatives with passive acceptance.

The difficulties of generalising about the appearance of outback women are highlighted by accounts of dress on the goldfields. One is tempted to suggest that working women in these areas deviated from the norms of conventional dressing for their class. Certainly they are sometimes described as caring little for their appearance, and looking sunburned, crass and slovenly. Smoking and drinking were common and their general appearance was said to be somewhat masculine.[70] Tattered and 'draggled' gowns were worn 'kilted' high enough to show the tops of thick 'stock keeper's' boots; bonnets were thrown far back; and some women wore gold ear-drops as massive as cattle bells.[71] The vulgarity of diggers' wives became legendary. George Lacy's watercolour of *A Digger's Wife* shows her promenading before a group of male spectators in an elaborately patterned crinoline gown with ruched peplum and a small parasol, all quite unsuitable for the rough conditions (Plate 27).

On the other hand, travellers reported many women working on the goldfields to be fashionably clothed. In 1853 William Howitt found the women at Bendigo more neatly dressed in the afternoons than one would expect in London.[72] William Kelly echoed these sentiments. He had expected women at Sandhurst to wear blankets, but was amazed at the fashionable silks and satins worn on a Sunday. He noted that women were 'wearing their bonnets as if they had been wafered on to the backs of their heads by a Parisian modiste'.[73]

Women on stations were held to be responsible for sustaining bourgeois mores for

**27**    George Lacy, *A Digger's Wife*, watercolour (National Library of Australia).

their entire families, exerting an especially strong influence on the appearance of homestead men. Their men were allegedly persuaded into maintaining a degree of urbane social behaviour that would have been perfectly acceptable in town, and 'should there be a lady on the station, respectability and broadcloth assert themselves'.[74] In 1862 Rachel Henning described her brother, Biddulph, at Exmoor, a Queensland station on the Bowen River, as extremely punctilious and 'not the least roughened or colonialised by his long residence in the bush'. On Sundays, presumably in deference to his sister's wishes, he, 'arrayed in white trousers, white coat and regatta shirt (nobody ever sits in the parlour without a coat) is lazily reading in an armchair'.[75]

On the other hand men living without women in rural areas were acknowledged to be too preoccupied with physical tasks or station matters to have time for social niceties. They were reputed to accord a low priority to fashionable style, for a smart appearance was regarded as something of an encumbrance to men on the land. Robert Harrison, speaking of men who took up life in the bush, observed:

> the first idea of liberty which some seem to possess is to reject decent attire, and after an attempt to imitate a Guy, the next step to perfect freedom, is to discard clean linen, and when freedom begins to be fully developed, the utter rejection of the advances of the tailor and the blandishments of the washer-woman . . .[76]

Where women were not available to run homes and provide assistance with domestic work, men allegedly attended as little as possible to their appearance. Diggers were reputed to undress seldom and did only minimal mending and washing.[77] David Waugh, an unmarried settler near Goulburn, reported that he had an unreliable woman servant, and so he sometimes made his men wash his stockings. He went on to say, 'you would be surprised at the way some bachelors do with their stockings in the mending way— if the hole is at the toe, they tie a string round it.'[78]

During the colonial period in Australia, the bourgeoisie made concerted attempts to introduce and sustain the codes of social practice that operated in Britain. Rituals of social life were rigorously maintained and, if anything, Australians were so anxious about being judged 'colonial' that they worked harder at their behaviour than they would have done in Britain. Even so, visitors to the colonies were astounded at the lack of propriety, especially during the gold rush and in rural areas. In the bush and on stations, social circumstances were not as regulated as in town, and men and women did become less inhibited about clothing and behavioural niceties. Yet the strengths of bourgeois codes of formality were such that, wherever possible, conventional dress practices were maintained, controlled and indeed nurtured, sometimes by the expenditure of extraordinary effort and ingenuity, by women.

# 7

# MATERIAL NEEDS:
# SUPPLY AND DEMAND

Clothing functions within economic systems in complex ways, as does any cultural product. Variable relations of meaning are produced by the outward appearance of people, whilst garments themselves are produced or marketed within different forms of social regime, thus accruing other sets of values and meanings. The manner and conditions under which clothing products are commercially retailed are social practices which are specific to gender and class. Australian shops and retail outlets for clothing in the nineteenth century helped to encode the meanings of dress, and to characterise particular ways in which colonial forms of dress were denoted. The merchandise of stores, from high-class custom-made items to goods sold in outback stores, was shaped by local tastes and requirements.

Major developments in the structure of the dress retail trade, in advertising and mail-ordering, and in the local clothing industries occurred during the colonial period. These changes were interlocked with the growing demands and constructed needs of consumers. Australians of all classes who could afford to do so, both in town and country areas, were able to purchase an increasing variety of garments, custom and readymade. Desires for diversity and changing fashion styles were stimulated by vigorous advertising strategies, and from the 1880s by the expansive and sexualised culture of department store retailing.

Even in the 1820s observers of colonial life were astonished at the tasteful and civilised nature of Sydney, with its fine homes, degree of commercial activity and elegant retail facilities. In the following decade, although small tailoring and specialised garment businesses were increasingly common, often run by women, general stores still supplied clothing as they had done since the early settlement years. For instance in the mid-

1850s, James Gregg, draper, haberdasher, hosier, clothier and grocer of Pitt Street, Sydney, continued to provide customers with fabric and clothing as part of a wide assortment of commodities displayed in the crowded front windows of his store.[1] Similar kinds of shops selling a miscellany of hardware, slops and food were found in towns throughout Australia. Perhaps even more common than such small retail stores were public auction rooms handling mixed business, that included clothing for men, women and children. In 1842 Thomas Champion claimed in his diary that Sydney auction bells could be heard going all day.[2]

As the century progressed the nature of city dress retailing changed dramatically, although rural stores remained limited in their range of goods and their prices were high. By the 1870s mixed businesses, auction rooms and small retail outlets in urban areas were increasingly supplanted by department stores. The main city thoroughfares in Sydney, Melbourne and Brisbane had numbers of these architecturally palatial shops, with goods displayed on several floors. Some like Paterson, Laing and Bruce in Melbourne were serviced by the new device of hydraulic lifts. Advertisements in newspapers and magazines exhorted shoppers to visit stores like David Jones, Farmer's, Finney Isles and Co., and Buckley and Nunn, where in ostensible freedom they could browse through the fixed-price merchandise, unmolested by street touts. Ladies could use the quieter facilities on upper floors and examine millinery, mantles and imported 'fancy goods', elegantly displayed in the grand showrooms. Close by were private rest rooms, like the special suite at Farmer's in Pitt Street, 'of convenience to all lady customers in a climate where the heat is so intense'.[3]

The colonies depended heavily on imported clothing, as Australia does today, especially British goods. By the end of the century American shoes, French and German fancy accessories, haberdashery and other specialist items frequently supplanted British-made. Customers were able to choose between imported items that were varied, cheap and attractive, and the rather limited types of local clothing that were often more practical, but at the same time more expensive. Local manufacturers responded to the aggressive flow of imports, mainly from British sources, by establishing businesses that combined retailing of imported goods with local garment production. The resulting relationship between clothing stores, local tailors and dressmakers, and British agents reveals that the Australian market had its own specialised requirements.

## Local Tailoring and Menswear Retailing

There are few surviving records to show in any detail the working or distribution methods of early colonial tailoring businesses or clothing manufactories. We know that from the 1830s traditionally militant groups, such as tailors and bootmakers, were beginning to unionise, although in Victoria the tailors' union, like others, fell away temporarily after the gold-rush period.[4] New South Wales had a small number of garment manufactories in the 1820s, but the industry developed slowly and was far behind its counterparts in Europe and North America.

The economic growth of the 1830s brought about some increased production but the overall picture was not one of major growth. Competition with imported readymade clothing was fierce. In Sydney during the depressed economic circumstances of the 1840s local tailors railed against those who sold cheap imported London slops which were 'altered' and 'embellished' to give the impression that they were locally made.[5] All through the century wily manufacturers continued to use such ruses to enhance their custom in the colonies.

The few clothing manufacturers operating in Australia during the 1840s did not employ many workers and produced a fairly small range of goods, seemingly all for men. Most used imported cloth even though textile mills were established in all the colonies, and colonial cloth by this time had a reputation for quality, a reputation that lasted throughout the century. So-called Sydney tweed was considered to be more hard-wearing than English tweed and was recommended for men's riding trousers, waistcoats, coats and jackets.[6] The problem for customers was that local cloth lacked the variety and 'finish' of British cloth and was less attractive.

Prices and rates of growth in the clothing trades differed in each of the colonies. An advertisement placed by the Journeymen Tailors' Society in 1846 gives a useful comparative table of the variable tailoring prices in Sydney, Melbourne and Van Diemen's Land.[7] The table demonstrates the regional diversity in Australian tailoring even at this early date, with overall charges highest in Sydney and lowest in Van Diemen's Land.

Some New South Wales tailoring firms expanded into the area of men's readymade clothing in the 1840s, as a way of combining the business of quality custom-made goods with the advantages of ready-to-wear dress. For instance, in 1842 Pite and Preston extended their drapery business in Sydney by establishing a separate Tailoring and Cloth Department. At this period they were catering to 'gentlemen' clients, but they also supplied slops to the public.[8] This followed similar contemporary practices of large London tailoring companies, like E. Moses and Sons, who advertised their services as wholesalers as well as 'made to measure' tailors. It was much the same throughout North America.[9] But in Australia, underlying this form of expansion was the competitiveness of English imports and a diversification within the retailing business, no doubt essential when the economy was so precarious during the 1840s.

In 1842 the Sydney tailoring firm of Henry Haynes was advertising readymade 'Bush Clothing', consisting of tweed coat, waistcoat and corduroy trousers, for which it charged 65s.[10] This was a substantial amount, given that an average jacket, trousers and waistcoat cost between 20s. and 30s., indicating that a sophisticated trade for readymade clothing was being solicited. The same applied to Smith's Colonial Shirt Manufactory in Sydney, which prided itself on its specialised cutting methods. By the 1850s their ready-to-wear shirts, such as 'Eureka' (a type of shirt invented in Britain but also manufactured by other companies), were advertised as well-fitting and respectable, and looking as if a personalised service had been rendered.[11] Readymade items in Australia were thus garments not just for working men but available for gentlemen 'not disposed to purchase the common readymade slop clothing'.[12] In other words, by the 1840s and 1850s a two-tiered, though fairly limited, ready-to-wear industry for male clothing was in place.

Numerous tailoring shops and retail outlets for menswear operated in urban areas by mid-century. Following traditional trade practices, custom tailors like I. Fawcett of Fitzroy, Melbourne, continued to supply women as well with tailored clothing like riding

28  Davies and Co., *I. Fawcett, Tailor*, 1861, photograph (La Trobe Collection).

habits. His shop was photographed c. 1861 with its bales of imported fabric and fashion plates for both sexes displayed in the window. Staff and neighbourhood children crowd together in front of the shop to participate in this event (Plate 28). Tailors like Fawcett often operated mail-order services for their customers. These were important for maintaining commercial contacts and for the distribution of clothing to customers far from central business districts. Marketing strategies of this kind, as well as diversity in the garment trades, were ways in which businesses could survive when competition with imports was intense. Both custom-made clothing and ready-to-wear items could be ordered by mail. Tailors would sometimes travel to customers on receipt of postal directives. William Charles Smith, a Hobart tailor, habit- and pelisse-maker, announced a visit to the country every second month.[13] The firm of Henry Haynes advertised that, on receiving a post-paid letter, gentlemen living within six miles of Sydney would be 'waited on at their own residence' for tailoring requirements.[14]

To assist mail-order customers, and to obviate the need to measure and fit them personally, detailed self-measuring guides were published by tailors, shirt-makers and outfitters. These guides were ultimately replaced by proportional clothing sizes, identified at first by figure types—proportionate figure, stooping figure, corpulent figure, etc.—and later by a numerical system.

By mid-century customers could select from fabric swatches sent by mail, and illustrated catalogues of both readymade and custom-tailored items were available. Morris Jacobs and Co., Sydney general outfitters, published illustrated designs from which numbered items such as frockcoats, shirts and trousers could be ordered by both town and country buyers.[15] This readymade clothing service catered only for men, children, male servants (livery), and women's riding habits. More extensive mail-order services for women's clothes were not in common use until the 1870s, since there was little readymade women's dress manufactured until then.

Mail-orders continued to play a crucial part in Australian dress retailing. By the latter part of the century desirable images of cultured, urban, middle-class commodities were extended widely into remote rural and regional areas and the practice continued into the twentieth century.[16] In the 1870s big department stores like Farmer's and David Jones published seasonal 'fashion book' catalogues for customers of both sexes, and ran extensive postal departments for despatching mail-order goods to the country. Madame Weigel's, a Melbourne business based on postal distribution, developed its mail catalogue in the 1870s, and produced paper patterns of international women's fashions for rural and urban home dressmakers.

## The Clothing Industry

Australia struggled throughout the nineteenth century to develop a viable garment manufacturing industry. Undercapitalisation, the force of British imports and the high cost of labour combined to create major problems for these endeavours. Competition with imports and the small size of the local market inevitably reduced possibilities. Local industries expanded unevenly until the 1870s, marginally increasing colonial self-sufficiency. Loss of impetus in the economy by the mid-1870s was paralleled by an inability to establish further productivity growth, especially in high-quality goods, and the garment industry continued to languish.

The manufacture of clothing on a large scale did not expand to any degree until the mid-1860s, after some mechanisation was introduced and 'outwork' became an established practice. The industry was still limited chiefly to making men's dress. Rates of progress varied from colony to colony and the structure of the industries varied as well. In New South Wales, for instance, the factory system as a whole appears to have been smaller than in Victoria, with more outworkers employed. By comparison, in Victoria the clothing industry was heavily protected by tariffs, and this may have been the main reason for the manufacturing progress in this state.[17] Endemic to the industry in each of the colonies were swings between stagnation and progress, and the inevitable seasonal periods of high and low production.

In 1881, evidence to the Royal Commission on the Tariff indicated that 1873-7 were good years for the Victorian clothing industry, but subsequently the situation changed. After 1877 wages of female workers, who were most numerous in the industry, declined between 20 and 30 per cent.[18] Mostly women and youths were employed in clothing factories, in low-paid unskilled positions. During the 1880s, especially in Victoria, the industry was changing from a craft to a fully mechanised factory process. Working arrangements became looser and apprenticeships fell into disuse.[19] The seasonal nature of the apparel trades contributed to shifts in patterns of consumption and exacerbated the precarious nature of the industry, whilst the cheapening of the methods of production undermined the market for finely crafted, more expensive goods.

Despite something of a boom at the end of the 1880s, manufacturing failed to progress during the depressed 1890s. Factory sizes were reduced, with the expansion of sweated labour practices, and many establishments closed. Prices for local garments dropped substantially and foreign competition remained high, chiefly in specialist lines like ties, socks and underwear. The falling off in the clothing manufacturing industry was partly attributed at the time to high tariffs on imported fabrics, of which there were no comparable high-quality local equivalents.[20] Some industries like shirt-making in Sydney failed to expand at all, in comparison to coarse slop-making, which to an extent held its ground. A report to the New South Wales Legislative Assembly in 1891 attributed the problems in the shirt-making industry directly to competition with imported stock shirts, which were said to be better made, more highly finished but cheaper.[21] These were the same problems that had beset the industry early in the nineteenth century and in fact the situation has changed little even in the 1990s. The Australian retail market is still saturated with cheap, imported garments made not in Britain but in Asia.

## Footwear

Australia's footwear industry in the mid-nineteenth century faced similar problems to clothing manufacturing. Colonial-made shoes and boots commanded the local market in New South Wales from 1840 to 1852.[22] The period also recorded high productivity in South Australia, and shoemakers were able to provide much of the footwear for the local market.[23] Adelaide had four tanneries in full production in 1843, and colonial articles were reputedly preferred to imported ones.[24] One reason for this preference was that English shoes became mildewed on the passage out and were not suited to colonial conditions. Local manufacturers alleged that colonial boots were longer-lasting than English 'slops', and locally made working women's boots would last almost a month, rather than the two to three weeks said to be the average for an English pair.

Although they were more practical, colonial-made boots and shoes were expensive in comparison to imports, thereby reducing their competitiveness. In the late 1850s the prices ranged from 3s. 6d. to 6 or 7s. for an English pair of women's boots, to 12s. 6d. for a colonial pair.[25] It is important to compare the high cost of local footwear with the cheapness of imports, for not until later in the century is there any suggestion that imported goods were regarded as 'luxury' items.

There was a general slowing of the footwear industry in New South Wales during the 1850s and early 1860s. This was partly the result of high wages demanded during the gold rush. Indeed, wages for bootmakers in New South Wales doubled between the 1840s and the 1860s.[26] The sluggish nature of the trade was also partly due to large quantities of goods arriving from Britain. There was in fact an exceedingly strong push by British manufacturers to capture the clothing market in Australia at this period.

A survey of British imports into New South Wales shows that footwear imports rose dramatically in the 1850s, corresponding with a general slowing down of the local industry (see Appendix II).

One evident problem in relation to production costs and output within the footwear industry was that it was slow to mechanise. Once mechanisation was effected, larger quantities of items could be cheaply produced and unskilled boys could be used in the manufacturing process of hitherto uneconomic lines such as children's boots. Lower labour costs in Britain, plus the advantage of even greater mechanisation, meant that imports remained competitively priced even after allowing for transport costs.

The productivity of the industry had improved substantially by 1870. Shirley Fitzgerald estimates that the output of boots and shoes in Sydney reached fifteen thousand pairs a week in 1870.[27] Two articles in the *Sydney Morning Herald* in 1878 gave a full description of the trade at the time, indicating that boots and shoes were chiefly made for men and children rather than women.[28] Statistical data on the output of boot factories are available from 1886-7 onward. Between then and 1889-90 a 16.8 per cent increase was recorded.[29] Boot and shoemaking was one of the most successful of the garment industries. One of the reasons for this can be attributed to its concentration on producing profitable, hard-wearing footwear in preference to fashionable items.

By the 1890s the manufacturers had made a conscious effort to streamline workmanship, and produce a more competitive class of goods. In Melbourne, within a few years, the whole bootmaking industry converted to a modern system of mechanisation.[30] Yet the continuing preponderance of low-grade items made Australia particularly vulnerable to the influx of higher-quality American boots and shoes, with their fine leathers and attractive finish. Firms like John Guest (Sunbeam Trademark) of Fitzroy tried to counter the American push by producing their own wide range of items, including handsewn pumps. Bedggood and Co., a Melbourne firm, responded by introducing Kangaratta boots and shoes in 1895 (Plate 29). This brand used kangaroo skin tanned with a new process that made the leather resemble superior glacé kid. Despite these initiatives, the Americans had virtually captured the Australian market by the mid-1890s.[31] An article on the boot trade in Victoria in 1896 claimed that the outlook in the local trade was more doubtful than it had ever been in the past.[32]

## Imported Clothing

The problems faced by the local clothing industry, in regard to competition from imported readymade clothing, intensified during the gold-rush years. Due to labour shortages, local costs and prices rose. Moreover, the rapid export growth of 1851-3, occasioned by gold, made possible a large increase in overseas goods. In New South Wales, which was a free trade state compared to Victoria, the total amount of imported British-made clothing more than quadrupled between 1848 and 1853, in spite of only a minor increase in population. These figures match substantial increases of other British goods recorded in the 1850s. One long-term effect of the gold rushes was a rising population of prosperous consumers, which made Australia attractive to British exporters.[33] Local products became less competitive and goods, including clothing and fabrics, became more expensive.

**29** Kangaratta advertisement, *Australian Storekeepers' Journal*, August 1895.

Statistics concerning imports of apparel need to be used with care because of the nature of data collection and because clothing could be made locally yet crafted from imported cloth. There is the further likelihood that, until 1884, 'apparel' was partly subsumed within the class of imports designated as 'drapery'. Nevertheless, the New South Wales figures point to an increasing reliance on Britain as a source of clothing supplies from the end of the 1840s to 1853 (Appendix II). Subsequently the amount of imports appears to have diminished, remaining fairly steady in the 1860s and 1870s, although up again during the 1880s. Import figures for Victoria do not provide useful comparisons because of the added tariff.

Clothing imports during the century varied widely, indicating first of all that the dependency on Britain was not a static component of colonial dressing. Imports increased at a period when local clothing manufacture was at a low ebb, thus highlighting British imperialism within the colonial marketing structure at certain periods. At the same time, the dumping of exports on the Australian market militated against any colony expanding and modernising its industries.

Walsh has suggested that the superior quality of imported labour-intensive British goods caused colonial manufactures to suffer.[34] The situation was rather more complex. British imports of cloth, clothing and footwear were not always considered of superior quality, but were widely regarded as desirable because they were cheap.[35] Australian companies like Price, Favenc and Gwyn advertised their readymade colonial cloth clothing as far superior in quality to imported articles, being 'better adapted to the wants of consumers than shewy but worthless English slops, imported to sell only— wear being a subordinate consideration'.[36] By 'shewy' the company was referring to the glossy finish on the English product that was lacking in colonial cloth. According to local manufacturers, working-class customers preferred the inferior imported fabric for its appearance. The prejudice extended to the middle classes. Colonial tweed was worn by them only for stout suits for country or station wear, and tailors could not get the same price for a custom-made suit of hard-wearing local tweed as they could for one of English cloth.

The precise origin of imported goods is not always easy to detect. The complexities of the import trade are well illustrated by the copious correspondence between the Geelong drapers and clothiers, Bright and Hitchcock, and their London agent. These letters provide a detailed insight into the relationships between Australian retailers, their manufacturing contractors, and British agents. In 1870 the company's Australian branch decided to cease purchasing readymade clothes from Britain and buy only colonial goods. The London agent was quick to point out that this was a foolish decision. He indicated that British garments were in any case systematically imported into Australia with 'Warranted Colonial Made' tickets.[37] This reveals the difficulties in establishing the precise origins of colonial manufactures, and the complexity involved in disassociating Australian goods from imports. Ironically, this nineteenth-century problem is still with us: even in the 1990s we are often unable to identify Australian-made goods in our retail stores.

The London agent of Bright and Hitchcock was frequently at a loss to explain the difference between styles that sold well in England and sales in the colonies. He described taste in Melbourne and Geelong as being so consistently out of step with the latest London styles that the extent amazed him: 'the caprice of a colonial taste, often quite different in various parts of Melbourne, seems to fix your sale'. In this instance he was writing about hats, pointing to the variations in taste to be found even within the various shops of Melbourne. He noted as well in 1866 that Australia 'does not adopt everything that takes here'. He maintained that less variety was required in the colonies and that Australian fashion was often dead against the prevailing taste in Britain: 'crinolines—your lengths in front are really absurd now they are so much smaller'. The manufacturers 'cannot conceive what you do with skirts of 38 to 48 inches in front ... coats with broad lapels and 105 trousers generally worn and very fashionable are quite unsaleable with you'.[38] Clearly the Australian market for clothing manufactured in Britain was more selective than has been supposed, and frequently out of step with British styles.

Thus, although the local clothing industry and custom tailoring were firmly established by mid-century, there were complex relationships with British markets and European agents, as well as very decided local preferences in taste. Yet some wealthy settlers continued to import their clothes directly from British suppliers. The prosperous Biddulph Henning, who lived on a property south of Sydney, ordered straight from Manchester. 'Clothes are so dear and so bad out here that he wants a lot from England', wrote his sister Rachel in 1855.[39]

## Women's Readymade Imports

In Australia, as in Britain and America, development of the women's readymade clothing industry occurred more slowly than the comparable industry for men. Historians document differing time frames for the late emergence of the large-scale industry for women in Europe and America. Kidwell attributes the development of the American industry for men's dress, well before that for women, to two main factors. Firstly she maintains that by the 1840s there was a greater demand for men's clothing for purchase at short notice, and secondly that the relative uniformity of men's dress made mass production possible. It was not until the 1880s, when uniqueness was not so important in garments like cloaks, corsets and underwear, that the female industry took off, receiving further impetus in the 1890s when styles of easy-fitting blouses and skirts became popular.[40] Levitt, on the other hand, suggests that the beginnings of ready-to-wear women's clothing in England occurred earlier than this, in the 1850s and 1860s but still after that of men's slopwear.[41] None of these accounts entirely accords with recent documentation of a substantial output of readymade clothing, including women's and children's dress, produced during the consumer revolution of the late eighteenth century.[42]

In Australia a few types of imported readymade items for women and children were on sale in the first decades of the century. They grew somewhat in extent and variety over the years but there is no evidence that either women's or children's ready-to-wear clothing was manufactured locally in any quantity until the late 1870s. A study of newspaper advertisements of imported garments from the period of first settlement supports the picture of a British readymade industry well under way early in the century, although it may not have qualified for the description of 'mass-production'. All the same, there were imports of readymade underwear, stays, spencers, bonnets, shoes, informal gowns and cloaks, and children's dresses which were worn by very young boys as well as girls.

By the 1850s an increasing variety of imported, readymade garments for ladies could be purchased in Australia. These were chiefly informal, outerwear or leisure garments and little in the way of stylish gowns. In 1853, Mary Allport of Hobart recorded in her journal having bought 'a great many ready made clothes at Waterhouses'. She added that this would relieve her of some trouble, probably that of preparing her daughter's trousseau.[43] At this time, garments for sale included ladies' morning robes of cashmere and silk, flannel gowns and invalid wrappers, mantles, ottomans, skirts, nightdresses and riding drawers.[44] Part-made evening and walking gowns (the skirts readymade) and some so-called 'made up' gowns were also available.[45] Many types of readymade children's clothes were also on sale in the 1850s, such as school suits, juvenile caracos and polka jackets.

One reason for the lack of stylish readymade clothes manufactured commercially for bourgeois women and their children was that making clothes, or having them made, was a pleasurable pastime. Participating in the discussion of clothes with dressmakers and milliners, and paying visits to specialist shops to purchase fabrics, were events enjoyed by women as a way of interacting with their own sex. Shopping allowed women to exercise their consumer skills and to pass on knowledge of fashion to their adolescent daughters. The acceptance by women of sewing as an appropriately feminine pastime, the taste for specialised well-fitted garments, and the relative lack of choice in readymade clothing meant that large amounts of clothing had to be made by dressmakers or at home. In fact, the extent of domestic sewing may have actually acted to discourage the market for women's ready-to-wear clothes. Alternatively, but perhaps less likely, the lack of readymade clothing for women made it imperative for them to undertake sewing tasks.

## Hidden Workers

Although scarcely acknowledged by historians, a vast private economy of home dressmaking and tailoring provided a further dimension of the Australian market. Its extent reveals the important place of locally crafted garments in colonial dressing. More significantly, it points to the likely effect that home dressmaking had on retarding expansion in the market for readymade women's clothing until the end of the century.

The role of all classes of colonial women in the manufacture and maintenance of clothing and footwear was significant, although the numbers of tradeswomen actually employed are likely to have been underenumerated by census data. Thus any attempt to gain a clear picture of the 'invisible' spheres of female occupational groups, including needlewomen, dressmakers and milliners, is frustrated by the likely distortion of the official figures.

Throughout the century women undertook sewing tasks as part of their household chores, ranging from mundane repairs to making bedlinen and curtains, as well as fine-quality work such as embroidery. Domestic sewing was strongly associated with mid-nineteenth-century prescriptions for femininity, and it was in the home that truly feminine activities such as housework and the maintenance of family welfare, including sewing, were pursued. Feminine grace was held to be at its most attractive when women were engaged in the domestic activity of making clothes. The various forms of needlework were seen as class-specific, with plain needlework an activity more suited to the lower classes. By contrast, fine embroidery and home dressmaking were regarded as genteel and desirable activities for middle-class women, and were part of the emphasis placed on creative tasks centred on the home.[46]

Stores in Australia catered to women's dressmaking requirements from the early years of settlement, but by the 1850s and 1860s an increased emphasis on sewing instruction, sale of mail-order patterns, self-tuition studies and dressmaking lessons is revealed in journals and newspapers.[47] Specific dressmaking rooms and fabric showrooms appear in large stores by the 1860s.[48] Farmer's 'New Show Room', illustrated in their trade and fashion catalogue *The Great Drapery Emporium* in 1869, shows the section of the store devoted to the display of luxurious French and British silks for dressmaking. Women could choose their desired fabrics from a wide selection in stores such as these, perhaps basing their choice on an imported fashion print.

The introduction of graded, mass-produced dress patterns pioneered by Butterick, and later the firms of Worth and Madame Weigel, gave women ready access to international fashionable styles in the second half of the century. With the wide availability of sewing machines from the 1860s, it became increasingly possible for women to undertake more sophisticated forms of dressmaking in the home. Sewing machines in Australia cost ten pounds each early in the decade, and brands such as Singer, Wertheim, and Grover and Baker were frequently advertised.[49] An Australian-made lockstitch machine was also available by the 1880s. Sewing machines certainly had the potential to save women sewing time, but initially may have had the reverse effect, since dressmakers often used them for the elaborate detailing on gowns rather than long straight seams. Such a complicated style of machine-made dress, somewhat overly bold in its frontal draped section, was that worn by Hannah Prior for her wedding at Kelso near Bathurst in 1882. The gown suggests the work of a professional small-town dressmaker as it is almost entirely sewn by lockstitch machine, including the gauging or shirring across the front (Plate 30).

Women in Australian towns and country areas made clothes for themselves, their husbands and children, as well as repairing and altering garments and mending shoes. Women had to make their own clothes, especially in rural areas where professional dressmakers were few and the cost could not be supported, leading to a large burden of work within the family home. Alteration of clothing also played a substantial part in women's dressmaking tasks at this time, when fabrics were lasting and could be made over successfully.

Women frequently made clothes for men as part of their domestic duties. This was particularly the case in rural areas where women were expected to be capable of a wide variety of domestic tasks. They were not necessarily skilled at tailoring, but found

30   Hannah Prior's wedding gown, 1882 (Powerhouse Museum, Sydney).

themselves making garments for their men, as well as being overwhelmed with sewing tasks for themselves. The burdens of domestic needlework and tailoring for men were outlined by the Quaker, Margaret May, writing to an aunt in London from Fairfield, South Australia, in 1843:

> we have so very much needlework to do that we always feel to have more than we can get through: were it not for the tailoring, we should manage very well—besides mending all my brother's clothes, we plait and sew straw hats, make cloth caps, jackets, waistcoats, trousers and lately a few shirts.[50]

Men's readymade clothing was not always of good quality and at times necessitated further domestic stitching. Catherine Spence, in her novel *Clara Morison*, described readymade shirts bought especially for the goldfields having to be resewn, for they were only 'blown together'.[51]

Women in both towns and country areas mended boots and shoes, and even sewed slippers. Mary Allport, a painter who lived in Hobart, wrote in her diary on 28 June 1853: 'Miss Burgess and I sewed all morning, and then I put a pair of Gutta Percha soles on my old boots in a very clumsy way.' Two days later she noted that she mended another pair of boots and also a pair of shoes that the cobbler declined to repair.[52] Shoes and boots wore out very quickly in rough conditions. In 1863 Rachel Henning described how desperately everyone needed footwear at Exmoor station in Queensland: 'We are all nearly barefoot...I mend my boots with bits of leather everyday, and they will soon be beyond mending.' The following year she noted that her boots 'are a miracle of patching' and 'I stitch on a fresh piece of sheepskin about every other day.'[53]

Clearly a great deal of dressmaking, tailoring and leatherwork was undertaken by women. This was in addition to quantities of plain stitching and mending, as well as the finer crafts of decorative netting, crochet, tatting, beadwork, fancy embroidery and knitting. This leads to the conclusion that locally made clothing made up a far larger proportion of Australian dress than has previously been recognised. Although much domestic sewing made use of patterns copied from European prototypes, and Europe was undoubtedly the source of fashionable ideals, locally manufactured and home-crafted garments should be seen as a crucial aspect of colonial dressing.

## Shopping

The nature of shopping in Australia changed radically between 1850 and 1880. Clothing which earlier in the century had been sold by general drapers, hawkers, dressmakers, tailoring establishments and warehouses was increasingly distributed by large urban department stores. Overcrowded drapers and haberdasheries gradually gave way to more finely appointed facilities, where the middle classes could shop in greater privacy for an ever-increasing range of consumer items. Louisa Meredith described ladies shopping by carriage in the afternoons, visiting 'fashionable emporiums [sic]' which she understood to be a peculiarly Australian term.[54] Many of these stores dealt in specialised items for a select clientele, where the proprietors prided themselves on the discreet nature of their advertising and their lack of common ticketed goods.[55]

In the 1840s Sydney's George Street was the centre of the retail trade. It was reputed to be especially fine, being frequently compared with the best that central London had to offer. According to Frank Fowler, 'one part of George Street is as much like Bond Street as it is possible one place can resemble another'.[56] By 1854 Melbourne had also become a town vibrating with commercial enterprise. William Howitt maintained the shops were noticeably elegant with an extremely tasteful display of goods.[57] The main shopping thoroughfare was Collins Street, where there was a concentration of jewellers' shops, as well as milliners and drapers.

One of Sydney's earliest department stores was David Jones and Co., which opened in May 1838 as a drapery business, slopsellers and importers. In 1851 it listed thirty-one separate areas of departmental specialisation in the two-storey building. These included tailoring, straw bonnets and hats, parasols and umbrellas, slops, and a 'foreign' department.[58] By 1855 there were specialist sections for silk, shawls, mantles, lace, dress, and millinery, and showrooms as well.

More than merely large shops, stores like David Jones were significant cultural sites which shaped the nature of modern consumerism, and which were at the centre of new forms of social interaction between buyer and seller.[59] By the later part of the century, stores played a major role in promoting mass-marketing strategies to increase consumption. As well as this, according to Reekie, department stores, along with other urban spaces, became the stage for the development and enactment of specifically modern sexual identities and bodily regimes.[60] In such emporia customers were ostensibly free to contemplate or choose their goods in an unconfined space, unhampered by the former strictures of price negotiation. At the same time buyers in these vast, attractive stores were offered a wide selection of commodities, invested with meanings well beyond their usefulness by new methods of display and skilled advertising techniques.

Late in the century many of the department stores were architecturally ornate edifices and prominent landmarks of the city streets. It was a common practice for women's departments to be located on the second or third floor of such stores, with men's on the ground floor. Trade experts believed men to be more predictable customers than women, with little interest in shopping. It was believed men wanted to make quick purchases and disliked the need to 'push past' drapery goods.[61] Thus the ground floor became male territory. Men's outfitting departments were much more austerely appointed than those of women and lacked soft seating facilities, carpeting, decorative ceilings and mirrors.

Women, unlike men, were considered to have selective shopping habits, and store-owners considered that women had the time and inclination to go upstairs to browse for items. Women, it was believed, also preferred to shop in greater privacy where a more intimate service was offered and where there was an attractive ambience and rest rooms. The interior of the millinery and underclothing sections of Francis Giles and Co.'s store in Sydney, illustrated in *Sands' Directory* of 1863, shows the well-appointed, mirrored decor and the discreet displays of bonnets and hairpieces. Even more luxurious was the interior of the ladies' showroom at Farmer's, photographed in 1865, with its plush-buttoned sofas and large interior rotunda on which was displayed a fully clothed fashion model.[62]

Shopping for clothes and millinery was considered to be a particularly feminine activity, best conducted in a comfortable, salon-like atmosphere. If the store could boast the presence of a French dressmaker, it added further tone and an aura of exclusiveness. The editor of the *Australian Woman's Magazine,* who paid a visit to the newly appointed costumiére at Buckley and Nunn in 1882, was ceremoniously ushered up a private stair-case into a well-appointed, fully mirrored apartment solely for the use of the 'artiste'. The business with 'Madame' was conducted entirely in French.[63]

As well as imported goods, colonial department stores like David Jones and Farmer's (established in 1840) also provided ready-to-wear services to their clients by means of their own workrooms and, later, clothing factories.[64] They thus supplied locally made, medium-priced slops as well as offering bespoke tailoring and dressmaking services. Rural customers and their specific requirements were not forgotten either. Rossiter and Lazarus in Sydney kept chesterfields (overcoats) and Albert sacques (loose coats) in stock especially for men in town just for the wool season.[65] The modern division of importing, manufacturing and retailing did not exist: each of these different practices was combined in the one establishment. This combination of making and selling by the big stores continued throughout the century. It was to their advantage in uncertain economic times. Later, after the turn of the century, it was these successful large retailers who became the major innovators in the development of the local clothing-manufacturing industry.[66]

Stores like David Jones, G. C. Tuting and Farmer's in Sydney, Foy and Gibson in Melbourne, and Finney Isles in Brisbane all had agents overseas, which meant that their establishments had direct control over what was designed and ordered from abroad, and also control over the retailing of these goods.[67] The fact that they sold imported British cloth, clothing and accessories as well as locally made garments demonstrates the fallacy of assuming that Australians dressed exactly like their British counterparts. Furthermore, at any one time an outfit might be made up of a combination of items, some produced locally and others imported.

Shopping undertaken by respectable bourgeois clients at big stores and high-class drapery establishments, such as Farmer's and David Jones, was in marked contrast to many wholesale stores and lower categories of clothing shop. Compared to the discreet displays of goods in Pitt Street emporia, Sydney slopshops were festooned with clothing, boots and shoes, remnants and drapery, all overflowing onto the sidewalks. James Inglis commented on this style of shopping where the anonymity and spaciousness of the big stores was replaced by irritating shop runners, wheedling the passers-by in a manner 'suggestive of Burra Bazaar in Calcutta'.[68]

From the 1870s complicated advertising strategies lured customers into the large department stores. They included newspaper advertisements, trade catalogues and circulars, sales notices, posters and even invitation 'Show Days' when customers were allowed to inspect the new season's clothing in certain selected departments. Pictorial images became more intrusive in newspaper and magazine advertisements. These often incorporated a grandiose external view of the establishment or its sales interior. In 1878 J. L. Hordern used a frontal architectural view to advertise his Ladies Warehouse, suggesting that customers cut out the illustration as a reminder of the store.[69] Images like these were designed to extract the maximum dramatic effect. The upside-down advertisement of Anthony Hordern was equally eye-catching. His new shop in Pitt Street, where everything 'from a handsome hearthrug to a wedding dress' could be purchased, was advertised in the same year with the printing the wrong way round.[70]

From the 1870s, overseas journals containing fashion prints were increasing supplanted by local newspapers and magazines catering to women's dress interests. These ranged from fashion illustrations to quite lengthy clothing advice. The *Town and Country Journal* had a weekly 'Ladies Column' including fashion illustrations from the mid-1870s, as did papers such as *Castner's*. *Weigel's Journal of Fashions*, available from the 1880s, appears to have been the first completely Australian women's fashion magazine. It offered consumers fashionable American-style cut-paper patterns as its main attraction and these probably contributed to its long-lasting success.[71] In 1889 the Brisbane *Princess* introduced an innovative full-page photographic supplement of fashion models, posed in interiors constructed of studio props (Plates 20 and 24).[72] These images marked a temporary change of style in fashion illustration away from line engravings towards a new veracity in the advertising of fashionable garments. Such visual realism gave maximum impact to their publicity.

## Country Supplies

Some country areas had reasonably good stocks of clothing in the 1840s. After early irregularities in supply, towns on the goldfields rapidly expanded their retailing facilities. Bendigo in 1853 had shops and stores along all the main roads; these were either wooden warehouses or large tents, and some of the huts had glazed windows. Two years later Ballarat had hundreds of shops and all the characteristics of a market town. David Jones opened a branch there as a sign of confidence in its continuing prosperity. Mrs Ramsay-Laye noted, in 1861, that Bryant's Range shops displayed a conspicuous array of dresses and bonnets from London.[73]

On the other hand, in some remote bush areas shopping facilities remained limited. Clothing supplies were sparse and could take months to arrive. Garments for women were especially scarce. Most of the clothing stock in rural stores was for men; it included moleskin trousers, socks, vests, drawers and cloth caps. For women there were few readymade garments; the goods that were available were mainly either fabrics or accessories.

Many rural settlements had only itinerant suppliers; hawkers would travel with haberdashery and drapery goods to isolated areas at stated periods. Families living at Lynn Banks in Victoria had only two hawkers in the 1850s, who visited at regular intervals. One of these dealt in good-quality drapery, hats and sunshades, while the other, who came more frequently, stocked women's shoes and basic items.[74]

Many big stores extended their urban services to country customers in the 1870s and 1880s, to great effect. Travellers would visit small towns at certain times and display their sample goods for local storekeepers to order. In the 1870s Anthony Hordern distributed so-called clothing 'parcels' of assorted clothes at fixed rates, and Riley Brothers had clothing bales for sale that could be carried to customers on horseback.[75] Family parcels cost upwards of five pounds sterling and consisted mainly of dress materials or underclothing for women, and readymade shirts, trousers and hats for men.

Dressmaking and tailoring work in the country was more sporadic than in urban areas. In remoter parts, customers had to rely upon itinerant tradespeople for such services. Colonel Mundy, in his account of an area near Bathurst, observed the words 'Tailor and Habitmaker' simply chalked on a plank nailed against a tree.[76] River boats, such as the *Platypus* on the Darling, were said to be travelling dressmakers' shops. Orders for gowns were taken going up river, for delivery on the return.[77]

Clothes retailed in Australia in urban and country areas were a mixture of locally made garments and imported goods. The close links forged between manufacturing and retailing, along with the extensive use of mail-ordering, were important strategies to overcome the limitations of the colonial market. The complex mixture of imported items and locally produced goods, reflected particularly in the merchandise of city stores, offered customers a wide range of items that included garments and footwear from overseas as well as local sources. The large stores maintained the close relationship with manufacturing and importing that had existed in the early colonial period but their marketing became increasingly aggressive, directed toward rapid turnover and consumption.

The interrelationship between importing and local production in the clothing retail industry was an especial characteristic of the colonial market, and demonstrates the impossibility of ascribing a precise origin to many garments. Aside from the considerable emulation of imported fashion, the extensive amount of sewing undertaken by women in the home suggests that the local content of Australian dress was far more extensive than has been acknowledged. Significantly, even imported items were continually being adapted to suit Australian conditions, or simply in repair. Thus a garment to which an Australian distinctiveness can be ascribed could well have been an imported article originally, and similarly one that appears to be a fashionable overseas item could have been domestically produced.

There can be no question that clothes for both sexes, whether they were imported, adapted or colonial-made, were inflected by local tastes, preferences and imperatives.

# PART III

# An Australian Distinctiveness

# 8

# A LOOSE FIT:
# EMIGRATION AND ADAPTATION

The general perception of historians about Australian clothing is that it merely replicated the styles and colours of British attire and was in many respects quite unsuitable for colonial conditions. These views were prevalent even in the nineteenth century, although they can be related to many other misapprehensions about colonial dress. In fact so much misinformation circulated in Britain about Australian customs and clothing that emigrants were often baffled on arrival, and as a result, sometimes suffered considerable hardship in the new environment. It is important to analyse in detail the nature and extent of these misunderstandings, as they help to determine the ways and degree to which Australians dressed in ways that were quite distinctive.

Misconceptions about colonial attire can be attributed mainly to misleading data in emigration guides and manuals.[1] Information published in these sources, directed toward intending emigrants, often painted a picture of a land of rural felicity: the climate was equable, working conditions were favourable, and there were no social constraints. By the 1830s various agencies and publications portrayed Australia as virtually a new Arcadia.[2] These views persisted through the following decades. Authors like Samuel Sidney infused their popular accounts of the colonies with similar eulogistic impressions, describing an egalitarian working man's paradise in the peace and tranquillity of rural Australia.

It was a commonly held belief that Australia was so far from civilised society that appearance there was of little concern. Literature encouraging middle-class women's emigration considered it to be a society where fine clothes were not important and where casual dress codes would suit the impecunious. Commentators like Charles

Hursthouse, with his romantic view of colonial existence, felt that Australian life was 'not closely hedged in and trimly squared by rank, form and custom'.[3] He assured his bourgeois readers that it was an environment where etiquette was informal and where there were no restrictive social routines. This vision of a way of life supposedly free of the dissipation and 'corroding cares' of metropolitan living was particularly attractive, especially to potential middle-class emigrants.

Descriptions of this carefree life were to an extent quite apposite about pastoral Australia in the early 1820s, when emigrants departed to the penal colonies 'picturesque' in their 'Australian garb' purchased especially for the climate: the women in durable colonial dresses and the men in striped trousers and matching shirts.[4] It continued to be a realistic impression of life for men in the bush or small rural towns in later decades. But it was certainly a misapprehension in regard to metropolitan living. In fact, middle-class travellers arriving in the colonies discovered that rules of etiquette were studied assiduously by the urban bourgeoisie. Louisa Meredith found behaviour in Hobart society extremely punctilious in the 1850s. Nowhere, she claimed, are 'decent and becoming observances of social and domestic life more strictly maintained'.[5] Mrs Ramsay-Laye, travelling out to Australia as a new bride after the height of the gold rushes, was deceived when she felt that homespun would be more useful to her than her Paris trousseau.[6] She was genuinely surprised to find that by then there were 'gentlemen' and 'ladies' living in the Antipodes.

Working-class migrants also had to revise their expectations of life in Australia. Enticed by promises of a higher standard of living, a warm climate and a life where fewer clothes were required, they often discovered little opportunity to improve their conditions. Ultimately some found that the only significant change in their economic circumstances was one of location.

Even in the process of travelling to the colonies, emigrants had to come to terms not only with the changed circumstances of their life, but with the need to revise many of their concepts about clothing. For the middle-class traveller in particular, conditions on board ship were often such that familiar dress codes could not be maintained. Casual kinds of clothing were essential in order to manage in the difficult, cramped conditions. Both men and women of this class found out later that circumstances in the bush could be equally trying.

## Advice to Emigrants

The numbers of free emigrants from Britain entering the Australian colonies increased rapidly from the 1830s. Wealthy settlers had at first been attracted in the 1820s by pastoral investment potential and the lure of virtues supposedly engendered by an agricultural life. Later in the following decade this group was supplanted by a broader range of social classes, including working-class emigrants hoping to escape from lives of drudgery in factories and mills. Between 1831 and 1850 over 200,000 immigrants entered the colonies under the Government and Bounty Schemes.

Despite the plethora of literature, travellers lacked informed detail about conditions in Australia. For those planning to travel out to the new colonies the question of what clothes to take with them was particularly perplexing. An increasing amount of emigrant literature in the form of government regulations, guides, broadsheets, pamphlets, journals, and manuals circulated from the 1830s. Emigrant guides offered advice to prospective travellers of all classes. The suggestions proffered were often conflicting, and sometimes inappropriate, and it is by no means clear how many were actually followed. Nevertheless, published guides certainly purported to give travellers some idea of what to expect, both on board ship and in the new colonial environment. Information about clothing formed a significant part of the burgeoning emigration literature.

The guides took a number of different forms. Some advice was contained in general travel literature describing life in the colonies, including Australia and New Zealand, and dealt with geography, climatic and travelling conditions, prices, labour requirements and housing. Guides could be written by experienced emigrants like Charles Hursthouse, but others were by journalists like John Capper who, according to Golding, had never been to Australia.[7]

As most guides were written by men, the authors confidently advised on the subject of male clothing requirements, and occasional directives were given for children's dress. Yet even an experienced traveller like Hursthouse felt that to 'grapple with the slippery subject of a lady's outfit' was beyond him. Hursthouse considered that the choice of clothing for a lady was best left to the individual, and that it would be useless for him to advise on 'details of cambric trousers and horse-hair petticoats, nightcaps and violet-powder'.[8] It seems that he found the vagaries of women's fashions too arcane for serious discussion. Other texts, such as *Silver's Guide*, dealt with the subject of women's dress with ease, for Silver's were London outfitters who specialised in the emigration clothing market and were keen to advertise their 'Ladies Department'.

The guides and advertisements published by clothing firms like Silver's, E. Grove, and Moses and Sons targeted both middle-class and working-class customers and revealed the vested interests of their establishments.[9] On the other hand, many suggestions about dress contained in personal letters and journals sent back home were genuinely instructive. Such information was sometimes hidden within texts that followed a predictable pattern, including descriptions of storms, illness, activities on board, accidents and marine life.

Advice on appropriate dress to wear for the voyage, and for conditions in Australia, varied widely and depended on the social group to which it was addressed. Clothes recommended for 'superior' class, or cabin passengers, differed substantially from those suggested for steerage class, both in quantity and type.[10] For instance, ladies were encouraged by *Silver's Guide* in 1858 to take a dark silk dress with them for the voyage, shawls and mantles, and also muslin and cambric chemises, India gauze vests, dressing gowns, cambric sleeping trousers, and blue or brown veils. Steerage-class women on the other hand, were advised to take only a few garments, consisting of two strong gowns, two flannel petticoats and six shifts.

There was a marked difference between the quantities of clothes recommended to travellers in the 1820s and requirements suggested by many guides later in the 1850s. In 1824 William Wentworth advised well-to-do male passengers to take a complete bale of slop clothes to Australia.[11] A bale consisted of twenty blue drugget jackets and trousers, five dozen striped cotton shirts, five dozen canvas trousers and three dozen duck frocks. By the 1850s, with the occasional exception, passengers were increasingly urged to take a minimum of garments with them. Fewer clothes were recommended for emigrants partly because of the known damage caused in transit to wools and silks. More importantly, it was felt that suitable and competitively priced clothing was readily available for purchase on arrival, although it was admitted that clothing in bush areas could be almost twice the price of that in town.[12]

The reduced quantities of dress were to become fairly standard recommendations and remained much the same throughout the century. Thus the minimum outfit for a single, Free Passage man—one whose fare had been paid by his proposed employer— consisted of two suits of beaverteen or moleskin, comprising jacket, waistcoat and trousers, warmlined.[13] Two duck suits of trousers and frocks were also recommended, as well as a scotch cap or thresher's hat, a Brazil straw hat, six striped cotton shirts (occasionally coloured), a pair of boots and a pair of shoes, plus sundry items. One substantial woollen top coat was suggested for the rural interior and for watching sheep.[14] Children of the same class were advised to have nine shirts or shifts, two complete suits of exterior clothing and a cloak or outside coat.[15]

For single working women, a warm cloak plus cape, two bonnets, one small shawl, one stuff dress, two print dresses, six shifts, two flannel petticoats and one of stuff, two twill cotton petticoats, two pairs of shoes and one pair of stays were advised.[16] *Silver's Guide* suggested that working-class women take garments that were all serviceable and not showy.[17] Hursthouse offered similar advice for all classes.

From the 1820s complete emigration wardrobes were stocked by British ready-to-wear suppliers like Messrs Early of Minories.[18] These varied from basic working outfits to more extensive ensembles. Some firms supplied 'Emigration Outfits', which were all-in pack- ages including linen, hats, shoes and clothes of various kinds, bedding, cutlery and per- sonal items like brushes, combs, needles, thread and razors. E. Moses and Sons, London East End slop-sellers and outfitters, and E. Grove of Lower March, Lambeth, catered to both 'superior' and steerage passengers, adjusting content and price accordingly.

In 1852 the cheapest advertised Free Passage outfits for men, from E. Moses and Sons, came to £3 15s.[19] By comparison a 'superior' lady's emigration outfit from the same firm in 1857, at a cost of £47 6s. 6d., included thirty long cloth chemises, eighteen nightdresses, eighteen long cloth drawers and six musquito drawers, thirty nightcaps, and also domestic linen.[20] The readymade items in this outfit were practically all under- wear, as gowns for middle-class ladies were not readily purchased 'off the peg'. Thus there was a clear differentiation between classes of emigrants, one constructed and sustained by the kind of clothing and its cost as advertised and sold by manufacturers.

A noticeable spate of British advertising appeared in the 1840s and 1850s, for manu- facturers saw the new categories of 'emigration' customer as a welcome opportunity to increase local sales and to make an imperial marketing thrust into Australia. Outfitting firms placed considerable pressure on potential emigrants with aggressive marketing techniques. According to Hursthouse, 'this is the age of *puffs* and *highly imaginative* advertising'. He advised emigrants to deal only with respectable houses and keep aloof from all 'puffing and plate glass' establishments.[21]

Firms and warehouses like S. W. Silver and Co. and Thomas Capp's also had agents in Australia to co-ordinate business, and some acted as travel and shipping agents as well. In the late 1840s S. W. Silver and Co. advertised that they shipped clothing monthly to representatives in Australia.[22]

Most manuals emphasised the inadequacy of shoe supplies in the colonies. Some insisted on the need to take good stout shoes, and some advised well-to-do passengers to travel with personal shoe lasts.[23] Others included bootmaker's self-measuring guides for 'colonials' who might need to send back to Britain for their shoes.[24] This advice was somewhat misdirected, especially for future urban dwellers, because Australia had a flourishing industry for hard-wearing, basic footwear by the middle of the century.

## The Voyage

The sea interlude on emigration vessels severed links with the homeland and dramatically marked a period of difference from life in Britain for all classes of passengers. For emigrants, who had been offered promises of an improved standard of living and subjected to exaggerated advertising of colonial conditions, the trauma of departure and the chaotic arrangements of the early emigration schemes diffused many of their hopes. These were further challenged by the extreme discomforts of the arduous voyage. Even the substitution of regular steam vessels to replace sail from 1881 did not eliminate travelling problems.

The voyage by sail to the colonies took an average of four months, during which period (depending on the season) a ship could pass through the stifling heat of the tropics, the equatorial doldrums, and then the bitter cold of extreme southern latitudes.[25] Subsequently the introduction of steam vessels reduced the travelling time to about two months, and there were fewer climatic contrasts. All the same, the seas could be rough, the rains heavy, and intolerable heat could be experienced in the Suez Canal (opened in 1869) and the Red Sea. Thus travellers were normally told to take clothes for a range of temperature extremes. The heat of the voyage was something most commonly underestimated by British migrants, few of whom had even crossed the English Channel before. At times it was intense, particularly in the airless quarters below deck.

Manuals and other published guides dispensed a good deal of advice on dress requirements for the tropics. Male cabin passengers in the 1840s were directed to take a standard tropical outfit, consisting of white jackets, and trousers and vests of lightest jean.[26] These items would have served the traveller well in Australia, for tropical clothing was commonly worn in Adelaide and Sydney in the 1840s and 1850s. For working men, duck or canvas trousers were recommended. Despite the advice, passengers consistently underestimated the heat, finding their tweed and other wool fabrics far too hot for the tropics. Working men are recorded as improvising with bed sheets in hot weather as late as the mid-1880s, regretting that 'a whole Tailor's shop in light clothes' had not been packed.[27]

For hot weather, lightweight shoes or slippers of thinnest leather, buff and even canvas were recommended.[28] William Dorling, an emigrant to South Australia on the *Princess*

*Royal,* described the heat of the tropics in a letter to his family. He noted that most of the passengers went without shoes or stockings, and sheltered under canvas that shaded the decks.[29] Hugh Watson, a shepherd who also emigrated to South Australia, wrote, 'I went most of the way barefoot for salt water spoils my shoes.'[30]

First-class passengers on steamers like those of the Royal Mail and Steam Packet Company, which were like floating hotels with furniture and linen, were told to dress following normal requirements for a fair to ordinary summer.[31] For cold weather, a scotch plaid, a pea jacket (a short, heavy cloth jacket), a pilot cloth, or waterproof coat and leggings were considered essential for gentlemen.[32] By comparison, guides tended to advise against much in the way of warm clothing for working-class emigrants other than recommending a warm suit. Young working men en route to Queensland were told they need bring only an old coat which then could be sold to the blacks in Australia.[33] *Mackenzie's Guide* of 1852 suggested to all working-class male travellers that an old blanket could simply be cut up as a temporary measure and sewn inside the waistcoat or trousers to protect the joints from the cold.[34] Men were told to add cork soles inside their shoes and wear extra worsted stockings.

Working women were advised merely to pass a flannel bandage round the knees and to wear drawers and an extra petticoat for the cold.[35] This is somewhat curious advice, considering that by the 1850s many ships were taking a new and quicker route to Australia, pushing further and further south, sailing past the Cape of Good Hope and then circling around Antarctica. Travellers wrote of the snow piled up on the decks, and how they were unable to warm themselves.

Visual images of life on emigrant ships stressed the orderly, decorous and comfortable nature of the accommodation and the normality of social intercourse on board.[36] Yet the inference from available sources suggests that this was far from the truth. Whatever might have been desired as a social norm, it was not always possible to separate the various social classes or sustain conventional forms of behaviour and dress. For instance the wide crinoline, an article adopted by all classes of women as a standard part of female underwear from 1856 onward, could not have been worn in these conditions.

Everyday activities such as sewing, card games, even shooting, gymnastics and kite-flying were certainly undertaken, but there were times when it was impossible to maintain any semblance of conventional behaviour in terms of eating, dressing and social discourse. Accommodation was exceptionally cramped. Steerage class was especially confined, with no privacy at all.

On sailing vessels even first-class passengers were often so limited for space that there was room for only one person to dress at a time. One journal in 1848 suggested that all gowns should be able to be fastened in the front rather than the back for 'it is awkward in a gale of wind to be feeling for an eyelet hole'.[37] In married compartments it was sometimes difficult even to sit upright, and dressing adults and children confined closely together became a difficult task. Mrs MacPherson, on her voyage out to Australia, maintained that her husband had to act quite inappropriately as both her nurse and ladies' maid, as her own maid was ill and there was no stewardess.[38]

The overcrowded communal areas on board ship, together with the unpredictable motion of the vessel, made inevitable incidents such as spillages of food and greasy water, and breakages of storage jars. Passengers were frequently doused with water coming through companionways, and drying out was a perpetual problem.

Thus, contrary to the impression given by many illustrations, the arduous conditions on emigration vessels meant that men and women abandoned the cumbersome dress of their everyday life on land, adopting instead their most comfortable clothes. Men allowed their hair to grow uncharacteristically long and did not wear top hats. Frederick Mackie, who travelled out to Australia in 1852, noted that he did not have his hair cut for four months.[39] Shabby, worn-out articles, scorned ashore by the middle classes, were considered quite appropriate because of the general wear and tear, nautical tar, nails, and the effects of sea water itself.[40] Informal, loose jackets and wearing apparel in a 'negligé style' were acceptable for gentlemen, whilst coats and collars were completely discarded once the tropics were reached. According to the young emigrant Joseph Sams, 'I am going about with shirt all undone, showing my noble (never mind).'[41]

Difficulties and discomforts on emigration vessels were considerable, and it is hard to conceive of the cramped conditions, the lack of privacy and the primitive sanitary arrangements that had to be endured. According to Joseph Sams, 'most of the cabins are swarmed with bugs and some of the fellows are afraid to undress'.[42] Women found it impossible to maintain the sense of order and cleanliness with which they occupied themselves in normal domestic circumstances, and for which they were responsible. 'You cannot think how dirty everything gets; hands, clothes, everything is black', noted Rachel Henning on board the *Great Britain* in 1861.[43] On steam ships, coal dust might lie inches deep.

As well as lack of space and poor cooking facilities, there was the all too frequent nightmare of sea sickness, lack of ventilation, limited access to baggage, constant dampness, and restricted washing arrangements. Soon after the trauma of departure, voyagers, under acute stress from the crowded and unpleasant conditions, would become understandably peevish. Trifling things grew into large issues, and after a few weeks nothing was heard but complaints and lamentations about the ship's inadequacies, and the ever-present hardships. According to Rachel Henning in 1854, 'the noise is wearisome, the people are wearisome and life is wearisome'.[44]

Water was strictly rationed on migrant ships, and passengers could not depend upon being able to wash either themselves or their clothes in anything other than sea water. Men and groups of unaccompanied women could wash behind temporary, segregated partitions on deck, and showers were improvised from colanders and bed curtains.[45] According to accounts documented by Charlwood, married women, including those in cabin class, did not like to bathe in groups and remained unwashed for long periods.[46] Limited bathing facilities for 'ladies' were introduced in the early 1850s.

Two significant Passenger Acts were passed by the British government in 1828 and 1835, and four more in the 1840s, intended to define and control conditions on British-owned vessels.[47] A procedure was also established, between 1837 and 1839, to appoint surgeon-superintendents of government emigration ships who were to supervise selection of emigrants and accompany them to the colonies.[48] Specific instructions for the surgeons were published in regard to washing, the use of clean linen, luggage access, and mustering of passengers on Sundays to see that they were decently clothed.[49]

Prior to this, during the 1820s and early 1830s, steerage passengers had no regular periods at all for washing. When tropical storms occurred, they would emerge from below, throwing their dirty clothes on deck and stamping on them in order to get them clean. The fore and main shrouds, and fixed ropes, were subsequently decorated with hundreds of shirts, shifts, napkins, gowns and trousers drying in the sea breezes. Sometimes rain water could be caught as it dropped from the sails, or else clothes were simply towed over the bows in an effort to clean them, and 'scarcely a day but something went adrift of wearing apparel'.[50]

Subsequently, as part of general attempts to improve conditions on ships, rules were established on government vessels allowing steerage passengers to wash clothing on two days of the week. Washing and drying were still forbidden between decks.[51] Clothes washing was not normally undertaken at all by cabin passengers. This marked an important class difference, for the bourgeoisie were presumed to have the means to bring sufficient garments to last the voyage, plus the cost of coping with a backlog of four months' washing at the end of it.

One of the conditions of receiving a free passage to Australia was that emigrants brought their own clothing with them. They were also required to bring sufficient shirts and other linen to last the voyage, for this would obviate the need for laundering. Yet evidence tabled in the 1838 *Report on Immigration* claimed many working-class emigrants possessed so little clothing that they could not change during the voyage, and some women allegedly had to stay in bed until they were given clothes in Sydney.[52] For working-class emigrants, clothing was thus an important prerequisite for travel to Australia, and from the late 1830s maintenance of cleanliness throughout the journey was, supposedly, closely supervised.

If passengers had insufficient clothes to last the voyage, officials became anxious about health and there were fears of contagion. The Reverend Mereweather, for instance, claimed in his diary that the health of other passengers was being endangered by filthy steerage passengers and proposed that stricter rules should be enforced regarding cleanliness.[53] No consistent assessment of emigrant health was undertaken at this period, although factors of environment and overcrowding shaped current theories of disease. Nevertheless, health care and survival rates on ships did improve and strategies for maintaining the welfare of passengers to Queensland, for example, were by and large effective.[54]

As cabin passengers could not expect to do any washing, a large quantity of linen and underclothing was required in order to maintain any semblance of a fresh appearance. A clean shirt each day in the tropics was advised for gentlemen. This could mean an outlay on at least three to four dozen shirts. First-class passengers were told that Regatta shirts (normally striped but sometimes blue) were perfectly appropriate and could also be worn in the bush.[55] Moreover, if slop shirts were included it would cut down on expenses, since these could be used later for clothing convict servants.

To solve the washing problem, one guide recommended that the intending passenger collect the discarded linen of friends to take on the voyage.[56] In this way the traveller could have frequent changes of linen, and could subsequently discard the soiled garments. When the passenger was ready to throw away clothes, they were to be tied in neat bundles and slipped discreetly through the portholes. Storing soiled clothing for most of the long voyage was felt to be unsanitary.

The risk of infection and contagious disease on migrant ships was a real and fearful one, and the relationship between health and clean clothing comes up repeatedly as an issue in emigrant manuals. Garments washed in salt water did not dry properly (because salt retains moisture) and damp clothes were regarded as a health risk.[57]

For the most part soiled cabin-class linen was kept in bags and left till the end of the voyage for attention. Laundresses would crowd forward when a ship arrived at its destination, certain of doing a good deal of business.[58] This is likely to have been an important source of employment for women in colonial Australia. Clara Morison, Scottish heroine of the novel of the same name by Catherine Spence, was advised on her arrival in Adelaide that it would cost thirty shillings to have all her washing done, a considerable sum at the time.[59] Some passengers were in such a hurry to receive back their clean laundry that it could be damp and new arrivals were reputed to suffer from 'shuddering' chills, rheumatism and cramp.[60]

Clearly some passengers did do their own washing and this could present problems. Anna Cook, emigrant on the *Scottish Hero* in 1883, recorded the embarrassment of women who had to wash intimate garments like chemises and drawers in public. She herself simply found it amusing: 'Mine were hanging up just over the butcher's table, and when the purser went to serve out the meat, my drawers kept flapping in his face.'[61]

Only a minimum amount of baggage could be kept at a passenger's side in either the cabin class or the crowded steerage section of the ship. All other clothing and household needs had to be stored in strong chests in the hold. There they had to be tightly and correctly packed, to guard against the salt sea air and the damp. Access to baggage in the hold was generally limited to once a month, when linen bags of dirty washing were exchanged for clean items. Fanny Davis gives a vivid account of this event in her diary entry for 1858:

> Nobody can form any idea of the bustle and confusion there is on these days, especially today for all the people have something spoiled with the damp, but in many cases it is their own fault for in one box a bottle of jam had burst and spoiled a new dress. In another it had spoiled two new bonnets, and can anyone pity them if people will be so careless as to pack jam and clothes together?[62]

Chests for the hold had to be clearly marked either 'Wanted on the Voyage' or 'Not Wanted on the Voyage'. Emigrants were advised to cut or paint the directions on the lids of all boxes, as cards were easily rubbed off.[63] The Narryna Museum in Hobart owns a small wooden box that belonged to Captain William Langdon which is so labelled. Nevertheless, baggage was lost in transit. A letter to the Immigration Agent from Anna Marlow in 1855, claiming a total of eleven pounds and sixteen shillings for all her baggage lost en route from Southampton to Port Adelaide, gives a good idea of the limited clothing possessions of a domestic servant at the time. Her luggage consisted of a large box, covered with black oilcloth, one small box covered with paper, and a workbox. The total contents of her stored luggage are listed in her letter of claim. One straw bonnet, trimmed; three shawls; five yards of black silk; four dresses (probably fabric);

two old dresses and underclothing; four pairs of stockings; sundries including night-clothing, aprons and soap.[64]

Such rare insights into the nature of a migrant's possessions reveal something of her priorities, as well as a fascinating glimpse of clothing as it related to a particular social group. The garments which passengers like Anna Marlow brought for the voyage and their accommodation and washing arrangements marked the class to which they belonged.

Despite a preponderance of literature available to them, travellers to Australia were seldom well prepared for their journey; they had to make many adjustments, not only in the use of clothes but in the meanings attached to them. Their familiar dress codes were constantly disrupted and confused by the crowded and uncomfortable conditions.

## Arriving and Adjusting

After the long, tedious, and exceedingly uncomfortable voyage to Australia, it was understandably a moment of great excitement when the destination was finally sighted. Many are the accounts of the shabby clothes of the voyage being packed away with great delight, and the passengers' best clothes brought out for the arrival: 'ladies, whose bronzed and scorched straw bonnets would have been discarded long before by a matchgirl, now appeared in delicate silks and satins of the latest London fashion. Gala dresses and holiday faces were the order of the day.'[65] An engraving of *Migrants Arriving*, c.1860s (Plate 31) shows newly arrived passengers in their fashionable attire. The men are almost uniformly clothed in top hats and there is an air of prosperity in their general appearance, quite different from the way they would have dressed on board ship.

The joy and gaiety of the moment of arrival was often shortlived. Some ladies dis-embarking at Port Phillip Bay in 1857, wearing silks and satins, were dismayed at having to wade through deep mud when landing.[66] Mrs MacPherson noted that men generally adopted high waterproof boots to cope with the conditions, and such protective footwear is portrayed in Von Guerard's lively drawing *A Melbourne Man and Woman* of 1854 (Plate 25). Mrs MacPherson said that the women arriving in long dresses looked pitiable: 'I really think they will have eventually to adopt the Bloomer costume, which, if allowable under any circumstances, would certainly be there for the purposes of traversing these terrible quagmires.'[67]

Men newly arrived in Australia found their British clothes were a distinct disadvantage, especially for rural and goldfields conditions where old garment stock of 'antiquated pattern, shape and material' was sometimes more appropriate.[68] By the 1840s, before undertaking the journey to the interior, they purchased more suitable local clothing made from hard-wearing colonial tweeds and leather. Rosamond Smith, an emigrant to Queensland in 1861, described the problems that faced men on arrival. She alleged that working-class emigrants found their European Sunday outfits of black cloth suit and black beaver hat entirely unsuitable for Australia. They invariably viewed such clothes with distaste, comparing them with the more practical colonial garments of jumpers and duck or moleskin trousers worn by others, and finally either packed up the suits to rot away out of sight, or gave them to a 'blackfellow'.[69] There is some

**31**  *Migrants Arriving,* c.1860s, wood engraving (National Library of Australia).

irony in the fact that Aborigines may sometimes have looked more like British models of middle-class dressing than the new arrivals. It is also important to note that colonial attire, even for working men, was often quite different from that of Europeans.

Many images and literary texts from mid-century highlight the differences between the fashionable appearance of new arrivals and more sensibly dressed local men. The ridicule displayed about dress reflects a perceived and particular difference between the experienced colonial man and the 'new chum'. The attempt to use dress as a way of marking out the local man from the stranger was part of the conscious formation of an all-male Australian identity. In the 1870s and 1880s this self-consciousness about the constituents of national distinction became more pronounced, and it gathered momentum with the nationalism of the 1890s. Its legacy remains in some respects even today.

By contrast, women made fewer changes to their clothing after arrival, although in the bright, clear sunshine of Australia 'everything requires to be very clean and fresh looking'.[70] Even 'Parisian summer colours' were suitable.[71] Ellen Moger, an emigrant to South Australia in 1840, described the gaiety of local dressing and how elegant people looked in church.[72] Sophie Cooke, who lived in Adelaide in the early 1850s, noted that 'people at home think we colonists do not dress much. Miss Grocer thought my light silk dress would be useless out here but she was much mistaken, for people dress as genteely and with quite as good taste as those at home.'[73]

In rural areas the situation was somewhat different and the practical considerations of life inevitably affected the priorities of women. There was little readymade clothing for them in country stores and so they needed to make many clothes at home. This occasioned requests for sewing materials from emigrants like Fanny Bussell in Western Australia: 'Belts are very useful, jean stay-binding, needles of the best description, buttons of every sort . . . Thimbles,—as we wear them out very quickly where we have so much hard work . . . in fact nothing can be useless.' Coloured and small-patterned cottons were found to be more suitable for gowns than plain fabrics. They washed easily and did not show marks. 'Although things are coarse, let them be good, genteel and small patterns', wrote Bessie Bussell. 'Shoes can never be too regularly despatched, stout and neat', noted Fanny in 1834.[74] Clogs for the winter were also requested.

Many emigration guides suggested that colonial clothing supplies were inadequate and shops were poorly stocked. In the early years this may well have been so. Shoe supplies and children's clothes seem to have been a particular problem. A letter from Perth, begun in 1830, written to an intending immigrant suggests bringing out shoes for 'many respectable females with their children are going barefoot—not a shoemaker can be got to work'.[75]

Later in the century shopping facilities were found to be remarkably similar to those in English provincial towns, and newcomers discovered that goods and services could, at times, exceed their expectations. William Dorling, an emigrant to South Australia in 1848, considered Adelaide as fine a town as Bury St Edmunds, with nothing lacking—'here is a better choice of silks and many other things than at home'.[76]

Some mid-century commentators claimed that clothes were competitively priced in Australia, but this may have had a good deal to do with propaganda relating to the supposedly high standard of living for workers. Accounts of the price of clothing vary and it is impossible to make a useful comparison between clothing costs in Britain and those in Australia. New arrivals were sometimes surprised at the cheapness of colonial clothing. John Hadfield, who arrived in Melbourne in 1857, considered clothes to be similar to English items in price but much inferior in quality.[77] Yet he found it expensive to get shoes and garments repaired. Richard Skilbeck had a similar view of the cost of goods in Melbourne.[78] Other sources suggest that clothing may not have been so cheap as was claimed in the guides.

As it happened, the costs of clothing in Australia were not static. They rose quite substantially during the gold-rush period, contributing to problems of accurately assessing the living costs of workers. According to New South Wales government statistics, a working man's outfit of jacket, waistcoat, moleskin trousers, coloured shirt, boots, socks and straw hat cost £1 11s. 1d. in 1844. For a working woman, an outfit of wool dress, flannel petticoat, stockings, shoes, cap, shawls, shift, stays, apron and straw bonnet cost slightly more, at £1 18s. 10d. The outfit for a man had more than doubled in price by 1854, and one for a woman had also risen substantially. Even so, by the end of the decade the cost of clothing had gradually diminished again.[79]

In other words, according to the statistics, general clothing costs soared in the mid-1850s during a period of social dislocation, when labour was in short supply and local costs had increased, but it is not clear if such data drew on prices of colonial or imported clothing. One must assume that locally made garments were uncompetitively priced in comparison to imports, and that the wealth generated by the gold rushes made Australia an attractive market for British exporters. Thus immigrants were easily able to purchase British readymade clothing at a reasonable cost, even though colonial items were readily available and of reputable quality.

Conditions of life in the colonies were to prove many predictions about Australian dress and behaviour to have been misleading. Long before settlers had accustomed themselves to life in the Antipodes, the experience on migrant ships prepared them for difficulties and hardships. The clothes which they were advised to bring with them sustained the notion of the class to which they belonged and the conditions in which dress was managed and cleaned continued to be class-specific. But in many instances, middle-class travellers disregarded accepted dress practices; those passengers who wore cast-off or shabby clothes on board ship transgressed established codes of middle-class dressing for public occasions.

The shipboard experience foreshadowed a more casual attitude to clothing that existed already in rural areas. On the other hand, those who settled in Sydney and Melbourne encountered a superficial similarity to the dress habits with which they were familiar. Newcomers felt there were many subtle differences both in clothing and demeanour which were perplexing, especially in regard to determining their social status.

There was obviously an appreciable distinctiveness about colonial dress practices quite contrary to what migrants had been led to believe, not only in the bush where it was most evident, but also in the cities and towns.

# 9

# ALTERNATE THREADS:
# PERCEPTIONS AND STEREOTYPES

Immigrants to Australia brought with them many misconceptions, particularly in relation to clothing. Conversely, when Australians returned to Europe they felt their clothes were out of place there, just as many do today. For instance Marian Ryan, mother of the artist Ellis Rowan, visiting London in 1860, found ladies to be '*much* more plainly dressed than the Australians'.[1] In other words, despite obvious generic similarities in dress, there were numerous quirks of colonial taste and undoubtedly contemporary perceptions about differences of style.

There is little doubt that dress in the colonies was heavily influenced by Europe, but the transmission of fashion ideas was not simply a one-way flow from the dominant culture to the supposedly inferior one. To take one example, in 1855 when Rachel Henning was living with her brother on a property in New South Wales, she sent presents to her sister in England, including fabric and trimmings. Some of the items were not quite what she wanted, as her choice had been limited, but she noted that 'Amy sends you a cloth mantle. Also a scarf for the neck. You must not think the latter old-fashioned, it *is* an old fashion revived again, but everybody wears them here and I think them pretty.'[2] This is not to suggest that Australian fashions had any serious impact on British dress, but it does show that Australians did not passively accept all imported ideas and dress practices without any fashion sense of their own.

Previous accounts of Australian dress have tended to present colonial clothing as a kind of second-rate version of European attire, and any local distinctiveness in clothing has been regarded as minimal. Yet behaviour and preferences for certain fabrics and garments, regional tastes and factors—especially in tropical areas like Queensland— and the presence of Aborigines all contributed to quite specific differences in appearance.

These were more than enough to justify a challenge to traditional notions about the relationship between Britain and the colonies.

When one examines the literature on colonial dress, two recurring stereotypes emerge about the dress of Australians—views which were already being formulated in the nineteenth century. The first has to do with the supposed deference to British styles and thus the unsuitability for the warm climate. The second relates to the alleged egalitarian nature of Australian clothing. Both of these perceptions have been sustained well into our present century. In the case of the first, as late as 1952 the British export magazine the *Ambassador* was reporting, as if a new discovery had been made, that there was an important need to manufacture textiles specifically for Australian conditions. It seems that up till that time many manufacturers still had not realised that there was an Australian preference for bold, colourful designs and light fabrics.[3]

## Dress and the Climate

One of the more persistent myths about colonial dress is that heavy, dark British-style clothes were uncritically adopted with little regard for the climate. Joel maintains that 'the first settlers were certainly not going to start changing things just because of a little matter of sub-tropical heat . . . there was a determination not to give in to the land or its climate'.[4] Colonial women are alleged to have almost mindlessly continued to wear hot and uncomfortable clothing in tropical areas. Auliciems and Deaves have recently postulated that in the later part of the century, bourgeois women in particular suffered a semi-permanent state of hyperthermia because of the heavy, hot clothing they wore 'day in, day out, and seemingly irrespective of season, or location'.[5]

These views deny cultural agency to Australians; they are simplistic and incorrect. Certainly the imported British traditions and social practices were extremely strong. By mid-century much male urban dress replicated British dress and showed little regard for the weather. Yet throughout the nineteenth century the climate and environmental factors in Australia had their effect on many choices of clothing, giving particular nuances to colonial dress.

Ironically, at the time of first settlement it was not known that Australia had very cold winters. Officials, in fact, had a quite inaccurate picture of the nature of local climatic conditions. This may have been due to the fact that Cook's brief stay in the area had taken place between the end of April and early May. At this time it is autumn in the region and his stay was marked by fair to moderate weather for the time of year. Joseph Banks, in his report to the Select Committee of the House of Commons in 1779, had stressed the area's moderate climate, which he likened to the South of France.[6]

In the assumption that the weather would be consistently warm and temperate, officials supplied the Marines accompanying the First Fleet convicts with tropical gear only. Storekeepers at Portsmouth and Plymouth were given directives to issue 'light clothing' sufficient for two years.[7] A degree of cold weather was clearly anticipated on the voyage because male convicts were given serviceable woollen jackets and drawers, and the women petticoats of serge. Yet there were no 'foul weather' overcoats for the male transportees (or the Marines) and no cloaks for the convict women, so it seems officials expected the weather to be quite mild.

In fact later correspondence from the settlement included bitter complaints about the lack of warm clothing. Major Ross, writing to the Admiralty in July of 1788, drew attention to the wet weather and asked particularly for a supply of greatcoats for each of his men: 'Greatcoats is likewise an article which in my opinion every man should be supplied with as the rains in the winter and the night dews in the summer makes it impossible for a man to remain on his post without being wet thro.'[8]

The first official acknowledgement of the variable climatic conditions in the settlements came in 1803 when it was established, in theory at least, that convicts should be supplied with both winter and summer dress.[9] In 1814 a more direct correlation between convict health and warm clothing was more publicly declared in the major inquiry into convict health undertaken by Sydney's Assistant Surgeon William Redfern. In his report to Macquarie, Redfern pointed out that convicts were not being given coarse cloth or frieze greatcoats as they were in Britain, but only light clothes of a thin unbleached linen called harn.[10] This he claimed was thinner even than the duck fabric worn by English convicts, and quite unsuitable for a winter passage. Subsequently Macquarie recommended that convicts be given more appropriate woollen trousers and flannel waistcoats and drawers.[11]

It is not clear whether or not this recommendation was followed through. Complaints about the inadequacy of prisoners' clothing for cold southern latitudes continued to be made all through the transportation period. Yet by 1804 there are signs that different clothes for summer and winter were being issued, and at the time of Bigge's *Reports* the desirability of half-yearly issue was openly acknowledged, as well as cloth suited to the season. Until this time convicts must have suffered considerably on account of the cold, especially if they were not in a position to bring much in the way of their own clothing with them from Britain.

Although all classes of new settlers experienced many problems as a result of the misconceptions about the climate, the upper social classes are likely to have been better prepared for the conditions, especially the heat. Fears about the debilitating effects of tropical climates on the European constitution, in environments like colonial India, circulated widely in Britain. Thus manuals and handbooks designed to assist travellers to India, for instance, contained advice as well as prescribing suitable clothing and fabrics for tropical environments.[12] Affluent men in Australia appeared to have been aware of these ideas and tended to wear tropical gear for the hot weather, at least until the 1840s, and in some instances throughout the century. This consisted of white silk or cotton jackets, trousers and broad-brimmed straw hats. In such outfits they would have been clothed extremely sensibly for the climate. Sadly, no complete outfits of such suits seem to have survived. There is one exceedingly rare example of a loose-fitting, lightweight lounge jacket, specially designed for the heat made of very fine unbleached linen and fastened with a single button; it is now in the Western Australian Museum. It is thought to have belonged to Henry Princep, the artist, draughtsman and photographer, who was born in India and arrived in the colony in 1866.

For a number of reasons, mercantile men began to change from clothing of this kind into a sort of urban uniform of black and dark grey suits by the 1840s. These garments became extremely popular for professional men both in Melbourne and Sydney by mid-century. Working men, however, continued to wear the practical but coarse, readymade slop trousers and shirts that were common in the early years of settlement. Tradesmen in the colonies were also more practically attired than the middle classes and appeared somewhat different from their British counterparts. According to Annabella Innes, they did not wear hats; they preferred light caps with white calico coverings, 'which almost everyone wears for coolness'.[13]

In Queensland men of the entrepreneurial and professional class were slower to respond to conventional city dress than those of southern colonies. In 1890, Charles Allen, in his book *A Visit to Queensland*, noted that white suits were common in Queensland towns in 1870 but that 'considerable effort' was being made to introduce black coats and bell-toppers.[14] These heavy European fashions made rapid inroads, particularly in Brisbane. The power of the convention was such that in 1893 Francis Adams described this abhorred black dress for men travelling north like some royal progress, engulfing one town after another. He claimed that the Queenslander was cheerily pushing northward the black coat and shining topper of 'civilisation', and that Brisbane was a town where 'the charming costume of white cotton coat with mother-o-pearl buttons, and white cotton trousers bound up with a scarf of silk gives way everywhere before the hateful conventional black'.[15]

Yet in Brisbane, as has been pointed out, many men, even at the end of the century, went without coats and waistcoats on hot days, or continued to wear cool, stylish, readymade 'Indian clothing' of white or khaki drill for formal occasions. This clothing was sold readymade by men's outfitters like Mountcastle and Sons and Pike Brothers. Further north, white tropical clothing was retained as well, although even here changes were occurring. A newspaper report of 1890 claimed that in Townsville the white collarless patrol jacket, worn without a waistcoat and with light underwear, was no longer seen; nor was the outfit consisting of an Oxford shirt with sleeves turned up at the wrist, snow-white moleskins and loose bright tie.[16] In fact, tropical clothing became more formalised and was worn with tightly knotted ties and waistcoats.

All the same, for the remainder of the century men continued to use versions of tropical clothing for informal activities such as boating, tennis, cricket, beach holidays and for picnicking throughout Australia. Sometimes they wore sandals in place of shoes or boots. Voigt of George Street, Brisbane, sold special mail-order ventilating footwear of plaited leather, recommended for cycling, tennis and golf (Plate 32).

Leisure outfits often consisted of white tropical trousers and shirts, together with coloured cummerbunds and broad-brimmed straw boaters.[17] Nat Gould described Sydney men out picnicking: 'young men start out arrayed in white flannels, and broad-brimmed hats that would not be unlike Japanese sunshades if they had sticks in the centre. Collars are at a discount . . . a pair of white boots and a sash round the waist.'[18] These informal outfits are rarely illustrated, but one is worn by the man standing on the left in the photograph, probably of the Bauer family, Queensland, c. 1889, shown in Plate 33. Tropical gear was also used for tennis and boating although the cummerbund was normally not worn on these activities.

**32**   S. Voigt advertisement, *The Street*, 1900.

Toward the end of the nineteenth century the scientific community, seeking justification for sustaining a belief in racial superiority, became increasingly occupied with the idea that tropical climates were unfit for civilised European peoples. Long exposure to the sun was considered to be detrimental to the white physique and to cause moral and physical degradation.[19] It was popularly believed that whites were not suited to labouring in places like Queensland, thus rationalising the continuing economic subservience of non-Europeans and Melanesians.[20]

Some of the scientific concerns about hot climates were introduced into broader debates about male and female dress reform taking place at much the same time. Walter Balls-Headley, for instance, lectured the Australian Health Society on 'Dress With Reference to Heat' in 1876, theorising about the need for rational clothing and suggesting that men (and boys) wear white clothing in summer and ventilated straw hats. He recommended that labouring men wear light-coloured woollen shirts in summer and that they should introduce a cabbage leaf or layers of calico into 'wideawakes' to protect their heads from the sun.[21]

Inevitably, some increased awareness of the dangers of wearing inappropriate clothing resulted from medical opinions such as these, yet the retention of cool (and cheap) white or khaki washing suits in Queensland well into the next century should not

**33**   *The Bauer Family [?]*, Queensland, c. 1889, photograph (John Oxley Library, Brisbane).

be ascribed to any concern for male dress reform. Indeed, the subject of suitable dress for men was seldom widely discussed until the late 1920s, when it was taken up by groups such as the Men's Summer Dress Reform Committee in Queensland. Light clothing was retained as a convention and then overridden by the alternate convention of dark urban dress.

To combat the summer heat, Indian-style puggarees or scarves, often made of thin muslin or silk veil, wound round the crown of a helmet or hat and falling down as a shade, were common throughout Australia in the 1850s and 1860s. The Powerhouse Museum owns one of these neckshades of knitted cotton, probably made in India but worn in Australia c.1830-60. Such garments continued to be worn informally by men and boys in the 1870s and 1880s, as well as by country visitors to town, but gradually fell into disuse.

The more scientific preoccupations with health in the latter part of the century caused puggarees to be replaced by sturdier sun-helmets of white drill, straw boaters and protective sunhats. These actually became a more permanent feature of warmer climates, compared to tropical suits, which were seen less and less in major urban areas. The *Rockhampton Morning Bulletin* in 1877 cautioned all newcomers to Queensland against the damaging effects of the heat, advocating the use of lined sunhats to protect the head from the sun's rays.[22] This kind of warning sounds quite familiar in the 1990s, with our more informed environmental awareness. Such hats continued to be widely

**34**  Land and Water Hat advertisement, *Queensland Punch*, Nov 1881.

advertised in the popular press. In 1896 Mountcastle and Sons, a Brisbane firm, were pressing customers to buy new 'Tropo' shaped sunhats and patented air-chamber helmets medically recommended for wear in the tropics.[23] Their Gympie branch advertised Terrai hats, doe-skin helmets and camp and washing hats for the country sale.[24] Teleaven and Begg, also of Brisbane, sold practical folding 'Land and Water Hats' for outdoor activities and travelling, assuring readers that 'men in these hats are irresistable [sic]' (Plate 34).[25]

Aside from stylish tropical clothing, men, when they were relaxing and for beach activities, wore cool, informal garments of various kinds, including pyjama suits. A group of young men photographed on Christmas Day at Stradbroke Island, Queensland, in 1885 (John Oxley Library) shows them dressed in a motley assortment of garments. Amongst them there are what appear to be bathing shorts, as well as the ancestor of the 'Aussie stubbie'—trousers cut off at the knee.

By comparison, bourgeois women were not as regularised as men by the social imperative to wear dark and heavy, city clothes like a sort of uniform. Throughout the century they dressed more ornamentally and in response to seasonal variations. Light-coloured muslins and cotton prints made up into gowns were commonly worn for the hot weather, and silks, heavy satins and woollen poplins of darker shades were reserved for autumn and winter. Light straw bonnets were also worn. In the early years of settlement most fashionable high-waisted gowns, worn by women of the upper social classes, tended in any case to be made of light fabrics like muslins, and a variety of other fine Indian materials. These garments were therefore quite suited to the summer heat and were often worn with little waist-length jackets. The National Trust of Victoria has such a jacket, an extremely unusual one of light, coarse linen, datable to about 1815, which would have been worn over a thin gown. It is tailored in the style of a heavier jacket, but it has clearly been adapted by the tailor or dressmaker to take account of the warmer climate.

Seasonal gowns, underwear and fabrics were commonly sold by major department and drapery stores throughout the century. Finney Isles of Brisbane advertised the 'Gossamer Swan Bill corset' designed for warm climates; it combined the advantages of the stay and 'Joan of Arc belt', while imparting a graceful symmetry to the figure.[26] Indian muslins, Ceylon skirtings, Liberty cretonnes, zephyrs and embroidered silks (all lightweight cotton or silk fabrics) were recommended for wear in hot weather. A *Boomerang* article of October 1888, entitled 'Summer Toilettes', advertised novel light, white Japanese cotton gowns for ladies, printed with dull blue or red Japanese figures, including hieroglyphs, pavilions and birds, readymade in Paris for the hot days coming on.[27]

Despite readily available lightweight garments, the bourgeoisie maintained a semblance of stoic acceptance of warm climatic conditions in public. This kind of social formality still persists in current etiquette for certain occasions, such as weddings and official ceremonies. During the nineteenth century it was believed that in public the heat should be bravely endured. Anthony Trollope found that the subject of hot weather was of extreme delicacy in Queensland. 'One does not allude to heat in a host's house anymore than to a bad bottle of wine . . . You may call an inn hot, or a court-house, but not a gentleman's paddock or a lady's drawing room.'[28] This was a formality that constituted part of the ritual of bourgeois etiquette in public.

Probably for this reason many formal photographs of middle-class women posed in studios give the impression that they dressed exclusively in dark sweltering gowns. There are numerous Queensland and Western Australian portrait photographs of such cumbersome outfits, which simply reinforce the perception that Australian women were unsuitably clothed for the climate. Nevertheless, these images are statements of public decorum and are likely to have been far from reality. Those who publicly kept up the appearance of being unaffected by the heat did not necessarily maintain this in private.

Women's letters and diaries in Queensland are filled with complaints about the weather, especially between January and February, and the ways in which they coped with the conditions. Katie Hume noted, in a letter to her mother in January 1868, that attending church at Drayton (near Toowoomba) in the heat was a terrible trial, especially in mourning wear. 'As a rule we always undressed and lay down all the afternoon . . . Of course I cannot wear anything but a black barege skirt and white body in-doors . . . washing bodies are indispensible this weather'.[29] Katie Hume thanked her family in Britain for 'The Box' they had sent to her in 1870. She writes, 'Thanks Ally for the pretty "Fish'ook", it will do nicely to wear out of doors next Summer, the present fashion of "having nothing on" being very suitable for this climate.'[30]

Mary McConachie, living in Brisbane in 1882, wrote a vivid account of the steaming vapours of December weather and how languid she felt in the heat. In a letter back to Scotland she compared Queensland fashions on Christmas Day to those in Britain. She reported that in Brisbane there were

> no muffler gravats [sic] to be seen no worsted gloved hands, no overcoats no leggings but instead suits of almost silk netting through which many parts of the body could almost be seen, scarf of the lightest make, gloves like a net for the hair, shoes like dancing slippers a fan in the hand a parasol overhead.[31]

Working-class women also wore clothes suited to the warm climate. In 1825, imme-diately after arriving in Sydney as a new settler, Ann Hordern, a fashionable 'long stay and corset maker', wrote a letter to her mother in England. She was hoping to persuade her to despatch items, in exchange for wool, which she could then sell in her new drapery business. Her letter requests cotton ginghams, stays, bonnet shapes, printed muslins, checked skirts, satin, slops and waistcoats—the latter three items fetching, she says, a great price. Ann added the request, 'the stays must be from 24 to 30 inches, no children's and more 27 and upwards as women's run large and slops thin as it is a warm climate'.[32]

Women living in the bush adopted lightweight wear for summer where possible, although their garments had of necessity to be more practical than those of the city. Nor were the colours they wore as pale as those assumed by ladies of leisure. Women on stations wore light muslins and print gowns or ginghams which were just as cool as, but more durable than, muslin. Sunbonnets with wide side flaps or frills were commonly worn to shade the face from the detrimental effects of the heat, and broad felt hats were frequently used as an alternative to straw hats in the tropics.[33] A photograph of a group of Queensland picnickers in the bush, in the 1890s, shows a variety of informal outfits and headwear. One of the women and the little girl are wearing protective sunbonnets and several of the men have tropical helmets. Fly veils are worn by both sexes (Plate 35).

Although Australian women of the bourgeois class were constrained to keep up a sense of decorum and follow rules of etiquette, the climate and conditions on stations and in tropical urban areas certainly affected what they wore and the manner in which

**35**   *Picnic—Queensland*, 1890s, photograph (John Oxley Library, Brisbane).

they conducted themselves. To think that they continued to wear British clothes quite uncritically is to ignore the substantial body of literature which suggests otherwise.

## Egalitarianism

As well as the erroneous perception that colonial dress was unsuitable for the climate, there has been a long-standing belief that the dress codes of Australian men were a visible sign of their egalitarian political attitudes. This belief was generated initially in the mid-nineteenth century, when the British began to regard the lifestyle of the upper section of the working class in Australia with an unrealistic degree of approbation. At this time as well, descriptions of some men's rural and goldfields dress focused erroneously on its alleged unchanging naturalness and supposed communality. Later in the 1870s, commentators began to generalise about town dress as well, describing it as somewhat unkempt but virtually free of class differences.

Such remarks were never made about women's dress, although visitors were at times especially critical about its components. It is likely that the notion of a common form of dress being worn by men, not women, had more to do with the difficulties in reading the signs of class rather than any form of democratic dressing. Vernon Lee Walker noted in 1876 that in Melbourne, 'the people dress very queerly here, you cannot tell a gentleman till you speak to him for as a rule the gentlemen are dressed most common.

Of course I am recognised everywhere I go as a "new chum" as they call it, by the cut of my clothes, hat etc.'[34]

The myth about men's egalitarian dressing which was developing by mid-century coincided with the peak of the critique about emancipist dressing. At this time, those in 'good' society allayed their fears of encroachment by emancipists and the newly rich by verbally castigating the alleged vulgarity and extravagant dress of these two groups. William Howitt claimed that the extreme dress of emancipists and their love of show only widened the social gulf which they tried so ostentatiously to hide.[35] He declared as well that ex-convicts of both sexes in Melbourne could be identified at a glance by their hard and grim faces, and that neither clothing nor wealth could hide this ignominy.[36] Louisa Meredith felt similarly about Sydney emancipists. She was scathing about their vulgar display of wealth, their crass behaviour and their lack of education.[37]

Commentators accused colonial men (and women too) of wearing too much jewellery, citing ornamentation such as 'handcuffy' bracelets, shirt pins, large rings and chains.[38] Abbold's drawing of *Tom Jones as he Appeared Six Months After his Arrival in the Colonies* (Plate 36) shows not only an exaggerated and affected stance but also accoutrements such as a flashy watch-chain and fingers overladen with rings. Caroline Chisholm believed that the behaviour of such individuals, with their neck ribbons, pins and finger rings, was formed on board emigrant ships. She called them the 'Do nothings' or 'Black Ribboned Gentry'.[39] It was the excessive use of jewellery that contributed to the notion of Australia as a materialistic society, and the habit was viewed by commentators as an unfortunate sign of the lower classes aping the idle and fripperous habits of the gentry.

These kinds of criticisms began to be supplanted mid-century by comments about equality in dress, although such opinions were probably based more on the hope of witnessing true egalitarianism than on encounters in real life. In fact, visitors who succumbed to the myth of Australia's egalitarianism probably felt out of place in their own dress and uneasy at the lack of familiar signs of class distinction. In the 1880s Twopeny, a major commentator on colonial urban life, discussed in some detail the issue of egalitarian clothing. Although personal opinion is generalised as social fact in his text, revealing his thoroughgoing bourgeois bias, it does provide useful information on colonial dress.[40] He considered that all classes of Melbourne men had a well-to-do look but that everyone looked untidy. Other visitors agreed that most men in Australian towns were similarly but shabbily dressed. James Inglis felt that the 'common ruck of the Sydney populace' was about the worst-dressed section of the Anglo-Saxon race he had ever seen.[41]

In keeping with the evolutionary scale of progress which Twopeny used as a method of analysis, he believed that middle-class men deteriorated in dress and behaviour once they had settled in the colonies. Businessmen, he noted, 'look like city men whose clothes have been cut in the country'. He also contended that women's dress was not quite as tasteful as that of British women. Yet in the summertime, when dresses were made of light and cheap material, he felt that there was a greater semblance of equality between the classes than could be found in Britain.[42]

The views of Twopeny and Inglis raise a number of significant points regarding urban

**36**  Charles Abbold, *Tom Jones as he Appeared Six Months After his Arrival in the Colonies*, 1851–4, ink drawing (Dixson Library, State Library of NSW).

dress in Australia. Firstly, although businessmen in Sydney and Melbourne had taken readily to European fashions, British dress and behavioural codes were not simply translated into the colonial context. Differences existed which can be partly attributed to the somewhat limited kinds of clothing available. Protectionist duties and freight costs discouraged the purchase of high-quality imported goods and acted, according to Twopeny, like a kind of sumptuary tax.[43] What was regarded as a general lack of attention to clothing may have been due in part to the general use of inferior readymade suits, which did not fit like custom tailoring. Inglis described readymade clothing being worn by the bulk of the Sydney population with 'slop suits the prevalent style'.[44]

There is no doubt as well that the term gentleman had connotations in the colonies different from those understood in Britain. In some instances those trappings of social distinction, assumed as a correlation of birth rather than economic success, could be recognised, but certainly not as readily as in Britain. Yet identifiable stratification did exist between professional men and those of the working classes. There was also an important dividing line within the working class between skilled and unskilled workers. The distinctions were made evident by clothing and accessories which reflected earning capacities. The divisions between these social groups could thus be demonstrated by the type of fabric worn, the cut and fit of garments, the accessories and the price. For example, a cheap working man's suit of moleskin cost 35s. in 1880 compared to 42s. and upward for a gentleman's readymade 'International tweed suit' for city wear.[45]

Unquestionably, visitors to Australia had persistent difficulties in reading the signs of class, and this may have added strength to the myth of egalitarianism. The whole issue was exacerbated by the fact that, as in Britain, certain urban garments changed their status during the 1870s and 1880s. Some moved from being working-class garments to the dress of the bourgeoisie, and vice versa. For instance frockcoats and top hats, common for professional men in the 1860s and 1870s, were gradually being replaced for city wear in the 1880s by more casual morning coats. Looser-fitting lounge suits, or sac suits, and round felt hats were adopted for less formal wear and also by adventurous dressers and clerks.[46] This added a variety to the appearance of men in the city, as the general conversion to practical city suits systematically took place.

Tweed lounge suits, in use for informal wear in Britain by the 1850s, became popular in Australia by the 1860s. They could be purchased readymade, or else tailormade from a better-quality cloth for more wealthy clients. Urban working men adopted versions of this essentially middle-class garment, and by the early 1860s suits made of hard-wearing colonial tweed or imported shoddy had gained the stigma of an urban working-class costume. A cloth manufacturer, giving evidence to a New South Wales parliamentary committee investigating the state of manufactures in 1862, suggested that colonial tweed was used chiefly by the working classes.[47] This stigma lasted well into the 1880s. Evidence presented by a Victorian clothing manufacturer to the Royal Commission on the Tariff indicated that mercantile men and clerks did not want to wear tweed suits, presumably because of their association with workers, and that they preferred to buy black cloth coats.[48] These garments, like white, collared shirts, were more difficult to keep clean and therefore had the aura of respectability.

On the other hand, tweed, long in use by the higher classes for leisurewear, gradually changed its status. In Australia it had become acceptable for some upper-middle-class formal and city wear by the 1880s, thus further exacerbating the problems of interpreting the signs of class.[49] Like other types of working-class dress such as trousers, tweed changed its position in the hierarchy of acceptability: originally a lower-class fashion, it was adopted by the middle and upper classes.

The difficulties visitors had in relating men's dress to their social class in Australia had their counterpart in perception of women's dress as well. Here the problem of matching the visual signs of dress to the appropriate class took a different form. The dress of women was commonly regarded by bourgeois commentators as 'loud' and lacking in conformity with European models. Epithets such as brash, materialistic and provincial were, of course, not confined to Australia but generally applied to other new societies like Canada, the United States and South Africa.[50] Yet the issue of brashness in Australian dress is worth pursuing, for the claim did not suddenly appear in the 1850s as it did in America, but had an earlier provenance in generalisations about convict women being vulgar or overly fine in their appearance.

Accounts of the preoccupation with excessive dressiness of all classes can be traced back to the early years of settlement and continued throughout the century.[51] Ladies living in Hobart were observed by Ellen Viveash in 1834 to be extraordinarily extravagantly dressed.[52] Twenty years later the inhabitants were discussed in similar terms, and according to the commentator Daniel Ritchie, they seemed to have 'a less ladylike deportment' and 'greater display of showy colours' than their equivalent in British provincial towns.[53] Generally speaking, Australian ladies were alleged to be so preoccupied with elaborate or fussy clothing that its richness sometimes came dangerously close to being tasteless.[54] According to Twopeny in 1883, the overall appearance of all classes of women in Melbourne was pleasing, if somewhat 'flashy', but in detail it was 'execrable'. He states that 'whatever does not meet the eye is generally of the commonest'.[55]

Some of the criticisms focused on the excessive use of jewellery. Young Australian women were described as frivolous, talkative and overdressed. According to Frank Fowler in 1859, 'they wear as much gold chain as the Lord Mayor in his state robes. As they walk you hear the tinkle of the bunches of charms and nuggets, as if they carried bells on their fingers and rings on their toes.'[56] Jewellery was only one aspect of dress targeted in comments about the concern with elaborate and brightly coloured clothing.

Part of the reason that commentators complained so much about the garish jewellery and the bright colours worn in Australia was that both were uncomfortably similar to the dress of prostitutes.[57] In 1883 a young married Scottish woman, Mary McConachie, described a Brisbane street girl:

> vice flaunts itself in gaudy colours here. A common street girl's attire when out of doors is ruby velvet trimmed with cream lace, or perhaps peacock blue satin with cream lace, black satin or velvet with gold lace, white or cream silk, white hats with long drooping white feathers, and abundance of jewellery.[58]

In essence, clothes like these could almost equally have been worn by a fashionable, if flamboyant, colonial lady of the upper-middle classes.

Undoubtedly the subtext beneath these varied views of women's dress was a form of bourgeois moral chiding and fear of sexual deviancy from the norm. Attention to stylish dress could support the social status quo, but if pursued excessively could be a deleterious moral exemplar or a sign of unregulated social practices. As well as this, a direct link was being made between these colonial women, the instability of fashion and the decorative. In so doing, observers posited them as inferior, almost unacceptably different from the British norms of womanhood, and at times even morally degraded. This causal link between women and the triviality of fashion remains to an extent entrenched as a patriarchal attitude in Australia even today. Men's assumptions that women are non-cerebral and therefore to be defined by their clothes and appearance, rather than their productiveness or performance, still inform some corporate and workplace practices in the 1990s.

The relationship between Australian and British dress was by no means straightforward. Fashionable dressing in Australia arose out of social circumstances that were very different from those of Europe. The proportion of fashionably dressed people to those in working-class dress in the early years was significantly smaller than that in Europe. At the same time fashion and etiquette were accorded a position of almost exaggerated importance as social indicators. This is not to say that fashion was a reliable sign of class difference. Throughout the century visitors, quite certain of dress signifiers in Britain, were baffled by the difficulties in matching colonial clothing habits to social position.

On the other hand, a number of misconceptions about Australian dress have grown up over the years. Some of these perceptions had their origins in the nineteenth century. At this time British observers themselves had reasons for conveying less than accurate impressions to home readers. The myth of egalitarian dress is the most surprising of all, for it may have arisen more out of a nostalgic yearning for some unchanging rural utopia, than out of any real understanding of Australian life.

# 10

# ROUGH AND READYMADE: BUSH DRESS AND THE MYTHOLOGY OF THE 'REAL' AUSTRALIAN

From the middle of the nineteenth century, contemporary accounts of colonial dress began to claim that the most distinctive Australian clothes were those worn by outback men. The belief was that the 'real' Australian was a man of the bush, defined in part by his physique and attire; it needs evaluation, for the concept of this ideal national character—an almost heroic type of Crocodile Dundee—still persists in the realm of popular culture. It informed depictions of many of the Australian film heroes of the 1980s, and 'bushman' outfits for men and women are still being successfully marketed as truly Australian attire by the firm of R. M. Williams. Although one could argue that, within the context of its wearing, almost all colonial dress had its own distinctiveness, it was a dominant perception at the time that only the dress of men in the bush could qualify as truly unique.

What has to be considered is why Australian culture has been shaped by dominant myths of the bush and mateship, and why this tradition has been so resolutely blind to women. These issues have recently been brought to the fore by feminist historians, like Marilyn Lake and Kay Schaffer, who have queried the manner in which male history has been elevated to a universal position and accorded the legitimacy of being an all-embracing history.[1] The same critical questioning can be applied to the ways in which dress history has been, and continues to be, mythologised. For instance, Alison Lurie defines Australian dress as masculine yet worn by both sexes. She claims that garments suggesting the pursuit of kangaroos across the outback, such as khaki shirts and jackets and the famous bush hat, are worn by women as well as men.[2]

The origin of this dress mythology lies in perceptions about colonial life published from the 1840s onward. Richard Howitt, in his account of a four-year residence in

Australia, published in 1845, defined his concept of a colony as an environment that tested human nature and fully developed the character of men. Here, he claimed, old opinions, old habits and shackles were replaced by a new order of things—'in colonies men cast off all disguise'.[3] The idea that a man could be his natural self only in a colony like Australia subsequently elided with the belief that this freedom resided in the bush. There men, unfettered by domesticity, could share common ideals and behaviour, and dress in garments suited to outdoor life.

During the gold rushes of the 1850s, the concept arose that the bush was a place where men (not women) could shun convention, and it was futher romanticised by texts and images. The physical prowess and mateship of diggers, explorers and pastoral settlers, living lives of hardship on the land, was idealised as truly egalitarian. The years leading up to the centennial celebrations of 1888 provided an additional context for identifying unique colonial features and for national myth-making.[4] The definition of Australian culture, marking out that which was distinctive from Britain, was to centre on the egalitarian life of the bush. Commentators at the time, like Douglas Gane, alleged that here in the outback was the location where the 'true' Australian character was most noticeable.[5] Gane, and many of his nineteenth-century contemporaries, associated Australian national identity fundamentally with the outback, while at the same time regarding it as something almost exclusively masculine.

As the mythology about outback dress is of such longevity, it is useful to examine in detail the nature of actual rural dress and its relationship to the mythic construct. In doing so, it is important to consider the forces which operated in the negotiation between urban and bush dress codes and the exclusion of Aborigines and Chinese from the outback definitive, as well as the masculinisation of women within it. As the 'real' Australian has been conceived in terms of an ideal national character, it is also worth considering reasons for the lack of an official, culturally endorsed Australian national costume for either sex.

## Bush Dress for Men

In order to evaluate the role of dress in the mythology of the typical Australian, it is necessary to examine the actual evolution of men's clothing in rural areas. As practically no garments survive, texts and images are the primary source of information. Both Alexandra Joel and Marion Fletcher claim, somewhat questionably, that outback dress was indigenous to Australia, and Fletcher argues that it changed little between the 1840s and the 1890s.[6] The view that some relatively unchanging and 'typical' form of dress existed in rural Australia contributes to the idealisation of bush dress, for it fails to take into account the complexities and the varied forms of clothing actually in use.

In Europe, long before the nineteenth century, a dichotomy existed between town and country dress. In Australia accounts of bush clothing being distinct from urban dress do not occur until the late 1830s. This separation occurred at much the same time as Australia's essentially urban social character began to receive clear definition, coinciding with the pastoral push into the interior. In contrast to the white tropical gear, or coats of Parramatta cloth and trousers worn in Sydney during the late 1830s, the clothes of an overlander appeared very different. Mention is made in a letter from Thomas Darton of one such traveller arriving back in Adelaide in 1838: 'we understand he made the natives of Sydney stare with his knee breeches and top boots'.[7]

The specific form of bush dress which had evolved by this time, derived from European working-class clothing, was well adapted to the harsh living conditions in outback and pastoral areas. Little subject to fashionable change, it was practical, coarse and durable. Its special character was commended to emigrants, who were told that they should not bring fancy waistcoats, dandy boots or other idle vanities to Australia.[8] All that a male station dweller would require in summer were common slop trousers, such as the linen fall-front trousers belonging to Thomas Muir (Western Australian Museum), a blue guernsey, and a leather belt 'to keep the trousers up and the guernsey down'.[9] Clothing of this kind was worn fairly uniformly throughout rural Australia as men moved freely from one job to another. Goods, people and information were highly mobile in the pastoral age. Louisa Meredith found rural labouring dress in Van Diemen's Land monotonous and drab, compared to English country costume. She attributed this to the amalgamation of the various trades in the colonies.[10]

Yet bush dress was not always readily distinguishable from some working men's garments worn in urban areas during the 1840s and 1850s. Alexander Harris, writing about Sydney in the 1830s, described quite vividly the 'lowest class' in a public house, where he saw clothing that was to all intents and purposes similar to country dress. Of course one has to bear in mind that Harris was well educated and likely to have had little understanding of the life of working men. As he recorded it, there was:

> The blue jacket and trousers of the English lagger, the short blue cotton smock-frock and trousers, the short woollen frock and trousers, fustian jacket and trousers, and so forth, beyond my utmost power of recollection. Some wore neck-handkerchiefs; some none. Some wore straw hats some beavers, some caps of untanned kangaroo skin. And not a shin in the room that displayed itself to my eyes had on either stocking or sock.[11]

Both urban and rural working men wore special clothes on Sundays. Harris described these two forms of dress worn by bush sawyers at Lane Cove. Their working dress consisted of lace-up boots, duck trousers, check shirts, coloured silk neckerchiefs and straw hats; a combination of garments that was to become fairly standard for all classes on the land over the following years. Yet Harris observed that they sometimes varied their outfits on Sundays with 'whity brown socks and pumps, with a stylish blue jacket and waistcoat and black hat'.[12] These occasion-specific garments would have brought them almost in line with tradesmen living in either London or Sydney. This similarity between some urban and rural dress during the 1830s and 1840s indicates that, in certain instances, the strong demarcation between the two was still under negotiation.

In addition to the problems of defining bush dress too narrowly, there are many indications that rural clothing was not the static costume Joel and Fletcher claim. Several surviving smocks, worn in Australia, range in quality from those evidently worn for Sunday best and those clearly used for practical work.[13] More than simply varying in quality, dress worn by squatters and stockmen evolved over the course of the century. For instance in the 1840s the footloose and independent male squatters appeared to the gentry extremely rough in their country dress, with an unkempt personal appearance. According to the Scottish squatter Neil Black, who lived in Victoria, the bachelor squatter lived very much like his men, 'half-savage, half-mad . . . half-dressed, half-not, unshaven, unshorn, shoes never cleaned'.[14]

By the end of the 1840s the way of life of the squatter had altered. William Westgarth observed in 1848 that during the previous three to four years many squatters had taken wives, put up substantial mansions, and become the recipients of more home comforts.[15] These changed circumstances were to add a 'civilising' dimension to the squatters' existence and to their dress. Similarly, in Queensland changes were recorded, and an increasingly sober-coloured costume evolved for stockmen over the progress of the century.

By the early 1860s a marked differentiation existed between the clothes of squatters, stockmen and boundary riders. At this time a squatter on a station would be quite richly attired and wear the finest felt hat, or black-ribboned straw, and the best-quality thigh boots, compared to his boundary riders in red flannel shirts, cord breeches and cabbage-tree hats.[16] In the 1870s, at a time when there was considerable public interest and debate about the nature of 'Australian Types', the *Illustrated Sydney News* ran a series of articles on 'Types of Colonial Life'. Here the texts conform to a consciousness about the historical and evolving nature of local rural clothing. In contrasting the Early Squatter with the Modern Squatter, dress played a key part.[17] The Early Squatter was rough, unlettered and dressed in riding boots and a coarse straw hat. The modern squatter was educated, liked his home comforts and had a fine house. His dress was a sac suit and a low-crowned hat, both of which would have been quite appropriate for town wear.

There are some indications that bush dress was subject to regional variations. Louisa Meredith's view that rural clothing lacked the differentiation of European regional dress is contradicted by other accounts of life on the land. An article in the *Adelaide Examiner* drew attention to a very noticeable clothing distinction in South Australia during the early 1840s. The passage suggested that bushmen to the north of Adelaide dressed in red shirts, and those to the south and east generally wore blue.[18] Similarly, Dr John Dunmore Lang described squatters on the Darling Downs in 1851 wearing red shirts while those at Moreton Bay wore blue.[19]

The steamy conditions in Queensland also caused minor regional modifications in style. Bush dress in the tropics often consisted simply of a pair of light trousers and either a short-sleeved, open-necked shirt or a coloured flannel waistcoat.[20] Duck and cord trousers were sometimes too warm for the tropics; lighter cotton moleskin garments were more likely to be worn in the north. Constance Ellis, an extremely adventurous woman, in recalling outback Queensland of the later part of the century in her auto-biography, notes 'all men wore white moleskins for bush work in those days'.[21]

## Goldfields Dress

A number of the most colourful aspects of the dress of bush workers were appropriated by men on the goldfields. Garments worn by these men included brightly coloured

**37**  Ludwig Becker, *A Gold Holding, Bendigo*, 1853, watercolour (La Trobe Collection).

guernsey shirts (often broadly striped) or so called zebra-coloured jerseys. There were jumpers, 'horrid tartan things' in blue and scarlet, or with tawdry stripes of red and white or blue and white; in fact 'all sorts of strange and flaming colours'.[22] S. T. Gill's popular images of life on the goldfields consistently show men in striped shirts, vivid red and blue overshirts, straw hats and working men's caps. In addition to brightly coloured jumpers and shirts, miners wore broad buckled belts, monkey jackets (short, cropped coats), jaunty neckerchiefs and gay silk scarves. Not all goldfields dress was so debonair. Beef boots and moleskin or fustian trousers were just as common, since they were deemed to be most suitable for the rough conditions. Becker's illustration of *A Gold Holding, Bendigo* in 1853 shows men in strong, practical trousers, heavy-duty working jackets, leggings and cabbage-tree hats (Plate 37).

Casual hats were a key part of both bush and goldfields costume, from sugarloaf hats to 'currency hats', wideawakes, and Californian headwear. Many Californians were attracted to the Australian gold rushes and brought with them supposedly colourful mannerisms and a recognisable way of dressing. In the country, cabbage-palm hats, 'as large as an umbrella', tied under the throat and sometimes burnt black by the sun, were especially common.[23] Practical and cool, they were plaited from the plant *Livistonia australis* that grows in semi-coastal rainforest areas. Convicts and their associates in the early settlement years made and used hats of plaited straw.[24] Later the making of these hats from cabbage palm became a form of cottage industry, and many extant examples are of fine craftsmanship. By mid-century they could be very expensive. For instance in 1855 they cost 10s. each compared to ordinary straw hats at 1s. 3d.[25]

Cabbage-tree hats were not primarily a rural garment. They were worn in town as much as in the country, certainly in mid-century, and by both sexes.[26] At this time they were the mark of unruly town roughs—'The Cabbage Tree Mob'—who stressed their native origins and poked fun at more conservative male headwear.[27] Considerable cultural meaning has subsequently been invested in this form of headgear. Cabbage-tree hats have been described as significant emblems of outback Australia and erroneously associated only with men of the bush.[28] It is not clear why they have been so singled out. In this regard, their importance has been overdrawn, allowing them to become part of the general mythology of rural men's dress.

## The Mythology of Bush Dress

In spite of some regional and occupational differences associated with country and goldfields clothing for men, by the 1840s and increasingly from the 1850s, 'bush' dress became invested with connotations of communality and mateship. It came to be a signifier of ideals shared by men living closely together in harsh conditions. It was this perception, fuelled by literary anecdote and visual imagery, that helped to constitute the dress mythology of the typical Australian. Egalitarianism was to some degree an actual characteristic of rural dress. Yet considerable romanticism accrued to this form of clothing.

In itself the idealisation implicit in the egalitarian mateship ethic was partly a self-conscious response to the high degree of urbanisation in Australia during the nineteenth century.[29] As urban dress for men became progressively more drab, so bush clothing, and later that of the goldfields, became invested with messages of freedom and lack of inhibition for convention-burdened, middle-class town dwellers. In Australia, as in New Zealand, 'posh' clothes, that signified class distinctions and urban values, were a disadvantage within the supposed communality of frontier life.[30] The bearded *Squatter on the Nowhereataboo Creek*, illustrated in *Sydney Punch* (Plate 38), offers a visual example of this popularly perceived, egalitarian informality, with his rolled shirt sleeves, casually unbuttoned riding trousers, boots without stockings and a cabbage-tree hat.[31]

At times the casual, often itinerant, life of workers in the bush did foster an unusually casual attitude toward dress. Attributes of outback men that were admired were adaptability and the strength to endure physical hardship, rather than social position. To a degree this was reflected in their clothing. Bush workers were required to turn their hand to many trades and skills, thus lessening distinctions of status and occupation. Opportunities for class mixing existed that would have met with strong disapproval in urban environments. According to John Hood, a male acquaintance, when passing a station, would

> dress himself in the settler's garments, as a fresh rig-out, and leave his own till some other occasion; nay I have heard of the dress so left being found on the back of a second caller as better than his own, and so passed through different hands before its original proprietor saw it again.[32]

**38**   *Squatter on the Nowhereataboo Creek*, illustration from *Sydney Punch*, Jan 1857.

As the Reverend Mackenzie pointed out in his guide to the colonies, 'if in some countries the people can boast of their relays of horses, here we can boast of our relays of shirts'.[33] This could be construed as part of the mateship of bush life, but it would be misleading to overemphasise such supposed egalitarianism. Sharing arrangements of this kind reduced travelling expenses among the upcountry, mobile workforce. Although organised as a form of bush hospitality, it may have been no less than imperative for the survival of men in rural areas.

Notions of communality in bush dress were strengthened by the fact that rural garments were worn by squatter and labourer alike. The Governor's entourage, as well as pastoral workers, could assume such clothing. George Fitzroy, son of Sir Charles Fitzroy, Governor-General of Australia (1846–55), deliberately wore rural dress when travelling to New England in the late 1840s. He is described as wearing 'long boots, with a great piece cut out under the knee, and dark cornered unutterables, a stable jacket and waistcoat of small black and white check, and a coloured shirt and neckerchief, and in this behold a bushman's costume of the year 1847'.[34]

Although rural dress was quite commonly worn across all classes on the land, there were subtle differences in degree that reflected class distinctiveness, rather than lack of class implicit in this kind of clothing. A gentleman landowner could be readily distinguished from one of his employees, and other forms of difference in status were frequently noted. Mrs Meredith, describing workers at Port Sorell in Van Diemen's Land in the 1840s, indicated that she had observed various social levels, each with their own distinct dress. Labourers wore red or blue flannel shirts belted like blouses, while stock-keepers, who were virtually a class apart, purposefully indicated their position by wearing what she described as highly distinctive, oddly-cut coats and very strange hats.[35] Lieutenant Colonel Mundy, travelling in the Bathurst area, found that rural inhabitants wore a range of garments that accorded with their social position. He recorded:

> 'gents' in green cutaways and cords; 'parties' in black dress coats, and satin vests à la Doudnay, and white Berlin gloves and one or two old soldier-like figures, with stiff socks, formal whiskers and upright seats contrasted well with many gradations of the real 'currency cavalier', handsome looking men in loose tunics and blouses . . .[36]

Other forms of distinction included speech differences, general conduct and the degree of cleanliness.[37] Christopher Hodgson observed that 'you see master and man arrayed in no other vestments, save shirt and handkerchief "à la Byron", and trousers supported round the waist by a scarf or belt: the only difference is that the master's dress is scrupulously clean, while the men indulge in a change only at periodical intervals'.[38]

Rural and goldfields dress was more than merely an established set of garments reserved for rough country wear, with some regional and occupational differences. The manner in which it was worn, combined with perceptions of this form of dressing and visual and literary images came to constitute a clearly defined and popular mythology. From the 1840s, rural dwellers were increasingly regarded in colourful and romantic terms as the legend of the typical Australian began to gather momentum. By the following decade the bearded and unkempt appearance of outback men was already being described as picturesque in its disregard for convention. The lack of neatness and fashionable style was said to give rural men the appearance of being 'a swell out of luck'.[39] More importantly, the perceived disdain for social conventions, and disregard for elegant clothing, were invested further with the concept that they went hand in hand with an assertive kind of masculine vigour. This matched current idealised views about the masterful physical type of Australian bush workers, which portrayed them as manly in deportment and not loutish like the English labourer.[40]

Aside from their 'rough' mannerisms 'clinging like the burr of the fleece', rural men quite self-consciously adopted garments like boots, broad belts and open-necked shirts to emphasise their physicality. In the opinion of Louisa Meredith boots, worn by hirsute and smokey men, were a colonial epidemic.[41] Trousers were lined outside with kangaroo leather and fastened with a broad buckled or embossed belt at the waist or perhaps a bright silk scarf. Alternatively they were of ticking (heavy linen or cotton) or tight moleskin, 'cut so much to the quick that your dread of their bursting keeps you in a state of uncomfortable nervous apprehension'.[42] Lacy's *A Digger and Family* shows a woman accompanied by two such assertively dressed men. Her immediate companion has his thumb hitched into his belt in a nonchalant and overtly masculine gesture (Plate 39).

In some cases outback men appeared almost like gaucho poseurs in their loose over-tunics, bright neckerchiefs, monkey jackets and occasionally a gay waistcoat. According to Mary Macmanus, during the winter pastoral workers in the Maranoa district wore heavy rugs or ponchos in gaudy colours, that 'resembled the skins of the tiger or leopard'.[43] These were reputed to have been introduced into the colonies by Spanish gold-diggers.

The effect of a vigorous masculinity in bush and goldfields dress was increased by the common practice of cultivating an excessive amount of hair on the face, as well as on the head. Even ringlets were common. At a time when untrimmed beards were unusual in fashionable society, rural and goldfields men sported long beards of 'Samson-like' vigour and moustaches of 'Turkish' luxuriance.[44] Vernon Lee Walker described this long hair in the late 1870s. At Gisborne, halfway to Castlemaine, he found the people 'most awfully countrified with their hair half way down their backs'.[45] Whilst hairiness may have been due to the scarcity of barbers as much as anything, it carried explicit overtones of masculine strength.

By mid-century, the supposed egalitarianism of rural dress was closely linked to the notion that this clothing signified colonial experience. The pervasive belief that 'old hands' looked substantially different from 'new chums' saturated colonial literature from this period onward.[46] New arrivals immediately sought to participate in the prevalent ethos. This meant the prompt acquisition of rough clothes and equivalent manners.[47] Readymade smock-frocks, hard-wearing trousers, boots and a slouch felt hat were necessary purchases for newcomers to make them feel less conspicuous, and discourage the customary ridicule from 'old hands'. Merchants at the height of the gold rush were kept busy with the task of outfitting new emigrants. 'There was no business doing in Adelaide but the sale of outfits for the diggings' (Plate 40).[48]

It was up country where 'new chums' in city outfits were most noticeably out of place. There they betrayed themselves by their speech and the cut of their 'swell' clothes.[49] Clearly, in the country Australian dress had developed a distinctiveness that marked it out very readily from European styles. Yet this distinction was not confined to outback areas. New British emigrants, like Vernon Lee Walker, found they were identifiable by their clothes even in well-populated cities like Melbourne.[50] According to George Sutherland in 1886, few city men 'like to follow very closely the latest fashions of England or the Continent for fear of being contemptuously regarded as "new chums" '.[51]

The belief that a rural dress existed as typically Australian gained further cultural endorsement with the development of a pictorial tradition of images of the gold-digger

**39**    George Lacy, *A Digger and Family*, watercolour (Dixson Galleries, State Library of NSW).

and the bushman. A new emphasis on the imagery of ordinary working men, both visual and literary, began in the early 1850s as a result of the gold rushes.[52] Yet the highly colourful dress of miners in bright striped shirts, codified by S. T. Gill and others, is contradicted by written accounts. Goldfields dress was often dirty and unpleasant.

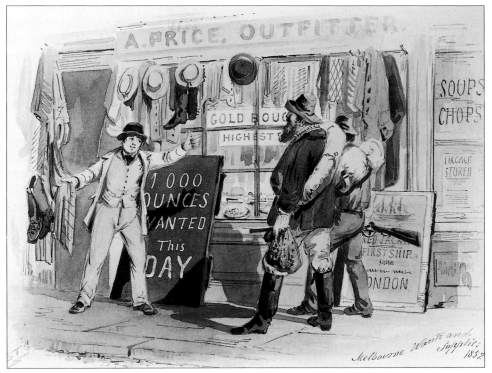

**40**   S. T. Gill, *Melbourne Wants and Supplies*, 1852, watercolour (Collection: Ballarat Fine Art Gallery).

According to William Kelly, diggers emerging from shafts were covered in grime and clay as if they were clothed in complete suits of yellow chamois leather.[53]

Whatever the truth, popular images of bush and goldfields life became entrenched in the illustrated press by the 1870s. The idealisation implicit in these images was given further impetus in the next decade with the monumental paintings of the Heidelberg school, proffering selected views of bush life through the eyes of city-based artists. The goldfields and bush mythology, as perpetrated in the illustrated press and by Tom Roberts and McCubbin, not only presented a romanticised view of outback life but ignored the historical changes that had occurred in rural dress, and also class and regional differences. Paintings like McCubbin's *Down on his Luck*, 1889 (Art Gallery of Western Australia), or *On the Wallaby Track*, 1896 (Art Gallery of New South Wales), portray a popular but heroicised image of bush life. The garments worn by the lone bushman are representative of the popular conception of bush clothing rather than the precise clothes that would have been worn.

It is impossible to disentangle entirely reality from myth, although undoubtedly most everyday dress worn in rural areas differed substantially from that of the legendary bushman or gold-digger as portrayed in literary accounts and popular imagery. Some of the mythology stems from the perception that rural dress represented wholesome, non-urban values. As such, rural clothing was increasingly regarded as picturesque, and by the 1880s invested with the same nostalgia that was applied to other rural activities.[54] Twopeny believed that it was an admirable and sensible kind of dress, although out of place in townships. He noted that the bushman made some concessions to urban styles when coming to town, by wearing a slop coat and a wide-brimmed, soft felt hat and a collar, but baulked at a tie. More significantly, he suggested that in town the slop clothes of the bushman appeared 'picturesque from the cavalier fashion in which he wears them'.[55]

Given the cultural assumption that the Australian character is a male subject, the perception that bush dress represented a key aspect of masculinity and physical prowess made such clothing significant in the construction of an Australian national identity. It must be noted that only the rural attire and physique of the white man, not that of Aborigines or the Chinese, received the cultural approbation of being distinctly Australian. Douglas Gane, who travelled widely in Australia, considered that examples of this true Australian race, big in stature, with profuse hair and florid complexions, could only be found in the interior.[56] These were men engaged in hard, physical labour, and they wore boots, readymade slops and slouch hats.

This dress has become fixed into a set of stereotyped garments, including a broad-brimmed felt hat, riding boots and moleskin trousers and is a form of cultural building block, aiding in the nationalising of the past. Because it was allegedly indigenous, it accrued even further value as a symbol of the 'real' Australian. This process was well under way by the 1890s, when Australian nationalism was being promoted by the popular media, including literature, ballads and engraved prints. According to Francis Adams, in his account of *The Australians* published in 1893, the one powerful and unique national type so far produced in Australia, was 'The Bushman'.[57]

## Women's Dress

Francis Adams made no mention of a female counterpart to 'The Bushman' although by the later part of the century the native-born 'Currency girl' had become transformed into the 'Australian girl'. She was identified as being unaffected, fearless and frank. Gilbert Parker considered that she had a special litheness and a 'pretty breezy directness quite her own'.[58] The 'Australian girl' was never regarded as picturesque, nor associated with any particular form of dress. She was either portrayed as the negative of the bushman, or acquired a kind of second-rate masculinity by 'being clever with horses or being a "tomboy"'.[59] Joseph Furphy wrote disparagingly of the daughter of a selector who did not have the evidence of Australian nationality on her upper lip; a 'short silky moustache which is the piquant trademark of our country women'.[60] The apparent inference of Furphy's text was that the thoroughgoing Australian woman was a surrogate man.

During the nineteenth century the colonial bush was perceived as an alien land to be mastered. Reputedly the bush was no place for a woman alone. In histories and fictional accounts women are portrayed in their dependent roles as wives, mothers and daughters, rather than as individuals shaping their own destinies.[61] So while male bush dress was heroicised, not only was any distinctiveness in the clothing of women overlooked, but the romantic notions associated with rural life tended to ignore their presence entirely.

Unlike male garments, those of women are seldom recorded as altering in any way as a result of bush life. Nor is there any mention of women sharing clothes or having any communal attitudes towards dress. There are some accounts that admire the lack of finesse in the dress of young country women and see it as a sign of their healthy naturalness—the old debate between nature and art—but these texts are rare. A. W. Stirling described a bush girl in 1884 as 'a splendid example of nature untaught by art: badly dressed, unpowdered, sometimes . . . unaccomplished'.[62] The majority of descriptions are of middle-class women, and they tend to dwell on the degree to which fashionable dressing and social niceties were maintained in the country.[63] In comparison to Stirling, most travellers' accounts, and those of the women themselves, frequently testify to the attempts to keep up with some semblance of fashionable styles.

The only way in which fashion could percolate into remote areas was through the despatch of actual garments, personal visits to the city, letters from family and friends, trade or store catalogues, pedlars' goods, or via illustrated magazines like the *Illustrated London News* and the *Queen*. The lack of up-to-date fashion information meant that styles changed abruptly, albeit infrequently, in remote areas. Rachel Henning, living in North Queensland, commented, 'we get hold of a fashion when we go to Sydney, and wear it till we go down there again'.[64] This problem diminished somewhat in the 1880s. By then more readymade clothing for women was commercially available and mail-order services had improved, but the difficulties were still considerable.

Despite the alleged 'dressiness' of some bourgeois female attire in outback communities, accounts evade the realities of existence for most rural women. Life for all classes could be arduous. Women married early in life and had larger families than in the city.[65] Their labour was held in low regard. Many worked in dairies, vegetable gardens and even cleared land, ploughed and sowed. The heat, the rigours and the dirt of country life meant that rural women of all social groups wore washable, durable print gowns and pattens (clogs). Whilst rural women are sometimes dressed for the purposes of the photographer in tightly corseted bodices, crinolines and the accoutrements of the bourgeoise, in everyday life their gowns were very simple in style with long sleeves or worn with short, caracao jackets. Undoubtedly they unlaced their corsets when undertaking labouring tasks, and the nature of daily life on properties meant that their clothes were coarse, hard-wearing and possibly years behind city fashions. A watercolour of a station nurse, by Harriet Neville-Rolfe in 1884 (Queensland Art Gallery), shows her wearing a dark-coloured gown, apron and kerchief. The high-waisted gown and ringlets suggest that she is more than forty years out of date in style.

Women in rural areas wore wide felt hats, or more frequently, protective sunbonnets or hoods for many daily activities.[66] The Quaker Margaret May, who lived near Mount Barker, noted in her diary, 'we always wear cotton bonnets to trudge from one room to another in summer, to keep us cool, in winter warm, and a good curtain behind protects our necks'.[67] Sunbonnets were not, as might have been expected, simply Quaker dress, which had its own colours and characteristics.[68] They were a form of rural clothing found in Britain, and quite commonly worn in Australia throughout the nineteenth

**41**    Eugene Von Guerard, *Black Hill*, 1854, watercolour (La Trobe Collection).

century. There seems to be no evidence that they exhibited any regional features, although collections such as that of the Powerhouse Museum reveal a variety of different types, most of them made of cotton.

Mary Gilmore (whose memories seem to be somewhat highly coloured at times) recalled that women always harvested in hoods while the men wore hats.[69] She also described the hoods worn by the very poor. These, she said, were made from worn-out moleskin trousers and tied with kangaroo-skin bootlaces.[70] Sunbonnets worn on the diggings were a common sight and were described by William Howitt as having a full flap behind, at least a foot long.[71] Two goldfields women wearing these protective sunbonnets are illustrated by Von Guerard in his group of *Black Hill*, 1854 (Plate 41). They appear with a number of men in occupational dress, such as a carter with an ill-fitting coat, and a 'Californian' (actually labelled as such) differentiated in his outfit by his boldness and his boots from a 'Colonial' in a checked shirt and bowyangs below his knees.

Sunbonnets were most characteristic of dress for outback women in the nineteenth century, and commonly worn by urban women as well for outdoor recreation, such as picnics and visits to the beach (Plate 35). Yet no cultural acknowledgement has been accorded to this form of headwear or to any other female garments. It is worth noting that, during World War I, 'kappies' (bonnets), gowns and aprons of a similar type were orchestrated and codified into a South African national costume.[72] Despite their active productive and reproductive life in rural areas, women within patriarchal Australian society were entirely silenced within the masculine ideology of mateship. Notions of egalitarianism and romance were not associated with any aspect of women's bush clothing, and they were completely excluded from the folklore of the typical Australian and his dress.

## Aborigines

The mythology about the Australian bushman and his appearance grew more intense during the gold-rush years. This mythology was one constructed by and for Europeans, without reference to Aborigines. Black men had begun to be employed on pastoral stations as stockmen and drovers from the 1840s. They were encouraged to dress like Europeans in working-class slop clothes and brimmed hats. Aboriginal station workers in Gippsland, for instance, are alleged to have identified closely with their employers and followed their way of dress when they could.[73] Slop clothing was officially dispensed by various Aboriginal Protection Boards. Yet Aboriginal working men, whose dress was often very like that of whites, were excluded from the bushman myth and attendant national mystique. There are likely to have been many reasons why blacks acquiesced in the adoption of European dress, but they were never accorded any positive place within the imagery of nationalism.

The traditional appearance and adornment of Aborigines was not admired in the nineteenth century, other than as a form of ethnographic curiosity. Aboriginal scarification, body paint, ornamental belts and fringes, and decorated native opossum cloaks were indigenous forms of dress that could have been given status as an 'Australian' folk dress. This did not occur. Abortive attempts after 1847 to induce male and female inmates of Oyster Cove settlement to wear a kind of north European regional peasant dress proved entirely misdirected. James Bonwick, who visited the settlement in 1859, found that this folk dress provided by the government, consisting of loose blue garments, red caps, tam o'shanters and handkerchiefs, had been sold for liquor, and the polka jackets were worn only on festive occasions.[74]

White Australians had scant regard for the traditional accoutrements of the indigenous people, and when Aborigines did assume the common clothing of bush workers, they were denied any part in the attendant white legends. What is interesting is that Aborigines themselves eventually sought to participate in the mythology of bush dress. According to Tim Rowse, by the 1950s and 1960s male Aborigines held cowboy or bush clothes in great regard, in part because they symbolised a shared work ethos amongst black and white men and the fellowship of the stockyard.[75]

## Mythology and National Dress

The concept of an Australian national type, a rugged male wearing bush hat, moleskins, shirt and boots was a construct of the 1840s and 1850s, and given additional romantic gloss by the popular and high art imagery of the 1880s and 1890s. Finch-Hatton observed in 1886 that many people, whose ideas of Australia were chiefly gathered from reproductions of bushrangers in illustrated magazines, imagined the inhabitants as always wearing enormous long boots halfway up the thighs. This, he said, was a delusion and called into question the very nature of typical Australian dress. 'The whole time that I was in the Bush, I never in my life saw a man with long boots on, unless he was a very recent arrival in the country.'[76]

By this period the idealisation of the bushman dressed in a classless, unchanging form of male 'backwoods' dress had become a powerful legend for those who lived in the cities. Associated with this fictional bushman were attributes of masculinity and mateship perceived to be important constituents of the Australian type. Local men were held to be recognisably 'colonial' in appearance, fostering the belief that 'old hands' looked quite different from new arrivals. For visitors and commentators, the regional character of some Australian dress codes was less noteworthy than this supposedly characteristic dress.

Rural clothing in Australia cannot be correlated with folk dress and it was not legitimised as a true national costume. Australia, like Britain, did not have a traditional folk costume, although both Wales and Scotland developed their own forms of national dress. What emerged as a stereotyped image of typical Australian male bush dress cannot be considered a national dress in any real sense, and it received no official recognition as such. It was more a sign of male nostalgia for, and identification with, the land, than a costume commonly in use.

Neither did an equivalent and characteristic female dress arise as a counterpart to this masculine construct. A comparison can be made with South Africa where national sentiment was fervidly associated with the formulation of an indigenous folk costume. This sentiment accelerated in the early twentieth century after the Boer War and, together with the euphoria surrounding the centenary celebrations of the Great Trek in 1938, was a major factor in the formation of a national dress there for both men and women.[77] Its fate in the new South Africa is yet to be decided, along with that of vast edifices like the Voortrekker Monument.

That Australia did not produce an official national dress as a corollary to its bush myths is not addressed by Russel Ward in his influential thesis of the mid-1960s, *The Australian Legend*. Indeed, it is remarkable that Ward paid so little attention to imagery and dress. If a collectivist morality and an anti-authoritarian egalitarian outlook were major ingredients in the formation of the legendary bushman, then one would expect appearance which reflected them to be of prime importance.[78] Yet this aspect has received hardly any critical attention. One reason for this could well be that clothes have been regarded by historians of the colonial period, like Ward, as a mundane part of social life, with no significance to national political history.

The association of bush costume with the 'real' Australian has related to the symbolic connection this kind of clothing had with masculinity, physical prowess and practical experience. Its symbolism was strong enough to allow the class nature of Australian dress to become obscured. It fostered the notion of a sharp division between urban and rural dress which belied the complexity of both styles of dress and which reinforced the erroneous belief that Australian urban clothing was a mere replica of European styles. Indeed, the strength of the myth of the legendary frontiersman is such that this form of dress is still held to be the only genuine Australian costume. Yet 'bush' dress can hardly be classed as typically Australian, since most Australians lived then, as now, in towns. The myth can be seen as a nostalgic construction, promoted and sustained by urban dwellers.

As Australia moves toward republicanism, the legendary construct of the 'real' Australian as a man of the land is likely to need some revision. In a multicultural society, where women increasingly move to take up positions of power, this atavistic image will surely be less meaningful. Yet, as Hugh Mackay points out in *Reinventing Australia*, Australians of the 1990s seem more anxious than ever to turn to the perceived values of the bush as a source of comfort and reassurance.[79] A most interesting speculation is whether the nostalgia for the countryside, and supposed ideals of our rural 'heritage', will extend to a mode of dress with a truly national identity. Alternatively, will the 'authentic' Country Road style prevail as an international trademark, as it does today, common to retail outlets from Sydney to New York?

# Appendix I

Estimate and final price of convict clothing, 1786

| Estimate of cost for clothing a male convict | | | Contract price of actual items supplied | | |
|---|---|---|---|---|---|
| 2 jackets | @ 4/6 | 9/– | 2 woollen jackets | @ 4/6 | 9/– |
| 4 woollen drawers | @ 2/– | 8/– | 4 woollen drawers | @ 1/9 | 7/– |
| 1 hat | @ 2/6 | 2/6 | 1 hat | @ 1/6 | 1/6 |
| 3 shirts | @ 3/– | 9/– | 3 check shirts | @ 2/6 | 7/6 |
| 3 frocks | @ 2/3 | 6/9 | 3 check frocks | @ 2/3½ | 6/10½ |
| 4 prs worsted stockings | @ 1/– | 4/– | 4 prs yarn stockings | @ 11d. | 3/8 |
| 3 prs trousers | @ 2/3 | 6/9 | 3 prs trousers | @ 2/2½ | 6/7½ |
| 3 prs shoes | @ 4/6 | 13/6 | 3 prs shoes | @ 3/– | 9/– |
| **TOTAL** (for one year) | £2 19s. 6d. | | **TOTAL** (for one year) | £2 11s. 2d. | |

*Source:* 18 Aug 1786, T 1/639 [PRO]; 7 Sep 1786, *HRNSW* II, 368.

The female clothes were not specified but estimated to the same amount. The contract price was doubled in the final issue which was for two years.

For each male convict, contractors undercut the total clothing estimate for two years by 16s. 8d. As supplies were issued for 680 male convicts, the overall saving to the government amounted to £566 13s. 4d. Thus total cost for male clothing came to £3479 6s. 8d. For each female convict the estimate for two years was undercut by £1 11s. 11d. This was considerably more than for the men. This made a saving of £111 14s. 2d. for the initial seventy women supplied.

# Appendix II

Expenditure in New South Wales on clothing imports from Britain (in pounds sterling), 1848–1861

| Date | Population | Apparel £ | Footwear £ | Hats £ | £ per head |
|------|------------|-----------|------------|--------|------------|
| 1848 | 220,474 | 55,510 | 13,529 | 6730 | .34 |
| 1851 | 197,168 | 68,481 | 18,104 | 9001 | .48 |
| 1852 | 208,254 | 98,258 | 51,186 | 12,840 | .77 |
| 1853 | 231,088 | 268,719 | 200,632 | 56,092 | 2.3 |
| 1856 | 266,189 | 96,984 | 195,420 | 30,290 | 1.2 |
| 1859 | 336,572 | 147,857 | 241,975 | 47,718 | 1.3 |
| 1861 | 358,278 | 122,748 | 275,677 | 30,569 | 1.19 |

Figures compiled from the *Statistical Returns of Imports of New South Wales*, 1848–61.

# Abbreviations

| | |
|---|---|
| Alp | Allport Library, Hobart |
| CO | Colonial Office |
| FL | Fryer Library, Brisbane |
| JOL | John Oxley Library, Brisbane |
| *HRA* | *Historical Records of Australia* |
| *HRNSW* | *Historical Records of New South Wales* |
| LaT | LaTrobe Library, Melbourne |
| ML | Mitchell Library, Sydney |
| MM | Maritime Museum, Greenwich |
| Mort | Mortlock Library, Adelaide |
| MUA | Melbourne University Archives |
| NL | National Library, Canberra |
| *NSW V and P LA* | *New South Wales, Votes and Proceedings of the Legislative Assembly* |
| *NSW V and P LC* | *New South Wales, Votes and Proceedings of the Legislative Council* |
| PRO | Public Records Office, London |
| SA | State Archives of New South Wales |
| SA PRO | South Australian Public Records Office |
| TA | Tasmanian State Archives |
| *VPP* | *Victoria, Votes and Proceedings of the Legislative Assembly and Papers presented to Parliament* |

# Notes

## Introduction

1  Virginia Woolf, *A Room of One's Own* 1929 (Harmondsworth: Penguin, 1973) 74.

2  Philippe Perrot, 'A Different Approach to the History of Dress', *Diogenes* 114 (1981) 162.

3  Michel Foucault, *Discipline and Punish. The Birth of the Prison* (Harmondsworth: Penguin, 1977) and Biddy Martin, 'Feminism, Criticism and Foucault', *Feminism and Foucault. Reflections and Resistances* ed. Irene Diamond and Lee Quinby (Boston: North Eastern University Press, 1988).

4  Sandra Lee Bartky, 'Foucault, Femininity, and the Modernization of Patriarchal Power', in *Feminism and Foucault* 61-2.

5  For instance A. G. L. Shaw, *Convicts and the Colonies: A Study of Penal Transportation from Great Britain and Ireland to Australia* (London: Faber and Faber, 1966) and Russel Ward, *Finding Australia: The History of Australia to 1821* (Victoria: Heinemann, 1987).

6  Joan Fox, 'Designing Differences', *Making a Life: A People's History of Australia since 1788* ed. Verity Burgmann and Jenny Lee (Fitzroy, Victoria: McPhee Gribble, 1988).

7  G. P. Walsh, 'Factories and Factory Workers in New South Wales, 1788-1900', *Labour History* 21 (1971), Katrina Alford, *Production or Reproduction: An Economic History of Women in Australia, 1788-1850* (Melbourne: Oxford University Press, 1984) and Monica Perrott, *A Tolerable Good Success: Economic Opportunities for Women in New South Wales, 1788-1830* (Sydney: Hale and Iremonger, 1983).

8  Elizabeth Wilson, *Adorned in Dreams: Fashion and Modernity* (London: Virago Press, 1985) 2-3.

9  Kim Sawchuk, 'A Tale of Inscription/Fashion Statements', *Canadian Journal of Political and Social Theory* 11 (1987) 55.

10  Alexandra Joel, *Best Dressed: Two Hundred Years of Fashion in Australia* (Sydney: William Collins, 1984) and Elizabeth Scandrett, *Breeches and Bustles: An Illustrated History of Clothes Worn in Australia, 1788-1914* (Lilydale: Pioneer Design Studio, 1978).

11  Kylie Winkworth, 'Provenance "a Guarantee of Paternity" ', *The Australian Antique Collector* July/Dec (1984) 80.

12  Margaret Maynard, 'Terrace Gowns and Shearer's Boots: Rethinking Dress in Public Collections', *Culture and Policy* 3 (1992) 80.
13  As an example of this, the Australian National Gallery has, until the recent cutbacks, collected international couturier dress, wearable art, Australian fashion photographs and theatre costume. It has never seriously collected Australian fashion. Jane de Teliga, 'Twentieth Century Costume: A Focus for Australian Museums', *Art and Australia* 19 (1982) 348.
14  Penal dress is located in a number of collections including the Queen Victoria Museum, Launceston, the Hyde Park Barracks, Sydney, the Tasmanian Art Gallery, The Australian Museum and the Mitchell Library.
15  Tony Bennett, 'Out of Which Past? Critical Reflections on Australian Museum and Heritage Policy', *Cultural Policy Studies* Occasional Paper No. 3 (1988) 16.

# 1    *Irregular Patterns*

1  Beverely Lemire, 'Consumerism in Preindustrial and Early Industrial England: The Trade in Secondhand Clothes', *Journal of British Studies* 27 (1988).
2  Macquarie to Bathurst, 28 Feb 1820, Colonial Despatches CO 201/99 [PRO].
3  Diana de Marly, *Working Dress: A History of Occupational Clothing* (New York: Holmes and Meir, 1986).
4  Evidence of John Steven, *Report from the Select Committee on Secondary Punishments*, House of Commons 1832, 28 and 21 Dec 1843, *HRA* iii, 213.
5  John Bradley Hirst, *Convict Society and its Enemies: A History of Early New South Wales* (Sydney: Allen and Unwin, 1983) 127.
6  *Ibid.*, 82.
7  Robin Evans, *Fabrication of Virtue: English Prison Architecture 1750–1840* (Cambridge: Cambridge University Press, 1982) Introduction.
8  David Neal, *The Rule of Law in a Penal Colony: Law and Power in Early New South Wales* (Cambridge: Cambridge University Press 1991) 14.
9  *Report on Secondary Punishments*, 1832, 28.
10  7 Sep 1786, *HRNSW* II, 368, and Treasury Letters, 10 May 1787, ADM/OT [MM].
11  John Howard, *The State of the Prisons in England and Wales* (London: Warrington, 1777–84) 312.
12  Marine undress is described in Return of Slops Received and Issued, Port Jackson, 30 Sep 1788, ADM 1/3824 and Letters Relating to the Marines, Botany Bay, 1787, ADM 2/1178 [PRO].
13  Cyril Field, *Britain's Sea Soldiers* II (Liverpool: Lyceum Press, 1924) 21–2.
14  Fox, 'Designing Differences', 18.
15  John Cobley, *Sydney Cove, 1788* (London: Hodder and Stoughton, 1962) 123.
16  John Thomas Bigge, *Report of the Commissioner of Inquiry into the State of the Colony of New South Wales*, House of Commons, 1822, 49.
17  *Ibid.*, 61–2, and 30 Oct 1802, *HRNSW* IV, 875.
18  Hobart Public Notice, 16 Aug 1822, Soull Papers, 459. A 1352 [ML].
19  8 Aug 1791, *HRNSW* I, ii, 510.
20  18 Nov 1791, *HRA* 1, i, 308, and 26 Jun 1792, *HRNSW* I, ii, 629.
21  Contract for transporting convicts, 27 Aug 1789, Accounts and Papers Relating to Convicts on Board the Hulks and those Transported to New South Wales, 10–26 Mar 1792, 56, *House of Commons Reports and Papers* (83) 1791–2.
22  Phyllis Cunnington and Catherine Lucas, *Charity Costumes of Children, Scholars, Almsfolk, Pensioners* (London: A. and C. Black, 1978) 8.
23  15 Nov 1793, *HRNSW* II, 81.
24  15 Nov 1793, *HRA* I, i, 457.

25  Paula-Jane Byrne, 'Women and the Criminal Law: Sydney 1810-1821', *Push from the Bush: A Bulletin of Social History* 21 (1985) 4 and 17.

26  10 Sep 1801, *HRNSW* IV, 323.

27  8 May 1837, WO 47/1752 [PRO].

28  8 Aug 1810, Government and General Orders, NC 11/5 [SA].

29  The short government jacket is mentioned in Bigge, *Report* 63.

30  Linda Young, 'The Experience of Convictism: Five Pieces of Convict Clothing from Western Australia', *Costume* 22 (1988) 81.

31  17 May 1833, WO 47/1609 [PRO].

32  There is no direct evidence that the man wearing gray in the left background was either a ticket-of-leave man or an educated convict, nor that the man in blue was privately assigned as suggested by Joan Kerr and Hugh Falkus, *From Sydney Cove to Duntroon. A Family Album of Early Life in Australia* (Richmond, Victoria: Hutchinson, 1982) 32.

33  Sandra Blair, 'The Felonry and the Free? Divisions in Colonial Society in the Penal Era', *Labour History* 45 (1983) 13.

34  John Douglas Ritchie, *The Evidence to the Bigge Reports. New South Wales Under Governor Macquarie* II (Melbourne: Heinemann, 1971) 92-3.

35  Opinions on the Conduct of Convicts. Unpublished Appendix to Bigge's Reports. 20 Jan 1820, CO 201/118 [PRO].

36  *Report on Secondary Punishments* 1832, 28.

37  Government and General Order, *Sydney Gazette*, 10 Sep 1814.

38  Hirst, *Convict Society and its Enemies*, 111.

39  Young, 'The Experience of Convictism', 81.

40  Foucault, *Discipline and Punish*, 259-62.

41  Examples of complete suits or partial garments can be found in the following collections: Mitchell Library, Sydney; Tasmanian Art Gallery; Australian Museum, Sydney; Queen Victoria Museum, Launceston; Port Arthur; and Western Australian Museum.

42  Bigge, *Report*, 49.

43  *Ibid.*, 61.

44  Ritchie, *The Evidence to the Bigge Reports*, I, 17.

45  Margaret Maynard, 'A Form of Humiliation: Early Transportation Uniforms in Australia', *Costume* 21 (1987) 62.

46  William D. Forsyth, *Governor Arthur's Convict System: Van Diemen's Land, 1824-1836* (Sydney: Sydney University Press, 1970) 85.

47  17 Oct 1826, Memoranda for the Consideration of the Clothing Board CSO 1/34/599 [TA].

48  Augustus Prinsep, *The Journal of a Voyage from Calcutta to Van Diemen's Land* (London: Smith Elder, 1833) 112.

49  Brian Fletcher, *Ralph Darling. A Governor Maligned* (Melbourne: Oxford University Press, 1984) 122. Macleay to Hely, 10 Aug 1830, 4/3667 [SA].

50  *Report from the Select Committee on Transportation*, Appendix, House of Commons 1812, 109; and *Report* 1832, 352.

51  Byrne, 'Women and the Criminal Law', 12.

52  20 Apr 1828, CSO 1/34/599 [TA].

53  Rules and Regulations for the Management of Female Convicts at the New Factory at Parramatta, 31 Jan 1821, Unpublished Appendix to Bigge's Reports CO201/118 [PRO].

54  Rules for Regulation Dress, Female Factory, 26 Aug 1824, 4/1708 [SA].

55  Dress for Females in the Factory, 20 Apr 1828, Memoranda for the Consideration of the Clothing Board CSO 1/34/599 [TA].

56  'Rules and Regulations, House of Correction for Females', *Hobart Town Courier*, 10 Oct 1829.

57  Bigge, *Report* 11.

58   The letter enclosed in a despatch of 30 August 1823 is quoted in Kay Daniels and Mary Murnane, *Uphill All the Way: A Documentary History of Women in Australia* (St Lucia: University of Queensland Press, 1980) 9–10.

59   Elizabeth Fry, *Observations on the Visiting, Superintendence and Government of Female Prisoners* (London: J. and A. Arch, 1827) 60–1.

60   Michael Sturma, 'Eye of the Beholder: The Stereotype of Women Convicts, 1788-1852', *Labour History* 34 (1978) 4.

61   Daniel Mann, *The Present Picture of New South Wales* (London: John Booth, 1811) 80.

62   Female Factory, Report of Board, 2 April 1826, 255, 4/1791 [SA].

63   Evidence of the Police Magistrate, Tasmania, *Report from the Select Committee on Transportation*, House of Commons, 1838, 119.

64   Kay Daniels, 'Prostitution in Tasmania during the Transition from Penal Settlement to "Civilized" Society', *So Much Hard Work: Women and Prostitution in Australian History* ed. Kay Daniels (Sydney: Fontana, 1984) 33.

65   Byrne, 'Women and the Criminal Law', 17.

66   Daniels and Murnane, *Uphill All the Way*, 21.

67   Kay Daniels, 'Feminism and Social History', *Australian Feminist Studies* I (Summer 1985) 29.

68   Report, Police Office, Hobart, 14 Jan 1839, *Parliamentary Papers on Transportation* 6 (1810–41).

# 2   *Fraying at the Edges*

1   Eric Jones and Geoffrey Raby, 'The Fatal Shortage: Establishing a European Economy in New South Wales 1788-1805', *Studies from Terra Australis to Australia*, ed. John Hardy and Alan Frost (Canberra: Australian Academy of the Humanities, 1989) 158.

2   2 Oct 1827, *HRA* I, xiii, 534.

3   List of Articles Required by Private Individuals, Ordnance 4/1703 [SA].

4   Letter to the Editor, *Monitor*, 26 Jun 1826, 43.

5   *Monitor*, 30 Jun 1826, 52. This item appeared the year after Goulburn ceased his position as Colonial Secretary.

6   Lumber Yard List, 5 Feb 1829, CSO 1/34/599 [TA].

7   Aileen Ribeiro, 'Provision of Ready-made and Second-hand Clothing in the Eighteenth Century in England', *Per Una Storia della Moda Pronta*, CISST Conference Milan, 1990, 88.

8   26 Dec 1789, Navy Board Minutes, ADM 106/2622 [MM].

9   *Accounts and Papers Relating to Convicts on Board the Hulks and Those Transported to New South Wales*, March 1792, 53.

10   Roger Knight, 'The First Fleet: Its State and Preparation, 1786-1787', *Studies from Terra Australis*, 135.

11   David Mackay, *A Place of Exile: European Settlement of New South Wales* (Oxford University Press: Melbourne, 1985) 8.

12   'Estimate of Clothing to Serve a Male Convict for One Year' in Heads of a Plan, T1/639 [PRO]. Female dress was calculated to amount to the same value as the male clothing but was not specified by garment.

13   Phillip's Views on the Conduct of the Expedition, 1787, *HRNSW* I, ii, 53.

14   2 Sep 1787, *HRNSW* I, ii, 111–12.

15   *Sydney's First Four Years: Being a Reprint of a Narrative of the Expedition to Botany Bay*, introd. L. F. Fitzhardinge (Sydney: Angus and Robertson, 1961) 83.

16   Jul 1790, *HRNSW* I, ii, 388.

17   'Slop Clothing Received', Apr 1790–Dec 1792, NC 11/1 [SA].

18   Ken Buckley and Ted Wheelwright, *No Paradise for Workers: Capitalism and the Common People in Australia, 1788-1914* (Melbourne: Oxford University Press, 1988) 38–9.

19  Officers' petition to land goods and a small supply of clothing from Bengal, 13 Jan 1800, *HRNSW* IV, 19.

20  5 Jun 1802, *HRA*, I, iii, 527.

21  9 Nov 1812, *HRA* I, vii, 527.

22  Macquarie to Bathurst, 1 Sep 1820, CO 201/99.

23  Government Order, 29 Jun 1831, *Sydney Gazette*, 5 Jul 1831, fp.

24  Evidence of William Cox, 25 Nov 1819, Bonwick Transcripts, Box 5, 1962 [ML].

25  24 Feb 1803, *HRA* I, iv, 22, and 14 Jul 1804, *HRA* I, v, 90.

26  20 Jun 1801, *HRNSW* IV, 409.

27  Act for the More Effectively Preventing Persons from Purchasing or Receiving Clothing etc., 17 Jul 1828, Geo. IV n.10.

28  See Mollie Gillen, 'The Botany Bay Decision 1786: Convicts not Empire', *English Historical Review* 97 (1982) and Alan Frost, 'Botany Bay: An Imperial Venture of the 1780s', *ibid.*, 100 (1985).

29  Mackay, *A Place of Exile*, 64-5.

30  25 Apr 1787, *HRA* I, i, 13.

31  25 Apr 1787, *HRNSW* I, ii, 89.

32  Frost, 'Botany Bay', 323, and Geoffrey Blainey, *The Tyranny of Distance* (Melbourne: Sun Books, 1977) 34.

33  Gillen, 'The Botany Bay Decision', 764.

34  Margaret Hazzard, *Punishment Short of Death: A History of the Penal Settlement at Norfolk Island* (Melbourne: Hyland House, 1984) 20.

35  18 Oct 1796, *HRNSW* III, 154.

36  2 Mar 1798, *HRNSW* III, 375.

37  31 Jan 1797, *HRNSW* III, 191, and 14 Dec 1797, *HRNSW* III, 334.

38  29 Aug 1802, *HRNSW* IV, 825.

39  James Semple Kerr, *Design for Convicts: An Account of Design for Convict Establishments in the Australian Colonies During the Transportation Period* (Sydney: Library of Australian History, 1984) 22.

40  17 Sep 1803, *HRNSW* V, 221.

41  6 Apr 1804, *HRA* I, iv, 629.

42  Return of the Whole of the Cloth Manufactured at the Government Factory, 1814-1819, Unpublished Appendix to Bigge's Reports, CO 201/118 [PRO].

43  Female Factory, Report of Board, 12 Apr 1826, 255, 4/1791 [SA].

44  7 Mar 1828, *HRA* I, xiv, 20.

45  Annette Salt, *These Outcast Women: The Parramatta Female Factory, 1821-1848* (Sydney: Hale and Iremonger, 1984) 102 and 105.

46  Report of the Board of Management of the Female Factory, 31 Dec 1829, 4/2094 [SA].

47  Timothy A. Coghlan, *Labour and Industry in Australia* I (London: Oxford University Press, 1918) 129-30.

48  James Atkinson, *An Account of the State of Agriculture and Grazing in New South Wales* (London: J. Cross, 1826) 108 and 131.

49  Advertisement for Mr Browne's Store, *Sydney Gazette*, 6 May 1820, 859.

50  See the rather late account in David Waugh, *Three Years Practical Experience of a Settler in New South Wales: Being Extracts from Letters to his Friends in Edinburgh 1834-7* (Edinburgh: John Johnstone, 1838) 48.

51  Letter from Hugh Watson, 9 Sep 1839, D6075 (L), [Mort].

52  Advertisement, *Sydney Gazette*, 21 Oct 1815.

53  Bigge, *Report*, Commons 1823, 52, and Salt, *These Outcast Women*, 102 and 104.

54  Walsh, 'Factories and Factory Workers', 4.

55  *Australian*, 29 Aug 1842, 2.

56  'Hunter River Society', *Maitland Mercury*, 18 Mar 1843, 2.

57  'Hunter River Society', *Australian*, 14 Oct 1842, 3.
58  David-Thiery Ruddel, 'The Domestic Textile Industry in the Region and City of Quebec, 1792-1835', *Material History Bulletin* 17 (1983) 118.
59  Observations Made on Sundry Articles Sent Out to New South Wales, by Mr. Alexander Davison, 24 Mar 1791, CO 201/1 [PRO].
60  2 Oct 1792, *HRNSW* I, ii, 643. There were also 320 rotten and useless jackets as a result of damp on the *Resolution*, 10 Dec 1794, *HRA* I, i, 485.
61  Major Ross to the Admiralty, 10 Jul 1788, ADM I/3824 [PRO].
62  Hirst, *Convict Society and its Enemies*, 83.
63  17 Nov 1812, *HRA* I, vii, 614.
64  1 Jun 1829, *HRA* I, xv, 4.
65  'Work at the Government Factory', Vouchers to the Treasurer's Disbursements, I, 1824, 8, 2/855 [SA].
66  *Sydney Gazette*, 2 May 1829.
67  Record of Stores Issued, Ordnance Daybook, 1839-42, 4/483 [SA].
68  Ritchie, *The Evidence to the Bigge Reports* I, 16.
69  22 Dec 1827, *HRA* I, xiii, 662-4.
70  Alford, *Production or Reproduction?* 164.
71  7 Mar 1828, *HRA* I, xiv 22.
72  *The Sirius Letters*, ed. Nance Irvine (Sydney: Fairfax Library, 1988) 95.
73  26 Apr 1798, *HRNSW* III, 379.
74  1 Mar 1802, *HRA* I, iii, 439.
75  15 Oct 1805, *HRA* I, iii, 331-4.
76  Ritchie, *The Evidence to the Bigge Reports* I, 16.
77  31 Dec 1800, *HRNSW* IV, 280ff.
78  Hazel King, *Elizabeth Macarthur and Her World* (Sydney: Sydney University Press, 1980) 162.
79  See the list of samples of his manufactories submitted to Bigge, 1 Feb 1821, Unpublished Appendix to Bigge's Report vol. 129, 6107 and 6109 [ML].
80  *Monitor*, 21 Jul 1826, 79.
81  Editorial, *Hobart Town Courier*, 14 Mar 1834.
82  30 Jan 1833, Riley Papers 74a, A III [ML].
83  Margaret Steven, 'The Changing Pattern of Commerce in New South Wales, 1810-1821', *Business Archives and History* (Aug 1963) 142.
84  Quoted in Fletcher, *Costume in Australia*, 38.
85  See the auction for new and old wearing apparel advertised by S. Lyons, *Currency Lad*, 24 Feb 1833, fp, and the auction for readymade clothing, *Monitor*, 20 Apr 1840, 7.
86  *Sydney Gazette*, 17 Apr 1803.
87  *Ibid.*, 15 May 1803.
88  Advertisements, *Monitor*, 21 Jul 1826, 79, and *Launceston Advertiser*, 4 May 1829.

# 3   A Cut Above

1  Beverley Lemire, 'The Theft of Clothes and Popular Consumerism in Early Modern England', *Journal of Social History* 24 (1990-1).
2  Elizabeth Windschuttle, 'The New Science of Etiquette', *Push from the Bush: A Bulletin of Social History* 7 (1980) 61.
3  Mann, *The Present Picture*, 44.
4  Robert Burford, *Description of the View of the Town of Sydney, New South Wales* (London: J. and C. Adelard, 1829) 6.

5   Alan Frost, 'Going Away, Coming Home', *Studies from Terra Australis*, 221.

6   Tatiana de Fircks, 'Costume in the Early Years of Western Australia', *Journal and Proceedings of the Royal Western Australian Historical Society* 9 (1988) 28.

7   See descriptions of this life in Barrie Dyster, *Servant and Master: Building and Running the Grand Houses of Sydney, 1788-1850* (Sydney: New South Wales University Press, 1989).

8   M. Barnard Eldershaw, *The Life and Times of Captain John Piper* (Sydney: Australian Limited Edition Society, 1939) 124.

9   Louisa Meredith, *Notes and Sketches of New South Wales during a Residence in that Colony, 1839-44* (Harmondsworth: Penguin, 1973) 50.

10  Clara Aspinall, *Three Years in Melbourne, 1858-61* (London: L. Booth, 1862) 33.

11  Thorstein Veblen, *The Theory of the Leisure Class: An Economic Study of Institutions* (New York: Macmillan, 1912) 170.

12  Georg Simmel, 'Fashion', *On Individuality and Social Forms*, ed. Donald N. Levine (Chicago: University of Chicago Press, 1971) 308.

13  Robert William Connell and T. H. Irving, *Class Structure in Australian History* (Melbourne: Longman Cheshire, 1980) 51.

14  *Ibid.*, 62.

15  As quoted from King, *Elizabeth Macarthur*, 189-90.

16  Leonore Davidoff, *The Best Circles: Society, Etiquette and the Season* (London: Croom Helm, 1973) 14.

17  As quoted from Malcolm Henry Ellis, *John Macarthur* (Sydney: Angus and Robertson, 1955) 282.

18  As quoted from Windschuttle, 'The New Science of Etiquette', 2.

19  Peter Cunningham, *Two Years in New South Wales* I (London: Henry Colburn, 1827) 53.

20  Marian Aveling, 'Imagining New South Wales as a Gendered Society 1783-1821', *Australian Historical Studies* 98 (1992) 11.

21  *Sydney Gazette*, 14 Jul 1810.

22  Marsden Family Letters, 6 Sep 1799, 719 [ML].

23  *Sydney Gazette*, 22 Jul 1804.

24  William Bligh Correspondence, 10 Oct 1807, 105, Safe 1/45 [ML].

25  Perrott, *A Tolerable Good Success*, 96. At the Muster of 1806, out of a total of 818 ex-convict women, only one mantua-maker, one milliner and two seamstresses were listed.

26  *General Muster of New South Wales 1814*, ed. Carol Baxter (Sydney: Australian Biographical and Genealogical Record, 1987).

27  *Sydney Gazette*, 17 Apr 1803.

28  *Ibid.*, 19 Jun 1808.

29  Perrott, *A Tolerable Good Success*, 108.

30  Alford, *Production or Reproduction?*, 162.

31  Portia Robinson, *The Hatch and Brood of Time: A Study of the First Generation of Native-Born White Australians, 1788-1828* (Melbourne: Oxford University Press, 1985) 126.

32  *Sydney Gazette*, 7 Oct 1804.

33  *Ibid.*, 17 Aug 1811.

34  'The King's Birthday', *ibid.*, 29 Apr 1826.

35  *Sydney Society in Crown Colony Days: The Reminiscences of the Late Lady Forbes*, ed. George Forbes, typewritten (1914) 23 [ML].

36  Christiana Brooks, Diary, Feb 1827, Typescript 1559 [NL].

37  Cunningham, *Two Years* I, 48 and 54.

38  Handbill, 1827, Macarthur Clothing Accounts, A4288 [ML].

39  *Ibid.*

40  Alford, *Production or Reproduction?*, 197.

41  *Sydney Gazette*, 6 Jan 1827.
42  *Monitor*, 16 Jul 1826, 39, 3 Feb 1827, 303, and 20 Apr 1827; *Sydney Gazette*, 4 Nov, 1 Jul 1824 and 2 Jan 1823.
43  *Monitor*, 30 Mar 1827, 361, and 6 Apr 1827, 369.
44  Cunningham, *Two Years* I, 53.
45  Advertisement for fashionable Parisian book muslin dresses, *Hobart Town Courier*, 30 Aug 1828, and advertisement for French jewellery, *Sydney Gazette*, 3 Nov 1819.
46  Cunningham, *Two Years* I, 54.
47  *Australian*, 14 Feb 1827.
48  *Sydney Gazette*, 9 Sep 1820.
49  Accounts and Bills of Mrs John Macarthur, Macarthur Papers, vol. 13, A2909 [ML].
50  Anna Frances Walker Papers, 462/4 pt 2 [ML].
51  All Anna's wedding garments are owned by the Historic Houses Trust of New South Wales. My thanks to June Swann for her opinion on the shoes.
52  Anna's hobby and the silk 'shawl' are described in *Sydney Gazette*, 25 Feb 1826, 3.
53  Cunningham, *Two Years* I, 53.
54  Atkinson, *An Account of the State of Agriculture*, 29.
55  'London Fashions for March', *Monitor*, 21 Jul 1826, 75.
56  *Sydney Gazette*, 23 Sep 1804.
57  Helene Roberts, 'The Exquisite Slave: The Role of Clothes in the Making of the Victorian Woman', *Signs* 2 (1977).
58  Aileen Ribeiro, *Dress and Morality* (London: Batsford, 1986) 127.
59  *The Artist and the Patron: Aspects of Colonial Art in New South Wales* (Art Gallery of New South Wales, 1988) 20.
60  Elizabeth Windschuttle, 'Feeding the Poor and Sapping their Strength: The Public Role of Ruling-Class Women in Eastern Australia, 1788-1850', *Women, Class and History: Feminist Perspectives on Australia, 1788-1978*, ed. Elizabeth Windschuttle (Melbourne: Fontana/Collins, 1980) 24 and 54.
61  *Sydney Gazette*, 3 Apr 1827, 2.
62  Neal, *The Rule of Law*, 53.
63  *The Tanner Letters: A Pioneer Saga of Swan River and Tasmania, 1831-45* compiled by Patricia Statham (Nedlands: University of Western Australia Press, 1981) 75.
64  Meredith, *Notes and Sketches*, 51.
65  Alford, *Production or Reproduction?*, 39-41.
66  Valerie Steele, *Fashion and Eroticism: Ideals of Feminine Beauty from the Victorian Era to the Jazz Age* (New York: Oxford University Press, 1985) 102 and 105.
67  Brooks, Diary, Mar 1826 [NL].
68  Sturma, 'Eye of the Beholder', 4.
69  Fry, *Observations*, 60-1.
70  James Mudie, *The Felonry of New South Wales*, 1837, ed. Walter Stone (Melbourne: Lansdowne, 1964) 121.
71  *Report on Transportation*, 119.
72  Bigge, *Report* 11.
73  Cunningham, *Two Years* I, 68.
74  Letter from Thomas Gates Darton, 15 Jun 1838, PRG 456/1/57 [Mort].
75  Evidence of Samuel Marsden in Ritchie, *The Evidence to the Bigge Reports* II, 92-3.
76  Opinions on the Conduct of Convicts, Unpublished Appendix to Bigge's Reports, CO 201/118, 20 Jan 1820 [PRO.]
77  *Ibid.*

# 4   On the Fringe

1   W. E. H. Stanner, *White Man Got No Dreaming: Essays, 1938-1973* (Canberra: Australian National University Press, 1979) 180.
2   Ann McGrath, 'The White Man's Looking Glass: Aboriginal-Colonial Gender Relations at Port Jackson', *Australian Historical Studies* 24 (1990) 189.
3   'Particulars of Aid Given to Aborigines', *NSW V and P LA* 1882 (4) 1527.
4   Glyndwr Williams, 'Reactions on Cook's Voyages', *Seeing the First Australians*, ed. I. and T. Donaldson (Sydney: Allen and Unwin, 1985) 48.
5   15 May 1788, *HRA* I, i, 28.
6   John Hunter, *An Historical Journal of the Transactions at Port Jackson and Norfolk Island* (London: Stockdale, 1793) 57.
7   Alan Frost, *Arthur Phillip, 1738-1814: His Voyaging* (Oxford: Oxford University Press, 1987) 185.
8   Neville Green, *Broken Spears: Aboriginals and Europeans in the Southwest of Australia* (Perth: Focus Education, 1984) 32.
9   Williams, 'Reactions', 40.
10  Green, *Broken Spears*, 46.
11  Richard Wright, 'A Modicum of Taste: Aboriginal Cloaks and Rugs', *Australian Institute of Aboriginal Studies Newsletter*, New Series, Mar (1979) 54.
12  Henry William Haygarth, *Recollections of Bush Life in Australia* (London: John Murray, 1850) 105.
13  Wright, 'A Modicum of Taste', 56-8.
14  Joseph P. Townsend, *Rambles and Observations in New South Wales* (London: Chapman and Hall, 1849) 94.
15  N. J. B. Plomley, 'Pictures of the Tasmanian Aborigines', *Art Bulletin of Tasmania* (1983) 44.
16  Meredith, *Notes and Sketches*, 72.
17  Jeanette Hoorn, *The Lycett Album: Drawings of Aborigines and Australian Scenery* (Canberra: National Library of Australia, c.1990) 10-11.
18  5 Jul 1788, *HRA* I, i, 45.
19  10 Jul 1799, *HRNSW*, III, 691.
20  *Account of the English Colony at Botany Bay* (London: 1809) 65.
21  Henry Reynolds, 'Racial Thoughts in Early Colonial Australia', *Australian Journal of Politics and History* 20 (1974) 48.
22  Jean Woolmington, 'The Civilisation/Christian Debate and the Australian Aborigines', *Aboriginal History* 10 (1986) 92.
23  Raymond Evans, Kay Saunders and Kathryn Cronin, *Race Relations in Colonial Queensland* (St Lucia: University of Queensland Press, 1988) 119.
24  *Friendly Mission: The Tasmanian Journals and Papers of George Augustus Robinson, 1829-1834*, ed. N. J. B. Plomley (Sydney: Halstead Press, 1966) 64.
25  *Ibid*.
26  Cunningham, *Two Years* II, 8.
27  John Bull, *Early Experiences in Life in South Australia* (Adelaide: Wigg, 1884) 36.
28  Penelope Selby, Letters, 1839-44, 31, 9494 [LT].
29  Brooks, Diary, Jul 1825 [NL].
30  *Ibid*.
31  Bob Reece, 'Laws of the White People: The Frontier of Authority in Perth in 1838', *Push from the Bush* 17 (1984) 6.
32  Henry Reynolds, 'Aborigines and European Social Hierarchy', *Aboriginal History* 7 (1983) 2.
33  *Aborigines in Colonial Society, 1788-1850*, ed. Jean Woolmington (North Melbourne: Cassell, 1973) 24.
34  Evidence of Archibald Bell, 27 Nov 1819, Bonwick Transcripts, Box 5, 2032 [ML], and *Report from the Select Committee on the Condition of the Aborigines, NSW V and P LC* (1845) 29.

35 R. H. W. Reece, 'Feasts and Blankets: The History of Some Early Attempts to Establish Relations with the Aborigines of New South Wales 1814–46', *Archaeology and Physical Anthropology in Oceania* 2 (1967) 196.

36 Evidence of Mahroot, Botany Bay area, and evidence of William Thomas, Assistant Protector of Aborigines, Yarra and Port Phillip Tribes, *Report* 1845, 3 and 55.

37 John Henderson, *Excursions and Adventures in New South Wales* (London: Shobere, 1851) 107.

38 Reece, 'Feasts and Blankets', 200.

39 *Report*, 1845, 17.

40 *Aborigines in Colonial Society*, 88.

41 John Tregenza, 'Two Notable Portraits of South Australian Aborigines', *Journal of the Historical Society of South Australia* 12 (1984) 26.

42 Derek Mulvaney, *Encounters in Place: Outsiders and Aboriginal Australians, 1606–1905* (St Lucia: University of Queensland Press, 1989) 153.

43 A number of King Plates are illustrated in Susanna Evans, 'Kings without Kingdoms', *Australian Connoisseur and Collector*, 2 (1982) 86ff.

44 S. Wood, 'The British Gorget in North America', *Waffen und Kostum Kunde* 1 (1984) 5.

45 Reece, 'Feasts and Blankets', 192.

46 Meredith, *Notes and Sketches*, 100.

47 James O'Connell, *A Residence of Eleven Years in New Holland and the Caroline Islands* (Boston: B. B. Mussey, 1836) 66.

48 *Friendly Mission*, 50.

49 Lyndall Ryan, *The Aboriginal Tasmanians* (St Lucia: University of Queensland Press, 1981) 126.

50 James Backhouse, *A Narrative of a Visit to the Australian Colonies* (London: Hamilton, Adams, 1843) 83–4.

51 *Ibid.*, 172 and 174.

52 James Bonwick, *Daily Life and Origins of the Tasmanians* (London: Sampson, Low, Marston, 1898) 276.

53 Richard Broome, *Aboriginal Australians: Black Responses to White Dominance, 1788–1980* (Sydney: Allen and Unwin, 1982) 61.

54 Bonwick, *Daily Life*, 24.

55 Bain Attwood, *The Making of the Aborigines* (North Sydney: Allen and Unwin, 1989) 68.

56 *Report*, 1845, 55.

57 Townsend, *Rambles and Observations*, 92.

58 *Aborigines in Colonial Society*, 73.

59 *Ibid.*, 195.

60 Rachel Henning in 1862 indicated that it was usual for Aboriginal men and women in North Queensland to wear nothing more than a shirt: *The Letters of Rachel Henning*, ed. David Adams (Sydney: Angus and Robertson, 1963) 92.

61 Sharman Stone, *Aborigines in White Australia* (South Yarra, Vic: Heinemann Educational, 1974) 41.

62 Meredith, *Notes and Sketches*, 99–100. For another account see O'Connell, *A Residence of Eleven Years*, 84.

63 Another version of *Native Dignity* by S. T. Gill represents the Aborigines as more degraded and foolish: *Deutsche Fine Art Catalogue* (Apr 1985) 23.

64 'Art and Nature', *Melbourne Punch*, 5 Jan 1860, 192.

65 Evans, Saunders and Cronin, *Race Relations*, 89.

## 5   Dressing the Part

1 Robert V. Jackson, *Population History of Australia* (Victoria: McPhee Gribble, 1988) 3.

2  Colin Kerr, 'A Excelent Coliney': The Practical Idealists of 1836–1846 (Adelaide: Rigby, 1978) 161.
3  William Howitt, Land, Labour and Gold, or Two Years in Victoria with Visits to Sydney and Van Diemen's Land, 1855 (Kilmore: Lowden Publishing, 1972) 158.
4  See for instance the Chinese field coat c.1860 and 'coolie' hat, originating from Smeaton, Victoria, now in the Museum of Victoria.
5  Jackson, Population History, 4–5.
6  Richard Howitt, Australia: Historical, Descriptive and Statistic (London: Longman, Brown, Green and Longmans, 1845) 118.
7  Robert V. Jackson, Australian Economic Development in the Nineteenth Century (Canberra: Australian National University Press, 1977) 99.
8  Extrapolated from the Victorian Censuses of 1871 and 1881.
9  Wilson, 'Fashion and City Life', Adorned in Dreams.
10  Richard Sennett, The Fall of Public Man (London: Faber and Faber, 1986).
11  Graeme Davison, The Rise and Fall of Marvellous Melbourne (Melbourne: Melbourne University Press, 1978) 12 and 152.
12  Jackson, Australian Economic Development, 103.
13  James Inglis, Our Australian Cousins (London: Macmillan, 1880) 39, and Richard Twopeny, Town Life in Australia, 1883 (Harmondsworth: Penguin, 1973) 80.
14  Twopeny, Town Life, 21.
15  Diana de Marly, Fashion for Men (London: Batsford, 1985) 90.
16  Marion Fletcher, Costume in Australia, 1788–1901 (Melbourne: Oxford University Press, 1984) 49 and 151.
17  See the individual items of dress for men and women in New South Wales described in 'Prices of Provisions and Clothing', Statistical Returns, NSW V and P LA (1857) 1.
18  David Kennedy, Kennedy's Colonial Travel (London: Edinburgh Publishing Company, 1876) 14.
19  George Sutherland, Australia, or England in the South (London: Seeley, 1886) 15.
20  Letter from Thomas Gates Darton, 15 Jun 1838 [Mort].
21  Margaret May, Letters, 5 May 1845, 270, Typescript, 1363 [Mort]. Advertisement for India silk to make men's summer blouses and jackets, Adelaide Examiner, 20 May 1843, 2.
22  Charlotte Godley, Letters from Early New Zealand, 1850–53, quoted in Alan Birch and David Macmillan, The Sydney Scene, 1788–1960 (Sydney: Hale and Iremonger, 1982) 141.
23  Douglas Gane, New South Wales and Victoria in 1885 (London: Sampson Low, Marston, Searle and Rivington, 1886) 196.
24  Samuel Mossman and Thomas Banister, Australia Visited and Revisited: A Narrative of Recent Travels and Old Experiences in Victoria and New South Wales, 1853 (Sydney: Ure Smith, 1974) 80.
25  Alison Lurie, The Language of Clothes (New York: Vintage Books, 1983) 187.
26  William Kelly, Life in Victoria in 1853 and Victoria in 1858 I (Kilmore: Lowden Publishing, 1977) 268.
27  Howitt, Land, Labour and Gold, 395.
28  Kelly, Life in Victoria I, 268.
29  Edwin Booth, Another England: Life, Living, Homes and Homemakers in Victoria (London: Virtue and Co., 1869) 269.
30  Vernon Lee Walker Letters, 8 Feb 1876, 7568, Box 454/1 (a) 4 [LaT].
31  Fergus Hume, The Mystery of a Hansom Cab, 1887 (Melbourne: Sun Books, 1971) 138.
32  Walter Balls-Headley, 'Dress With Reference to Heat', Australian Health Society Lecture, Melbourne, 1876, pamphlet [LaT].
33  Judith Thompson, 'Lifestyle and Fashion in Nineteenth Century South Australia', Australasian Antique Collector 20 (1980) 112.
34  Lois Banner, American Beauty (New York: Alfred Knopf, 1983) 29.
35  Elizabeth Ramsay-Laye, Social Life and Manners in Australia (London: Longman, Green, Longman and Roberts, 1861) 2.

36  P. Just, *Australia, or Notes Taken During a Residence in the Colonies from the Gold Discovery in 1851 till 1857* (Dundee: Durham and Thomson, 1859) 303.

37  As quoted in Penny Russell, 'Significant Pauses: The Language of Class and Femininity in Nineteenth-Century Melbourne, 1860-80', unpublished Roger Joyce Lecture, History Department, University of Melbourne, 1988, 30.

38  *The Princess: A Lady's Newspaper* I (1889) 1.

39  *Queenslander*, 7 Jul 1888, 14.

40  Twopeny, *Town Life* 75.

41  *Trade With the United Kingdom, NSW V and P LA* (1896), 4, 56.

42  Margaret Maynard, 'Dress and the Urban Experience', *Brisbane in 1888: The Historical Perspective*, Brisbane History Group Papers, 8 (1989) 147.

43  Twopeny, *Town Life* 76.

44  'As Others See Us', *Queensland Figaro* 26 Jun 1886, 1022.

45  'As Others See Us', *Queensland Figaro* 24 Oct 1885, 667.

46  Twopeny, *Town Life* 74.

47  Webb's comments are quoted from *Australia Brought to Book: Responses to Australia by Visiting Writers, 1836-1939*, ed. Kaye Harman (New South Wales: Boobook, 1985) 149.

48  This gown is illustrated in Fletcher, *Costume in Australia*, 133.

49  Teresa Dean, *How to Be Beautiful* (Melbourne: J. E. Mitchell and Co., 1890) 2 and 64-5.

50  See the discussion in Anita Rush, 'Changing Women's Fashion and its Social Context, 1870-1905', *Material History Bulletin* (14) 1982.

51  'Our Ladies' Corner', *Illustrated Sydney News*, 7 Jul 1890, 210.

52  'In Fashion's Path', *The Woman*, 15 Feb 1892, 3.

53  *Australian Etiquette or the Rules and Usages of the Best Society in the Australian Colonies*, 1885 (Victoria: J. M. Dent, 1980) 350.

54  *Cole's Correct Conduct: Being the Etiquette of Everyday Life* (Sydney: E. W. Cole, 189?) 78.

55  'Taste in Dress', *Dawn*, 1 Jul 1889, 15.

56  'The Coming Woman', *Dawn*, Jan 1890, 12, and 'Dress Reform', *Court* 3 (1895) 48.

57  *The Woman's Voice*, 22 Sep 1894, 1.

58  Gail Reekie, *Temptations: Sex, Selling and the Department Store* (Sydney: Allen and Unwin, 1993) 21.

59  'The Rational Dress Question', *Australian Storekeepers' Journal* (Nov 1895) 198.

60  For descriptions of these occupations see John Freeman, *Lights and Shadows of Melbourne Life* (London: Sampson Low, Marston, Searle and Rivington, 1888).

61  Richard Kennedy, 'Charity and Ideology', *Australian Welfare History. Critical Essays*, ed. Richard Kennedy (South Melbourne: Macmillan, 1982) 55.

62  Freeman, *Lights and Shadows*, 144.

63  James Murray, *Larrikins: Nineteenth Century Outrage* (Melbourne: Lansdowne, 1973) 78, and Chris McConville, 'Outcast Children in Marvellous Melbourne', *The Colonial Child*, ed. Guy Featherstone (Melbourne: Royal Historical Society of Victoria, 1981) 40 and n.13.

64  Gane, *New South Wales and Victoria*, 97.

65  Freeman, *Lights and Shadows*, 77.

66  Mark Kershaw, *Colonial Facts and Fictions: Humorous Sketches* (London: Chatto and Windus, 1886) 98. *The New Australia: Edmond Marin La Meslee*, ed. Russel Ward (London: Heinemann, 1973) 63.

67  *The World Moves Slowly: A Documentary History of Australian Women*, ed. Beverley Kingston (Stanmore, Australia: Cassell, 1977) 15.

68  Freeman, *Lights and Shadows*, 47.

69  Gane, *New South Wales and Victoria*, 41.

70  *The New Australia*, 67.

71  Jackson, *Australian Economic Development*, 22.

72  Shirley Fitzgerald, *Rising Damp: Sydney, 1870-90* (Melbourne: Oxford University Press, 1987) 228.

73  Richard White, *Inventing Australia: Images and Identity, 1688-1980* (Sydney: Allen and Unwin, 1981) 45.

74  Aspinall, *Three Years*, 33-5.

75  Quoted from the *Bathurst Free Press*, 1851, in *Gold and Colonial Society, 1851-1870*, ed. G. R. Quaife (Stanmore, NSW: Cassell, 1975) 193.

76  Geoffrey Serle, *The Golden Age: A History of the Colony of Victoria, 1851-61* (Carlton, Vic.: Melbourne University Press, 1963) 378.

77  Penny Russell, 'The Relationship between Family Life and Class Formation in Nineteenth-century Melbourne', *Lilith* 5 (Spring 1988) 115.

78  Jackson, *Australian Economic Development*, 11 and 22.

79  Veblen, *The Theory of the Leisure Class*, 75.

80  Twopeny, *Town Life*, 93-4.

81  Kelly, *Life in Victoria* II, 63.

82  Journal of Mary Morton Allport, 11 Jan 1853, 19 [Alp].

# 6    *From a Different Cloth*

1   Bartky, 'Foucault, Femininity', 64.

2   Leonore Davidoff and Catherine Hall, *Family Fortunes: Men and Women of the English Middle Class, 1780-1850* (London: Hutchinson, 1987) 181.

3   Aspinall, *Three Years*, 65.

4   *The World Moves Slowly*, ed. Kingston, 14.

5   *Australian Etiquette*, 152.

6   Davison, *Marvellous Melbourne*, 193.

7   *Australasian*, 24 Jan 1885, 151.

8   Hume, *The Mystery*, 59.

9   *Ibid.*

10  Aspinall, *Three Years*, 8.

11  Hume, *The Mystery*, 59.

12  Birch and Macmillan, *The Sydney Scene*, 154.

13  Hume, *The Mystery*, 98.

14  An Old Housekeeper, *The Australian Housewives' Manual: A Book for Beginners and People with Small Incomes* (Melbourne: A. H. Messina, 1885) 77.

15  *Ibid.*, 78-9.

16  'The Ladies Column', *Castner's Rural Australia*, 1 Nov 1875, 18.

17  *Dawn*, 5 Feb 1890, 25.

18  An Old Housekeeper, *The Australian Housewives' Manual*, 93.

19  Inglis, *Our Australian Cousins*, 236.

20  Roslyn Otzen, 'Recovering the Past for the Present: the History of Victorian Calisthenics', *Lilith* 5 (1988) 99-100.

21  Bright and Hitchcocks Trade Card [MUA]; *Queensland Figaro*, 14 Jan 1888, 68 and 74.

22  *Australian Etiquette*, 357.

23  'The Ladies Column', *Castner's Rural Australia*, 1 Nov 1876, 16.

24  'A Vista of Fashion', *Worth's Australian Fashion Journal* 2 Oct 1899, 164.

25  Windschuttle, 'The New Science of Etiquette', 3.

26  Davidoff and Hall, *Family Fortunes*, 398.

27  Beverley Kingston, 'The Lady and the Australian Girl: Some thoughts on Nationalism and Class', *Australian Women: New Feminist Perspectives*, ed. Norma Grieve and Ailsa Burns (Melbourne: Oxford University Press, 1986) 29 and 32.

28  Karen Halttunen, *Confidence Men and Painted Women: A Study of Middle-class Culture in America, 1830–1870* (New Haven: Yale University Press, 1982) 1.

29  Windschuttle, 'The New Science of Etiquette', 2.

30  *Hints on Etiquette and the Usages of Society with a Glance at Bad Habits* (Hobart: William Gore Elliston, 1838) 34–5.

31  *Australian Etiquette*, 342.

32  Patricia Clarke, *The Governesses: Letters from the Colonies, 1862–1882* (Melbourne: Hutchinson, 1985) 56.

33  Mrs D. McConnel, 'Queensland Reminiscences, 1848–1870' 2/1623 [FL].

34  Davison, *Marvellous Melbourne*, 206.

35  Just, *Australia*, 302.

36  Kelly, *Life in Victoria* II, 60.

37  Louisa Meredith, *Over the Straits: A Visit to Victoria* (London: Chapman and Hall, 1861) 124.

38  Aspinall, *Three Years*, 64.

39  Meredith, *Notes and Sketches*, 51.

40  Deborah Gorham, *The Victorian Girl and the Feminine Ideal* (London: Croom Helm, 1982) 8.

41  Edna Ryan and Anne Conlon, *Gentle Invaders: Australian Women at Work, 1788–1974* (West Melbourne: Nelson, 1975) 31.

42  Beverley Kingston, *My Wife, My Daughter and Poor Mary Ann: Women and Work in Australia* (Melbourne: Nelson, 1975) 18.

43  Catherine Spence, *Clara Morison: A Tale of South Australia During the Gold Fever*, 1854 (South Australia: Wakefield Press, 1986) 193.

44  Charlotte Godley, *Letters from Early New Zealand* (Plymouth: private printing, 1936) 335 and 364.

45  Clarke, *The Governesses*, 56.

46  Joseph Elliott, *Our Home in Australia: A Description of Cottage Life in 1860* (Sydney: Flannel Flower Press, 1984) 29–32.

47  Margaret Kiddle, *Men of Yesterday: A Social History of the Western District of Victoria, 1834–1890* (Melbourne: Melbourne University Press, 1961) 88 and 89.

48  Comparative figures compiled from the New South Wales Census of 1856, *NSW V and P LA* (1857) I, 687ff.

49  *The Letters of Rachel Henning* (1986) 148.

50  Forman Letters, 23 Nov 1856 [MUA].

51  *Katie Hume on the Darling Downs: A Colonial Marriage*, ed. Nancy Bonnin (Toowoomba: Darling Downs Institute Press, 1985) 64.

52  Lucy Frost, *No Place for a Nervous Lady: Voices from the Australian Bush* (Melbourne: McPhee Gribble, 1984) 175.

53  Louisa Meredith, *My Home in Tasmania, or Nine Years in Australia* (New York: Bunce and Broker, 1853) 291–2.

54  *The Letters of Rachel Henning* (1963) 238.

55  Penelope Selby, Letters, 22 [LaT].

56  *The Letters of Rachel Henning* (1963) 204.

57  *Katie Hume*, 125.

58  *The Letters of Rachel Henning* (1963) 91.

59  Charles Eden, *My Wife and I in Queensland* (London: Longmans Green, 1872) 79.

60  Forman Letters, April 1858 [MUA].

61  Frost, *No Place*, 158.

62  *Sydney Punch*, 17 Jan 1857, 32 and 33.

63  Judith Godden, 'A New Look at the Pioneer Woman', *Hecate* 5 (1979) 11.

64  Constance Ellis, *I Seek Adventure* (Sydney: Alternative Publishing Co., 1981).

65  Katrina Alford, 'The Drover's Wife and Her Friends: Women in Rural Society and Primary

Production in Australia 1850-1900', *Working Papers in Economic History* 75 (Canberra: Australian National University, 1986) 29.

66  Godden, 'A New Look', 13.

67  *Katie Hume*, 26.

68  *The Letters of Rachel Henning* (1986) 105-6.

69  *Ibid.*, 152.

70  William Shaw, *Land of Promise: or My Impressions of Australia* (London: Simpkin, Marshall, 1854) 297.

71  Meredith, *Over the Straits*, 252, and Shaw, *Land of Promise*, 297.

72  Howitt, *Land, Labour and Gold*, 210.

73  Kelly, *Life in Victoria* II, 217.

74  Percy Clarke, *The 'New Chum' in Australia: or the Scenery, Life and Manners of Australians in Town and Country* (London: Virtue, 1886) 228.

75  *The Letters of Rachel Henning* (1963) 109.

76  Robert Harrison, *Colonial Sketches; or Five Years in South Australia* (London: L. Hall, Virtue, 1862) 76.

77  Mossman and Banister, *Australia Visited*, 52-3.

78  Waugh, *Three Years*, 40.

# 7   Material Needs

1   James Gregg, Handbill, 1854, A177 [ML].

2   Thomas Champion, Diary, 30 Mar 1842, 1093 [NL].

3   H. Mortimer Franklyn, *A Glance at Australia in 1880* (Melbourne: Victoria Review Publishing Co., 1881) 347-8.

4   Bradon Ellem, *In Women's Hands? A History of Clothing Trades Unionism in Australia* (Sydney: New South Wales University Press, 1989) 22.

5   Advertisement for S. & E. Scrase, tailors, *Sydney Morning Herald*, 20 Jan 1842, 1.

6   Advertisement for Pite and Preston, *Sydney Morning Herald*, 24 Sep 1842, 3 and *Australian*, 9 Jun 1842, 3.

7   *Argus*, 9 Jun 1846, 3.

8   Advertisement, *Australian*, 9 Jun 1842, 3.

9   Claudia Brush Kidwell, 'Transformation of the Women's Wear Industry into the Fashion Industry: Gender and the Ready-Made Industry in the United States', *Per Una Storia della Moda Pronta* (Milan: CISST, 1990) 220.

10  Advertisement, *Sydney Morning Herald*, 20 Sep 1842, 1.

11  Advertisement, *Sydney Post Office Directory* (1857)

12  Advertisement for Robert Mather and Son, *Wood's Tasmanian Almanack* (1857) 156.

13  *Hobart Town Courier*, 18 Aug 1837.

14  Advertisement for Henry Haynes, *Sydney Morning Herald*, 20 Sep 1842, 1.

15  Advertisement, *Sydney Punch*, 24 Jan 1857.

16  Ann Stephen, 'The Mail-Order Catalogue: From Family Bible to Junk Mail', *West* 3 (1991).

17  W. A. Sinclair, 'The Tariff and Manufacturing Employment in Victoria 1860-1900', *The Economic Record*, May (1955) 101.

18  *Royal Commission on the Tariff 1881, VPP* 4 (1883) 79.

19  Jenny Lee and Charles Fahey, 'A Boom for Whom? Some Developments in the Australian Labour Market, 1870-1891', *Labour History* 50 (1986) 18.

20  *Factories Act Inquiry Board First Progress Report, VPP* 2 (1893) 16.

21  *New South Wales Census and Industrial Returns Act of 1891*, NSW *V and P LA* (1891-2) 7, 24.

22  Walsh, 'Factories', 7.

23  E. S. Richards, 'The Genesis of Secondary Industry in the South Australian Economy to 1876', *Australian Economic History Review* 15 (Sep 1975) 121.
24  'Colonial Manufacture', *Adelaide Examiner*, 20 May 1843, 2.
25  *Progress Report on the State of Manufactures and Agriculture in the Colony, NSW V and P LA* (1862) 5, 1104.
26  Walsh, 'Factories', 7.
27  Fitzgerald, *Rising Damp*, 149.
28  'The Boot Trade' I and II, *Sydney Morning Herald*, 1, 8 Oct 1878.
29  *New South Wales Statistical Register 1892 and Previous Years*.
30  Davison, *Marvellous Melbourne*, 67-8.
31  'American v. English and Australian Boots', *Australian Storekeepers' Journal* (Mar 1895) 8.
32  'The Boot Trade in Victoria', *ibid.* (Aug 1896) 28.
33  Buckley and Wheelwright, *No Paradise for Workers*, 99.
34  Walsh, 'Factories', 7.
35  *State of Manufactures*, 1862, 1059.
36  *Australian Almanack* (1851).
37  London Letters, Bright and Hitchcock, 27 Jan 1870 [MUA].
38  *Ibid.*, 28 Aug 1865, 24 Nov 1866, 5 Nov 1868, 18 Jun 1868 and 25 Feb 1869.
39  *The Letters of Rachel Henning* (1952), 21.
40  Kidwell, 'Transformation', 220-1.
41  Sarah Levitt, *Victorians Unbuttoned: Registered Designs for Clothing, Their Makers and Wearers* (London: Allen and Unwin, 1986) 11 and 76.
42  Beverley Lemire, 'Developing Consumerism and the Readymade Clothing Trade in Britain, 1750-1800', *Textile History* 15 (Spring 1984), and *Per Una Storia della Moda Pronta* 1990.
43  Allport Journal, 13 Sep 1853 [Alp].
44  Advertisement, *Illustrated Sydney News*, 15 Oct 1853, 15.
45  Advertisement for Cook and Co., *Sydney Morning Herald*, 7 Sep 1855, 6.
46  Rozsika Parker, *The Subversive Stitch: Embroidery and the Making of the Feminine* (London: Women's Press, 1984) 174.
47  Advertisement for dressmaking lessons, *Wood's Tasmanian Almanack* (1857).
48  Advertisement for Northmore and Co., *Adelaide Almanack* (1864), and Francis Giles and Co., *Sydney Morning Herald*, 23 May 1863, 7.
49  Fletcher, *Costume in Australia*, 135-6.
50  Margaret May, Letters, 5 Nov 1843 [Mort].
51  Spence, *Clara Morison*, 221.
52  Allport Journal, 28 Jun 1853 [Alp].
53  *The Letters of Rachel Henning* (1986), 173 and 198.
54  Meredith, *Notes and Sketches*, 38.
55  *Ford's Australian Almanack* (1851).
56  Frank Fowler, *Southern Lights Being Brief Notes of Three Years' Experience of Social, Literary and Political Life in Australia* (London: Sampson Low, 1859) 13.
57  Howitt, *Land, Labour and Gold*, 395.
58  David Jones, Tradelist, inserted in *Ford's Australian Almanack* (1851) [ML].
59  David Chaney, 'The Department Store as a Cultural Form', *Theory Culture and Society*, I, 3 (1983) 24 and 27.
60  Reekie, *Temptations*, xiii.
61  Susan P. Benson, 'Palace of Consumption and Machine for Selling: The American Department Store, 1880-1940', *Radical History Review* (Fall 1979) 210.
62  Farmer and Co.'s Store, 1865, V1/SHO/Farm 4 [ML].
63  'A Visit to Buckley's and Nunn', *Australian Woman's Magazine and Domestic Journal* I (1882) 25.

64  'Our Manufacturing Departments', Farmer and Co., *The Great Drapery Emporium* (Sydney: 1869).
65  *Ford's Sydney Directory* (1851).
66  Reekie, *Temptations*, 70.
67  G. C. Tuting of Pitt Street had agents in London, Paris, Vienna and Lyons: Tradelist, *Ford's Australian Almanack* (1851).
68  Inglis, *Our Australian Cousins*, 174.
69  *Town and Country Journal*, 4 May 1878, 859.
70  *Illustrated Sydney News*, 5 Oct 1878, 22.
71  The journal was published until 1950. Between 1915 and 1947 it was entitled *Madame Weigel's Journal of Fashions*. Weigel's published a *Catalogue of Fashions* and a monthly *Journal of Fashion* in the 1880s.
72  *The Princess: A Lady's Newspaper* I (1889).
73  Ramsay-Laye, *Social Life and Manners*, 36.
74  Katherine McKell, *Old Days and Gold Days in Victoria, 1851-73* (Melbourne: E. A. Vidler, 1924) 79.
75  Advertisement, *Town and Country Journal*, 7 Jul 1875, 250.
76  Godfrey C. Mundy, *Our Antipodes or Residence and Rambles in the Australian Colonies* I (London: Bentley, 1852) 191.
77  Michael Cannon, *Australia in the Victorian Age*, 2: *Life in the Country* (West Melbourne: Nelson, 1976) 203.

# 8   A Loose Fit

1   See the article on how emigrants were misled about conditions in New South Wales, in *The Emigrant's Assistant* (London: G. Jackson, 1832) 11ff.
2   White, *Inventing Australia*, 33.
3   Charles Hursthouse, *Emigration: Where to Go and Who Should Go* (London: Trelawney Saunders, 1852) 88-9.
4   Green, *Broken Spears*, 60.
5   Meredith, *My Home in Tasmania*, 35-6.
6   Ramsay-Laye, *Social Life and Manners*, 2.
7   John Capper's text published as *The Emigrant's Guide to Australia in the Eighteen-Fifties*, ed. D. J. Golding (Melbourne: Hawthorne Press, 1973).
8   Hursthouse, *Emigration*, 121.
9   *The Library of Elegance* (London: E. Moses and Sons, 1852).
10  Compare the information on dress recommended for a free passenger with that for a first-class passenger in *Emigration Guide to Australia and New Zealand, Cape of Good Hope and the Canadas* (London: S. W. Silver and Co., 1858) 12 and 39-40.
11  William Wentworth, *A Statistical Account of the British Settlements in Australia* (London: Whittaker, 1824) 184.
12  *Sydney's Emigrants Journal*, 5 Oct 1848, 10.
13  *The Emigrant's Handbook* (London, 1852) 59, and *The Emigrant's Almanack and Guide to the Goldfields* (London: Cassells, 1854) 53.
14  J. C. Byrne, *Emigrants Guide to New South Wales Proper, Australia Felix and South Australia* (London: E. Wilson, 1848) 6. This was the publication's sixth edition.
15  *Emigrant's Almanack and Guide to the Goldfields*, 53.
16  *Ibid*.
17  S. W. Silver's *Emigration Guide*, 10.
18  *Godwin's Emigrants Guide to Van Diemen's Land* (London: Sherwood Jones and Co., 1823) 69.
19  *The Library of Elegance*, n.p.

20    Alison Gernsheim, *Victorian and Edwardian Fashion: A Photographic Survey* (New York: Dover, 1981) 39.

21    Hursthouse, *Emigration*, 121.

22    Advertisement in J. C. Byrne, *Emigrants Guide*, 17.

23    Thomas Tegg, *Handbook for Emigrants* (London: Thomas Tegg, 1839) 9. Reprinted in 1844.

24    S. W. Silver's *Emigration Guide*, 6.

25    During the gold rush, 1852-8, much faster travelling times were recorded: Don Charlwood, *The Long Farewell* (Ringwood, Vic.: Allen Lane, 1981) 37.

26    John Hood, *Australia and the East* (London: Murray, 1843) 36.

27    Helen Woolcock, *Rights of Passage: Emigration to Australia in the Nineteenth Century* (London: Tavistock Publications, 1986) 196.

28    Joseph Delpratt, Diary, 3 May 1870, F 224 [FL]; Shaw, *The Land of Promise*, 44.

29    Letter from William Dorling, 1 Aug 1848, D 6800 (L) [Mort].

30    Letter from Hugh Watson, 9 Sep 1839 [Mort].

31    S. W. Silver's *Emigration Guide*, 12.

32    *Ibid.*

33    *Letters from Emigrants to Queensland*, 14.

34    Eneas Mackenzie, *Mackenzie's Australian Emigrants' Guide* (London: Clarke Beeton, 1852) 3.

35    *The Diary of Joseph Sams, an Emigrant in the 'Northumberland'* ed. Simon Braydon and Robert Longhurst (London: HMSO, 1982) 85.

36    Susan Casteras, 'Victorian Images of Emigration Themes', *Journal of Pre-Raphaelite Studies* 6 (1985) 12.

37    *Sydney's Emigrants Journal*, 9 Nov 1848, 44.

38    Mrs A. MacPherson, *My Experiences in Australia: Being Recollections of a Visit to the Australian Colonies in 1856-7* (London: J. F. Hope, 1860) 8.

39    *Traveller Under Concern: The Quaker Journals of Frederick Mackie on his Tour of the Australasian Colonies, 1852-1855*, ed. Mary Nicholls (Hobart: University of Tasmania, 1973) 37.

40    Sidney Smith, *The Settler's New Home; or Whether to go and Whither?* (London: J. Kendrick, 1850) 36.

41    *The Diary of Joseph Sams*, 18.

42    *Ibid.*, 7.

43    *Letters of Rachel Henning* (1986) 67.

44    *Ibid.*, 21.

45    *The Diary of Joseph Sams*, 88.

46    Charlwood, *The Long Farewell*, 179.

47    See details on the Passenger Acts in Oliver Macdonach, *A Pattern of Government Growth, 1800-1860: The Passenger Acts and their Enforcement* (London: MacGibbon and Kee, 1961).

48    R. B. Madgwick, *Immigration into Eastern Australia, 1788-1851* (London: Longmans, Green, 1937) 121.

49    *Instructions for the Surgeon-Superintendent of Government Emigration Ships going to New South Wales* (London: W. Clowes and Sons, 1839).

50    Norman Plomley, *An Immigrant of 1824* (Hobart: Tasmanian Historical Research Association, 1973) 21.

51    *Instructions for the Surgeon-Superintendent*, 1839, 15 and 32.

52    *Report from the Committee on Immigration, NSW V and P LC* (1838) 42.

53    Rev. John Davies Mereweather, *Life on Board an Emigrant Ship: Being a Diary of a Voyage to Australia* (London: T. Hatchard, 1852) 30.

54    Woolcock, *Rights of Passage*, 220-1 and 329.

55    Rev. David Mackenzie, *The Emigrant's Guide, or Ten Years Practical Experience in Australia* (London: W. S. Orr and Co., 1845) 253, and Henry Capper, *South Australia: Containing Hints to Emigrants* (London: R. Tyas, 1838) 59.

56    Rosamond Smith, *Hints to Emigrants* (Braintree: E. C. Joscelyne, 1866) 8.

57  *The Emigrant's Almanack* (London: John Cassell, 1851) n.p.

58  Shaw, *The Land of Promise*, 2.

59  Spence, *Clara Morison*, 38.

60  Hood, *Australia and the East*, 103.

61  Frost, *No Place*, 24.

62  As quoted in Charlwood, *The Long Farewell*, 284.

63  Mackenzie, *Australian Emigrants' Guide*, 4.

64  Letter to the Immigration Agent, 24 Sep 1855, GRG 24/6-3174 CSO, Letters Received [SA PRO].

65  Meredith, *Notes and Sketches*, 34.

66  John D. Hadfield, 'A Letter from Melbourne', *LaTrobe Library Journal* 3 (Oct 1972) 26.

67  Mrs MacPherson, *My Experiences in Australia*, 323.

68  Smith, *The Settler's New Home*, 51.

69  Smith, *Hints to Emigrants*, 7.

70  *Ibid.*, 6.

71  *Sydney's Emigrants Journal*, 23 Nov 1848, 61.

72  Letter from Ellen Moger to her parents, 28 Jan 1840, 5919 [NL].

73  Maggie Weidenhofer, *Colonial Ladies* (South Yarra, Vic.: Currey O'Neil Ross, 1985) 42.

74  Alexandra Hasluck, *Portrait with Background: A Life of Georgiana Molloy* (Melbourne: Oxford University Press, 1955) 134.

75  Trigg Letters—Copy [Private Collection].

76  Letter from William Dorling, 1 Aug 1848. See also similar comments about Adelaide shops in 1840: *The Diary and Letters of Mary Thomas, 1836-1866*, ed. Evan Thomas (Adelaide: Thomas and Co., 1983) 155.

77  Hadfield, 'A Letter from Melbourne', 28.

78  *The Diaries of Sarah Midgley and Richard Skilbeck: A Story of Australian Settlers, 1851-1864*, ed. H. A. McCorkell (Melbourne: Cassell, 1967) 133.

79  'Prices of Provisions and Clothing', *Statistical Returns*, NSW V and P LC (1852) and NSW V and P LA (1857) 1.

# 9   *Alternate Threads*

1   Margaret Hazzard, *Australia's Brilliant Daughter. Ellis Rowan: Artist, Naturalist, Explorer, 1848-1922* (Richmond: Greenhouse Publications, 1984) 19.

2   *Letters of Rachel Henning* (1963) 34.

3   *Ambassador* 3 (1952) 93.

4   Joel, *Best Dressed*, 12.

5   Andris Auliciems and Stuart Deaves, 'Clothing, Heat and Settlement', *The Australian Experience: Essays in Australian Land Settlement and Resource Management*, ed. R. L. Heathcote (Melbourne: Longman Cheshire, 1988) 102 and 110.

6   Gillen, 'The Botany Bay Decision 1789' 743.

7   13 Jan 1787, ADM 2/1178 [PRO].

8   10 Jul 1788, ADM 1/3824 [PRO].

9   24 Feb 1803, *HRNSW* V, 43.

10  Redfern to Macquarie, CO 201/73 [PRO].

11  1 Oct 1814, *HRA* VIII, 281-4.

12  Jayne Shrimpton, 'Dressing for a Tropical Climate: The Role of Native Fabrics in Fashionable Dress in Early Colonial India', *Textile History* 23 (1992) 55-6.

13  As quoted from Annabella Boswell's Diary in Weidenhofer, *Colonial Ladies*, 79.

14  Charles H. Allen, *A Visit to Queensland and Her Goldfields* (London: Chapman and Hall, 1870) 161.

15  Francis Adams, *The Australians: A Social Sketch* (London: Fisher Unwin, 1893) 37.
16  'A Tropic City: Townsville North Queensland', *Illustrated Sydney News*, 20 Feb 1890, 22.
17  See the illustrations of picnicking and boating dress in the 'Christmas Supplement', *Sydney Mail*, 1895.
18  *Australia Brought to Book*, 120.
19  Ross Patrick, *A History of Health and Medicine in Queensland, 1824-1960* (St Lucia: University of Queensland Press, 1987) 359.
20  Evans, Saunders, Cronin, *Race Relations* 158.
21  Balls-Headley, 'Dress With Reference to Heat', 33.
22  'Editorial', *Rockhampton Morning Bulletin*, 22 Jan 1877, 2.
23  *North Queensland Register*, 13 May 1896, 28.
24  *Gympie Miner*, 26 Jun 1888, 1.
25  *Queensland Punch*, 1 Nov 1881, 14.
26  *Brisbane Courier*, 19 Sep 1877, 1.
27  'Summer Toilettes', *Boomerang*, 6 Oct 1888, 12.
28  *Anthony Trollope, Australia*, ed. Peter Edwards and Roger Joyce (St Lucia: University of Queensland Press, 1967) 67.
29  *Katie Hume*, 94.
30  *Ibid.*, 183. A 'Fish'ook' was probably a crocheted garment of some kind—in this case, evidently an overgarment.
31  Diary of Mary McConachie, 1882-5, OM 75-91 [JOL].
32  Helen Heney, *Dear Fanny—Women's Letters to and from New South Wales, 1788-1857* (Canberra, Australian National University Press, 1985) 85.
33  Eden, *My Wife and I*, 188.
34  Vernon Lee Walker, Letters, 8 Feb 1876 [LaT].
35  Howitt, *Land, Labour and Gold*, 420.
36  *Ibid.*, 118.
37  Meredith, *Notes and Sketches*, 51.
38  George B. Earp, *What We Did in Australia* (London: G. Routledge, 1853) 174.
39  Eneas Mackenzie, *Memoirs of Mrs Caroline Chisholm* (London: Webb Millington, 1852) 84.
40  Graeme Davison, 'R. E. N. Twopeny and town life in Australia', *Historical Studies* 16 (1974-5) 297-8.
41  Inglis, *Our Australian Cousins*, 174.
42  Twopeny, *Town Life*, 18 and 79.
43  *Ibid.*, 110.
44  Inglis, *Our Australian Cousins*, 174.
45  'Current Clothing Prices', *New South Wales Statistical Register of 1880*, and advertisement for David Jones, *Sydney Morning Herald*, 20 Mar 1880, 11.
46  Fletcher, *Costume in Australia*, 167.
47  *State of Manufactures and Agriculture in the Colony. Progress Report*, NSW V and P LA (1862) 5, 1059.
48  *Royal Commission on the Tariff, 1881*, 90.
49  Gane, *New South Wales and Victoria*, 108.
50  White, *Inventing Australia*, 47-8, and Banner, *American Beauty*, 73-5.
51  The first known comment of this kind is in Mann, *The Present Picture*, 44.
52  *The Tanner Letters*, 75.
53  As quoted from Peter Bolger, 'The Changing Image of Hobart', *Australian Capital Cities: Historical Essays*, ed. J. W. McCarty and C. B. Schedvin (Sydney: Sydney University Press, 1978) 161.
54  Ramsay-Laye, *Social Life and Manners*, 104.
55  Twopeny, *Town Life*, 77-8.

56  Frank Fowler, *Southern Lights and Shadows*, 1859, as quoted in Birch and Macmillan, *The Sydney Scene*, 156.

57  Hume, *The Mystery*, 98.

58  Diary of Mary McConachie, 1882–8 [JOL].

# 10   *Rough and Readymade*

1  Marilyn Lake, 'The politics of respectability: identifying the masculinist context', *Historical Studies* 22 (1986) 116–7, and Kay Schaffer, *Women and the Bush: Forces of Desire in the Australian Cultural Tradition* (Melbourne: Cambridge University Press, 1988) 3.

2  Lurie, *The Language of Clothes*, 105.

3  Howitt, *Australia: Historical, Descriptive and Statistic*, 169.

4  Schaffer, *Women and The Bush*, 39.

5  Gane, *New South Wales and Victoria*, 41.

6  Joel, *Best Dressed*, 14, and Fletcher, *Costume in Australia*, 86 and 96.

7  Letter from Thomas Gates Darton, 15 June 1838 [Mort].

8  *The Emigrant's Guide*, 2.

9  *Ibid.*, 25 and 103. The trousers (CH 71-181) were allegedly made and worn mid-century by Thomas Muir, a settler in the Albany region.

10  Meredith, *My Home in Tasmania*, 316.

11  Alexander Harris, *Settlers and Convicts or Recollections of Sixteen Years' Labour in the Australian Backwoods*, 1847 (Carlton, Vic.: Melbourne University Press, 1964) 5.

12  *Ibid.*, 88.

13  The Western Australian Museum owns a fine quality older boy's smock worn in the south-west of the colony at Jayes, the property of Lee Steere.

14  As quoted from Black's journal in Kiddle, *Men of Yesterday*, 57.

15  William Westgarth, *Australia Felix; or A Historical or Descriptive Account of the Settlement of Port Phillip, New South Wales* (Edinburgh: Oliver and Boyd, 1848) 245.

16  *Melbourne Punch*, 17 Jul 1856, and Kiddle, *Men of Yesterday*, 283–4 and 287.

17  'Types of Colonial Life', *Illustrated Sydney News*, 11 May 1870, 395, and illustration on page 401.

18  'Bush Fashion', *Adelaide Examiner*, 30 Nov 1842, 3.

19  Fletcher, *Costume in Australia*, 96.

20  *Letters from Emigrants to Queensland, 1863–85* (Brisbane: Queensland Family History Society, 1984) 9, and Eden, *My Wife and I*, 188.

21  Ellis, *I Seek Adventure*, 36.

22  *Australia Brought to Book*, 27, and Spence, *Clara Morison* II, 22.

23  Townsend, *Rambles and Observations*, 209, and Hood, *Australia and the East*, 114.

24  Ritchie, *The Evidence to the Bigge Reports* 1, 16.

25  *Victorian Government Gazette*, 9 Jun 1855, 69.

26  Townsend, *Rambles and Observations*, 169.

27  Mundy, *Our Antipodes*, 53.

28  Russel Ward, *The Australian Legend* (Melbourne: Oxford University Press, 1965) 12.

29  John Carroll, 'Mateship and Egalitarianism', *Intruders in the Bush: The Australian Quest for Identity*, ed. John Carroll (Melbourne: Oxford University Press, 1928) 153.

30  Jock Phillips, *A Man's Country? The Image of the Pakeha Male—A History* (Auckland: Penguin Books, 1987) 30.

31  *Sydney Punch*, 10 Jan 1857, 21.

32  Hood, *Australia and the East*, 115.

33  Mackenzie, *The Emigrant's Guide*, 197.

34  *Annabella Boswell's Journal,* ed. Morton Herman (Sydney: Angus and Robertson, 1965) 128.

35  Meredith, *My Home in Tasmania,* 316.

36  Mundy, *Our Antipodes,* 206.

37  E. W. Landor, *The Bushman, or Life in a New Country* (London: Bentley, 1847) 121. Differences in speech are noted by Eden, *My Wife and I,* 101.

38  Christopher P. Hodgson, *Reminiscences of Australia with Hints on the Squatter's Life* (London: W. N. Wright, 1846) 35.

39  Townsend, *Rambles and Observations,* 74.

40  Mossman and Bannister, *Australia Visited and Revisited,* 79.

41  Meredith, *Over the Straits,* 65 and 89.

42  Townsend, *Rambles and Observations,* 152.

43  Eve Pownall, *Mary of Maranoa: Tales of Australian Pioneer Women* (Carlton, Vic.: Melbourne University Press, 1964) 137.

44  Margaret May, Letters, 20 Mar 1844 [Mort], and Earp, *What We Did in Australia,* 58.

45  Vernon Lee Walker, Letters, 19 Feb 1877 [LaT].

46  The difference between an 'old hand' and a 'new chum' is described by Shaw, *The Land of Promise,* 104.

47  Serle, *The Golden Age,* 69.

48  Spence, *Clara Morison* I, 218.

49  Clarke, *The 'New Chum' in Australia,* 26, and Sutherland, *Australia or England,* 73.

50  Vernon Lee Walker, Letters, 8 Feb 1876 [LaT].

51  Sutherland, *Australia or England,* 15.

52  Frank Farrell, 'The Practical Politician', *Australian Cultural History* 8 (1989) 52–3.

53  Kelly, *Life in Victoria* I, 180.

54  *The New Australia,* 52 and 81.

55  Twopeny, *Town Life,* 80.

56  Gane, *New South Wales and Victoria,* 41.

57  Adams, *The Australians,* 165.

58  Gilbert Parker, *Round the Compass in Australia* (London: Hutchinson and Co., 1892) 80.

59  White, *Inventing Australia,* 83.

60  Joseph Furphy, *Such is Life: Being Certain Extracts from the Diary of Tom Collins* (London: Jonathan Cape, 1944) 263–4.

61  Schaffer, *Women and The Bush,* 62–3. See also Sue Rowley, 'Inside the Deserted Hut: The Representation of Motherhood in Bush Mythology', *Westerly* 4 (1989) 76 and 95.

62  A. W. Stirling, *The Never Neverland: A Ride in North Queensland* (London: Sampson Low, Marston, Searle and Rivington, 1884) 283.

63  Aspinall, *Three Years,* 32.

64  *Letters of Rachel Henning* (1986) 273.

65  Ellen McEwen, 'Family History in Australia: Some Observations on a New Field', *Families in Colonial Australia,* ed. Patricia Grimshaw, Chris McConville and Ellen McEwen (Sydney: Allen and Unwin, 1985) 189.

66  Eden, *My Wife and I,* 188.

67  Margaret May, Letters, 5 Mar 1845 [Mort].

68  See, for example, the extremely rare example in the Queensland Museum of a mid-century Australian Quaker outfit that belonged to Sarah Benson Walker.

69  Mary Gilmore, *More Recollections* (Sydney: Angus and Robertson, 1935) 89.

70  *Ibid.,* 24.

71  Howitt, *Land, Labour and Gold,* 1855, as quoted in *Australia Brought to Book,* 27.

72  Isabel Hofmeyr, 'Popularising History: The Case of Gustav Preller', *African Studies Seminar,* University of Witwatersrand, August 1987, 20–1.

73  Bain Attwood, 'Off the Mission Stations: Aborigines in Gippsland, 1860–1890', *Aboriginal History* 10 (1986) 134.

74  James Bonwick, *The Last of the Tasmanians or, the Black War of Van Diemen's Land* (London: Sampson Low, Son and Marston, 1870) 276.

75  Tim Rowse, ' "Interpretive Possibilities": Aboriginal Men and Clothing', *Cultural Studies* 5 (1991) 8.

76  Harold Finch-Hatton, *Advance Australia, an Account of Eight Years' Work Wandering, and Amusement in Queensland, New South Wales and Victoria* (London: W. H. Allen, 1886) 81–2.

77  See articles in the popular press during the 1930s: Mare Liebenberg, 'Voortrekkers Kleredrag', *Die Huisgenoot*, 9 Oct 1931.

78  Eleanor Hodges, 'The Bushman Legend', *Intruders in the Bush*, 6.

79  Hugh Mackay, *Reinventing Australia. The Mind and Mood of Australia in the 90s* (Sydney: Angus and Robertson, 1993) 211.

# Bibliography

## Primary Sources

### Manuscripts: United Kingdom

*Greenwich, Maritime Museum*
Navy Board Minutes [ADM 106/2622]
Treasury Letters 1783–9 [ADM/OT]

*London, Public Records Office*
Letter from Major Ross to the Admiralty, 10 Jul 1788 [ADM 1/3824]
Return of Slops Received and Issued, Port Jackson, 30 Sep 1788 [ADM 1/3824]
Letters Relating to the Marines, Botany Bay, 1787 [ADM 2/1178]
Observations Made on Sundry Articles Sent Out to New South Wales, by Mr Alexander Davison, 1791 [CO 201/1]
Redfern to Macquarie, 30 Sep 1814 [CO 201/73]
Macquarie to Bathurst, 28 Feb 1820, Colonial Despatches [CO 201/99]
Unpublished Appendix to Bigge's Reports [CO 201/118]
Heads of a Plan: enclosed in a Letter from Sydney to the Treasury, 18 Aug 1786, Treasury Documents [T1/639]
Board of Ordnance Minutes: WO 47/1516; WO 47/1609; WO 47/1686; WO 47/1694; WO 47/1737; WO 47/1752; WO 47/1821; WO 47/2282.

### Manuscripts: Australia

*Allport Library, Hobart*
Journal of Mary Morton Allport, 1852–4.

*Fryer Library, University of Queensland*
Diary of Joseph Henry Delpratt, 1870 [F224]

Mrs D. McConnel, *Queensland Reminiscences, 1848–1870* [2/1623]

*John Oxley Library, Brisbane*
Diary of Mary McConachie, 1882–8 [OM75-91]

*La Trobe Library, Melbourne*
Vernon Lee Walker, Letters [7568]
Penelope Selby, Letters [9494]

*Melbourne University Archives*
Bright and Hitchcock, London, Letters, 1864–70, and Trade Cards.
Forman Letters, 1856–60.

*Mitchell Library, Sydney*
Banks Papers [A78-2]
Bigge's Reports. Unpublished Appendix, vol.129.
Bligh, William, Correspondence [safe 1/45]
Bonwick Transcripts, Box 5.
Gregg, James, Tradecard, 1854 [A177]
Macarthur Clothing Accounts [A4288]
Macarthur Papers [A2909]
Marsden Family, Letters [719]
T. L. Mitchell, Field Book, 1828–30 [C42]
Riley Papers [A111]
Soull Papers [A1352]
Walker, Anna Frances, Papers [462/4 pt.2]

*Mortlock Library, Adelaide*
Letter from William Dorling, 1848 [D6800 L]
Letter from Thomas Gates Darton, 1838 [PRG 456/1/57]
Margaret May, Letters to her Aunt. 2 vols. Typescript [1363]
Letter from Hugh Watson, 1839 [D6075 L]

*National Library, Canberra*
Brooks, Christiana, Diary, 1825–8. Transcript [1559]
Champion, Thomas, Diary 1842 [1093]
'Life in an Emigrant Ship', 1863 [4145]
Letter from Ellen Moger, 1840 [5919]

*New South Wales, State Archives*
Vouchers to the Treasurer's Disbursements, (1) 1824 [2/855]
Ordnance Day Book, 1839–42 [4/483]
List of Articles required by Private Individuals. Ordnance [4/1703]
Rules for Regulation Dress, Female Factory [4/1708]
Female Factory Parramatta, Reports [4/1791]
Report of the Board of Management of the Female Factory, 1829 [4/2094]
Macleay to Healy [4/3667]
Government and General Orders [NC 11/5]
Slop Clothing Received, 1790–2 [NC 11/1]

*Private Collection*
Trigg Letters, Western Australia.

*South Australia, Public Records Office*
Letter to the Immigration Agent, 24 Sep 1855, CSO
Letters Received [GRG 24/6-3174]

*Tasmania, State Archives*
Memoranda for the Consideration of the Clothing Board [CS01/34/599]


## Published Records: British Government

*Accounts and Papers Relating to Convicts on Board the Hulks and Those Transported to New South Wales*,
    March 1792.
Bigge, John Thomas.
    *Report of the Commissioner of Inquiry into the State of the Colony of New South Wales.* House of Commons,
    1822.
———. *Report of the Commissioner of Inquiry on the State of Agriculture and Trade.* House of Commons,
    1823.
*House of Commons Reports and Papers.* (83) 1791-2.
*Instructions for the Surgeon Superintendent of Government Emigration Ships Going to New South Wales.*
    London: W. Clowes and Sons, 1839.
*Parliamentary Papers on Transportation* (6), 1810-41.
*Report from the Select Committee on Secondary Punishments.* House of Commons, 1832.
*Report from the Select Committee on Transportation.* House of Commons, 1812 (including Appendix);
    Appendices, 1837 and 1838.


## Published Records: Colonial Governments

*Act for the More Effectively Preventing Persons from Purchasing or Receiving Clothing etc.* 17 Jul 1828, George
    IV n.10.
*Factories Act Inquiry Board, First Progress Report, New South Wales, Votes and Proceedings of the Legislative
    Assembly*, (2) 1893.
*Historical Records of Australia*, 1787-1843.
*Historical Records of New South Wales*, 1786-1804.
*New South Wales Census and Industrial Returns Act of 1891. NSW V and P Legislative Assembly*, (7) 1891-2.
'Particulars of Aid Given to Aborigines', *NSW V and P Legislative Assembly*, (4) 1882.
'Prices of Provisions and Clothing', *Statistical Returns, NSW V and P Legislative Council*, (2) 1852.
New South Wales, *Census*, 1828, 1856.
*New South Wales Statistical Registers*, 1880, 1888, 1892.
*New South Wales Statistical Returns, 1847-56, NSW V and P Legislative Assembly*, (1) 1857.
*New South Wales Statistics, 1852-61, NSW V and P Legislative Assembly*, (3) 1862.
*Progress Report on the State of Manufactures and Agriculture in the Colony, NSW V and P Legislative Assembly*,
    (5) 1862.
*Report from the Committee on Immigration, NSW V and P Legislative Council*, 1838.
*Report from the Select Committee on the Condition of the Aborigines, NSW V and P Legislative Council*, 1845.
*Report into Conditions of the Working Classes of the Metropolis, NSW V and P Legislative Assembly*, (4)
    1859-60.
*Royal Commission on the Tariff, 1881, VPP* (4), 1883.
*State of Manufactures and Agriculture in the Colony, Progress Report, NSW V and P Legislative Assembly*,
    (5) 1862.
*Trade With the United Kingdom, NSW V and P Legislative Assembly*, (4) 1896.
Victoria, *Census*, 1854, 1857, 1861, 1871 and 1881.
*Victorian Government Gazette*, 1855.

## Newspapers and Periodicals

*Adelaide Examiner*, 1842-3.
*Ambassador*, 1952.
*Argus*, 1846.
*Australasian*, 1885.
*Australian*, 1827 and 1842.
*The Australian Storekeeper's Journal*, 1895-6.
*Australian Woman's Magazine and Domestic Journal*, 1882.
*Boomerang*, 1888.
*Brisbane Courier*, 1877.
*The Butterfly*, 1869-70.
*Castner's Rural Australia*, 1875-6.
*Court*, 1895.
*Currency Lad*, 1833.
*Dawn*, 1889 and 1890.
*Gympie Miner*, 1888.
*Hobart Town Courier*, 1828, 1834 and 1837.
*Illustrated Sydney News*, 1853, 1870, 1878 and 1890.
*Launceston Advertiser*, 1829.
*Maitland Mercury*, 1843.
*Melbourne Punch*, 1856 and 1860.
*Monitor*, 1826-7 and 1840.
*North Queensland Register*, 1896.
*The Princess: A Lady's Newspaper*, 1889.
*Queenslander*, 1888.
*Queensland Figaro*, 1885-6 and 1888.
*Queensland Punch*, 1881.
*Rockhampton Morning Bulletin*, 1877.
*Sydney's Emigrants Journal*, 1848.
*Sydney Gazette*, 1803-31.
*Sydney Mail*, Christmas Supplement, 1895.
*Sydney Morning Herald*, 1842, 1855, 1863, 1878 and 1880.
*Sydney Punch*, 1857.
*Town and Country Journal*, 1875 and 1878.
*Weigel's Journal of Fashion*, 1881-90.
*The Woman*, 1892.
*The Woman's Voice*, 1894.
*Worth's Australian Fashion Journal*, 1899.

## Almanacks and Directories

*Adelaide Almanack*, 1864.
*Australian Almanack*, 1851.
*Ford's Sydney Directory*, 1851.
*Ford's Australian Almanack*, 1851.
*Melbourne Directory*, 1864.
*Sydney Post Office Directory*, 1857.
*Wood's Tasmanian Almanack*, 1857.

## Contemporary Books

*Account of the English Colony at Botany Bay*. London, 1809.

Adams, Francis. *The Australians: A Social Sketch*. London: Fisher Unwin, 1893.

Allen, Charles H. *A Visit to Queensland and her Goldfields*. London: Chapman and Hall, 1870.

Aspinall, Clara. *Three Years in Melbourne, 1858-61*. London: L. Booth, 1862.

Atkinson, James. *An Account of the State of Agriculture and Grazing in New South Wales*. London: J. Cross, 1826.

*Australian Etiquette, or the Rules and Usages of the Best Society in the Australian Colonies*. 1885; Melbourne: J. M. Dent, 1980 (reprint).

Backhouse, James. *A Narrative of a Visit to the Australian Colonies*. London: Hamilton Adams, 1843.

Bonwick, James. *Daily Life and Origins of the Tasmanians*. London: Sampson Low, Marston and Co., 1898 (2nd edn).

———. *The Last of the Tasmanians or, The Black War of Van Diemen's Land*. London: Sampson Low, Son and Marston, 1870.

Booth, Edwin. *Another England: Life, Living, Homes and Homemakers in Victoria*. London: Virtue and Co., 1869.

Bull, John. *Early Experiences in Life in South Australia*. Adelaide: Wigg, 1884.

Burford, Robert. *Description of a View of the Town of Sydney, New South Wales*. London: J and C. Adelard, 1829.

Byrne, J. C. *Emigrants Guide to New South Wales Proper, Australia Felix and South Australia*. London: E. Wilson, 1848.

Capper, Henry. *South Australia: Containing Hints to Emigrants*. London: R. Tyas, 1838.

Clarke, Percy. *The 'New Chum' in Australia, or the Scenery, Life and Manners of Australians in Town and Country*. London: Virtue, 1886.

*Cole's Correct Conduct. Being the Etiquette of Everyday Life*. Sydney: E. W. Cole, 189?.

Cunningham, Peter. *Two Years In New South Wales*. 2 vols. London: Henry Colburn, 1827.

Dean, Teresa. *How to Be Beautiful*. Melbourne: J. E. Mitchell, 1890.

Earp, George B. *What We Did in Australia*. London: G. Routledge, 1853.

Eden, Charles H. *My Wife and I in Queensland: An Eight Years Experience in the Above Colony*. London: Longmans Green, 1872.

Elliott, Joseph. *Our Home in Australia: A Description of Cottage Life in 1860*. Sydney: Flannel Flower Press, 1984.

*The Emigrant's Almanack*. London: John Cassell, 1851.

*The Emigrant's Almanack and Guide to the Goldfields*. London: Cassells, 1854.

*The Emigrant's Assistant*. London: G. Jackson, 1832.

*The Emigrant's Handbook*. London: 1852.

*Emigration Guide to Australia and New Zealand, Cape of Good Hope and the Canadas*. London: S. W. Silver and Co., 1858.

Farmer and Co. *The Great Drapery Emporium*. Sydney: 1869.

Finch-Hatton, Harold. *Advance Australia, an Account of Eight Years Work Wandering, and Amusement in Queensland, New South Wales and Victoria*. London: W. H. Allen and Co., 1886.

Forbes, George (ed.). *Sydney Society in Crown Colony Days. The Reminiscences of the Late Lady Forbes*. Typewritten, 1914 [ML].

Fowler, Frank. *Southern Lights, Being Brief Notes of Three Years Experience of Social, Literary and Political Life in Australia*. London: Sampson Low, 1859.

Franklyn, H. Mortimer. *A Glance at Australia in 1880*. Melbourne: Victorian Review Publishing Co., 1881.

Freeman, John. *Lights and Shadows of Melbourne Life*. London: Sampson Low, Marston, Searle and Rivington, 1888.

Fry, Elizabeth. *Observations on the Visiting, Superintendence and Government of Female Prisoners*. London: J. and A. Arch, 1827.

Furphy, Joseph. *Such is Life. Being Certain Extracts from the Diary of Tom Collins.* London: Jonathan Cape, 1944.

Gane, Douglas M. *New South Wales and Victoria in 1885.* London: Sampson Low, Marston, Searle and Rivington, 1886.

Garnsey, Edward. *The Australian at Home. Notes and Anecdotes of Life at the Antipodes.* London: Leadenhall Press, 1892.

Gilmore, Mary. *More Recollections.* Sydney: Angus and Robertson, 1935.

Godley, Charlotte. *Letters from Early New Zealand.* Plymouth: Private Printing, 1936.

*Godwin's Emigrants Guide to Van Diemen's Land.* London: Sherwood Jones and Co., 1823.

Harris, Alexander. *Settlers and Convicts, or Recollections of Sixteen Years' Labour in the Australian Backwoods.* (first published in 1847) Carlton, Vic.: Melbourne University Press, 1964 (reprint).

Harrison, Robert. *Colonial Sketches: or Five Years in South Australia.* London: L. Hall, Virtue, 1862.

Haygarth, Henry William. *Recollections of Bush Life in Australia.* London: John Murray, 1850.

Henderson, John. *Excursions and Adventures in New South Wales.* London: Shobere, 1851.

*Hints on Etiquette and the Usages of Society, with a Glance at Bad Habits.* Hobart: William Gore Elliston, 1838.

Hodgson, Christopher P. *Reminiscences of Australia. With Hints on the Squatter's Life.* London: W. N. Wright, 1846.

Hood, John. *Australia and the East: Being a Journal Narrative of a Voyage to New South Wales in an Emigrant Ship in the Years 1841 and 42.* London: John Murray, 1843.

Howard, John. *The State of the Prisons in England and Wales.* London: Warrington, 1777–84.

Howitt, Richard. *Australia: Historical, Descriptive and Statistic.* London: Longman, Brown, Green and Longmans, 1845.

Howitt, William. *Land, Labour and Gold, or Two Years in Victoria with Visits to Sydney and Van Diemen's Land.* 1855; Kilmore: Lowden Publishing Co., 1972 (reprint).

Hume, Fergus. *The Mystery of a Hansom Cab.* 1887; Melbourne: Sun Books, 1971 (reprint).

Hunter, John. *An Historical Journal of the Transactions at Port Jackson and Norfolk Island.* London: Stockdale, 1793.

Hursthouse, Charles. *Emigration: Where to Go and Who Should Go.* London: Trelawney Saunders, 1852.

Inglis, James. *Our Australian Cousins.* London: Macmillan and Co., 1880.

Just, P. *Australia, or Notes Taken During a Residence in the Colonies from the Gold Discovery in 1851 till 1857.* Dundee: Durham and Thomson, 1859.

Kelly, William. *Life in Victoria 1853 and Victoria in 1858.* 2 vols. Kilmore: Lowden Publishing Co., 1977.

Kennedy, David. *Kennedy's Colonial Travel.* London: Edinburgh Publishing Co., 1876.

Kershaw, Mark. *Colonial Facts and Fictions: Humorous Sketches.* London: Chatto and Windus, 1886.

Landor, E. W. *The Bushman, or Life in a New Country.* London: Bentley, 1847.

*Letters from Emigrants to Queensland, 1863–1885.* Brisbane: Queensland Family History, 1984.

*The Library of Elegance.* London: E. Moses and Sons, 1852.

McKell, Katherine. *Old Days and Gold Days in Victoria 1851–73.* Melbourne: E. A. Vidler, 1924.

Mackenzie, David (Rev.). *The Emigrant's Guide, or Ten Years' Practical Experience in Australia.* London: W. S. Orr and Co., 1845.

Mackenzie, Eneas. *Mackenzie's Australian Emigrants' Guide.* London: Clarke Beeton, 1852.

———. *Memoirs of Mrs Caroline Chisholm.* London: Webb Millington, 1852.

MacPherson, Mrs A. *My Experiences in Australia. Being Recollections of a Visit to the Australian Colonies in 1856–7.* London: J. F. Hope, 1860.

Mann, Daniel. *The Present Picture of New South Wales.* London: John Booth, 1811.

Meredith, Louisa. *My Home in Tasmania or Nine Years in Australia.* New York: Bunce and Broker, 1853.

———. *Notes and Sketches of New South Wales During a Residence in that Colony 1839–44.* Harmondsworth: Penguin, 1973 (reprint).

———. *Over the Straits. A Visit to Victoria.* London: Chapman and Hall, 1861.

Mereweather, John Davies (Rev.). *Life on Board an Emigrant Ship: Being a Diary of a Voyage to Australia.* London: T. Hatchard, 1852.

Mossman, Samuel, and Banister, Thomas. *Australia Visited and Revisited. A Narrative of Recent Travels and Old Experiences in Victoria and New South Wales.* 1853; Sydney: Ure Smith, 1974 (reprint).

Mudie, James. *The Felonry of New South Wales.* 1837; ed. Walter Stone, Melbourne: Lansdowne, 1964.

Mundy, Godfrey C. *Our Antipodes, or Residence and Rambles in the Australian Colonies* I. London: Bentley, 1852.

Murray, Robert D. *A Summer at Port Phillip.* Edinburgh: William Tait, 1843.

O'Connell, James. *A Residence of Eleven Years in New Holland and the Caroline Islands.* Boston: B. B. Mussey, 1836.

An Old Housekeeper. *The Australian Housewives' Manual: A Book for Beginners and People with Small Incomes.* Melbourne: A. H. Messina and Co., 1885.

Parker, Gilbert. *Round the Compass in Australia.* London: Hutchinson and Co., 1892.

Prinsep, Augustus. *The Journal of a Voyage from Calcutta to Van Diemen's Land.* London: Smith Elder and Co., 1833.

Ramsay-Laye, Elizabeth. *Social Life and Manners in Australia.* London: Longman, Green, Longman and Roberts, 1861.

Shaw, William. *The Land of Promise: or My Impressions of Australia.* London: Simpkin Marshall, 1854.

Smith, Rosamond. *Hints to Emigrants.* Braintree: E. C. Joscelyne, 1866.

Smith, Sidney. *The Settler's New Home: or Whether to Go and Whither?* London: J. Kendrick, 1850.

Spence, Catherine. *Clara Morison: A Tale of South Australia During the Gold Fever.* 1854; Adelaide: Wakefield Press, 1986 (reprint).

Stirling, A. W. *The Never Neverland: A Ride in North Queensland.* London: Sampson Low, Marston, Searle and Rivington, 1884.

Sutherland, George. *Australia, or England in the South.* London: Seeley, 1886.

Tegg, Thomas. *Handbook for Emigrants.* London: Thomas Tegg, 1839.

Townsend, Joseph P. *Rambles and Observations in New South Wales.* London: Chapman and Hall, 1849.

Twopeny, Richard. *Town Life in Australia.* 1883; Harmondsworth: Penguin, 1973 (reprint).

Waugh, David. *Three Years' Practical Experience of a Settler in New South Wales: Being Extracts from Letters to his Friends in Edinburgh, 1834–7.* Edinburgh: John Johnstone, 1838.

Wentworth, William. *A Statistical Account of the British Settlements in Australia.* London: Whittaker, 1824.

Westgarth, William. *Australia Felix: or a Historical or Descriptive Account of the Settlement of Port Phillip, New South Wales.* Edinburgh: Oliver and Boyd, 1848.

## Secondary Sources

### Later Books

Adams, David (editor). *The Letters of Rachel Henning.* Sydney: Bulletin Newspaper Co., 1952.

———. *The Letters of Rachel Henning.* Sydney: Angus and Robertson, 1963.

———. *The Letters of Rachel Henning.* North Ryde: Angus and Robertson, 1986.

Alford, Katrina. *Production or Reproduction? An Economic History of Women in Australia, 1788–1850.* Melbourne: Oxford University Press, 1984.

*The Artist and Patron: Aspects of Colonial Art in New South Wales.* Sydney: Art Gallery of New South Wales, 1988.

Attwood, Bain. *The Making of the Aborigines*. North Sydney: Allen and Unwin, 1989.

Banner, Lois. *American Beauty*. New York: Alfred Knopf, 1983.

Bateson, Charles. *The Convict Ships, 1787–1868*. Glasgow: Brown Son and Ferguson, 1959.

Baxter, Carol (editor). *General Muster of New South Wales, 1814*. Sydney: Australian Bibliographical and Genealogical Record, 1987.

Birch, Alan, and Macmillan, David. *The Sydney Scene, 1788–1960*. Sydney: Hale and Iremonger, 1982.

Blainey, Geoffrey. *The Tyranny of Distance*. Melbourne: Sun Books, 1977.

Bonnin, Nancy (editor). *Katie Hume on the Darling Downs. A Colonial Marriage*. Toowoomba: Darling Downs Institute Press, 1985.

Brand, Ian. *The 'Separate' or 'Model' Prison, Port Arthur*. West Moonah: Jason, 1980.

Braydon, Simon and Longhurst, Robert (editors). *The Diary of Joseph Sams, an Emigrant in the 'Northumberland'*. London: HMSO, 1982.

Broome, Richard. *Aboriginal Australians: Black Responses to White Dominance, 1788–1980*. Sydney: Allen and Unwin, 1982.

Buckley, Ken, and Wheelwright, Ted. *No Paradise for Workers: Capitalism and the Common People in Australia, 1788–1914*. Melbourne: Oxford University Press, 1988.

Cannon, Michael. *Australia in the Victorian Age*, vol. 2: *Life in the Country*; vol. 3: *Life in the Cities*. West Melbourne: Nelson, 1976.

Charlwood, Don. *The Long Farewell*. Ringwood, Vic.: Allen Lane, 1981.

Clarke, Patricia. *The Governesses: Letters from the Colonies, 1862–1882*. Melbourne: Hutchinson, 1985.

Cobley, John. *Sydney Cove, 1788*. London: Hodder and Stoughton, 1962.

Coghlan, Timothy A. *Labour and Industry in Australia* I. London: Oxford University Press, 1918.

Connell, Robert William, and Irving, T. H. *Class Structure in Australian History*. Melbourne: Longman Cheshire, 1980.

Crowley, Francis. *A Documentary History of Australia*, vol. I: *1788–1840*. West Melbourne: Nelson, 1978.

Cunnington, Phyllis, and Lucas, Catherine. *Charity Costumes of Children, Scholars, Almsfolk, Pensioners*. London: A. and C. Black, 1978.

Daniels, Kay, and Murnane, Mary. *Uphill all the Way: A Documentary History of Women in Australia*. St Lucia: University of Queensland Press, 1980.

Davidoff, Leonore. *The Best Circles: Society, Etiquette and the Season*. London: Croom Helm, 1973.

Davidoff, Leonore, and Hall, Catherine. *Family Fortunes: Men and Women of the English Middle-Class, 1780–1850*. London: Hutchinson, 1987.

Davison, Graeme. *The Rise and Fall of Marvellous Melbourne*. Melbourne: Melbourne University Press, 1978.

Davison, Graeme, Dunstan, David, and McConville, Chris (editors). *The Outcasts of Melbourne: Essays in Social History*. Sydney: Allen and Unwin, 1985.

Dyster, Barrie. *Servant and Master: Building and Running the Grand Houses of Sydney, 1788–1850*. Sydney: New South Wales University Press, 1989.

Edwards, Peter, and Joyce, Roger (editors). *Anthony Trollope, Australia*. St Lucia: University of Queensland Press, 1967.

Eldershaw, M. Barnard. *The Life and Times of Captain John Piper*. Sydney: Australian Limited Edition Society, 1939.

Ellem, Bradon. *In Women's Hands? A History of Clothing Trades Unionism in Australia*. Sydney: New South Wales University Press, 1989.

Ellis, Constance. *I Seek Adventure*. Sydney: Alternative Publishing Co., 1981.

Ellis, Malcolm Henry. *John Macarthur*. Sydney: Angus and Robertson, 1955.

Evans, Raymond, Saunders, Kay, and Cronin, Kathryn. *Race Relations in Colonial Queensland*. St Lucia: University of Queensland Press, 1988.

Evans, Robin. *Fabrication of Virtue: English Prison Architecture, 1750–1840*. Cambridge: Cambridge University Press, 1982.

Field, Cyril. *Britain's Sea Soldiers*. II. Liverpool: Lyceum Press, 1924.

Fitzgerald, Ross. *From the Dreaming to 1915: A History of Queensland*. St Lucia: University of Queensland Press, 1982.

Fitzgerald, Shirley. *Rising Damp: Sydney, 1870-1890*. Melbourne: Oxford University Press, 1987.

Fitzhardinge, L. F. Introduction to: *Sydney's First Four Years: Being a Reprint of a Narrative of the Expedition to Botany Bay*. Sydney: Angus and Robertson, 1961.

Fletcher, Brian. *Ralph Darling: A Governor Maligned*. Melbourne: Oxford University Press, 1984.

Fletcher, Marion. *Costume in Australia, 1788-1901*. Melbourne: Oxford University Press, 1984.

Flower, Cedric. *Duck and Cabbage Tree: A Pictorial History of Clothes in Australia, 1788-1914*. Sydney: Angus and Robertson, 1968. Revised and republished as *Clothes in Australia: A Pictorial History, 1788-1980s*. Kenthurst: Kangaroo Press, 1984.

Forsyth, William D. *Governor Arthur's Convict System, Van Diemen's Land, 1824-1836*. Sydney: Sydney University Press, 1970.

Foucault, Michel. *Discipline and Punish: The Birth of the Prison*. Harmondsworth: Penguin, 1977.

Frost, Alan. *Arthur Phillip, 1738-1814. His Voyaging*. Oxford: Oxford University Press, 1987.

Frost, Lucy. *No Place for a Nervous Lady: Voices from the Australian Bush*. Melbourne: McPhee Gribble, 1984.

Gernsheim, Alison. *Victorian and Edwardian Fashion. A Photographic Survey*. New York: Dover, 1981.

Golding, D. J. (editor). *The Emigrant's Guide to Australia in the Eighteen-Fifties*. Melbourne: Hawthorne Press, 1973.

Gorham, Deborah. *The Victorian Girl and the Feminine Ideal*. London: Croom Helm, 1982.

Green, Neville. *Broken Spears: Aborigines and Europeans in the South West of Australia*. Perth: Focus Education, 1984.

Hainsworth, David Roger. *The Sydney Traders: Simeon Lord and His Contemporaries, 1788-1821*. Melbourne: Cassell, 1972.

Halttunnen, Karen. *Confidence Men and Painted Women: A Study of Middle-Class Culture in America, 1830-1870*. New Haven: Yale University Press, 1982.

Harman, Kaye (editor). *Australia Brought to Book: Responses to Australia by Visiting Writers, 1836-1939*. New South Wales: Boobook, 1985.

Hasluck, Alexandra. *Portrait with Background: A Life of Georgiana Molloy*. Melbourne: Oxford University Press, 1955.

Hazzard, Margaret. *Australia's Brilliant Daughter. Ellis Rowan: Artist, Naturalist, Explorer, 1848-1922*. Richmond: Greenhouse Publications, 1984.

——— . *Punishment Short of Death: A History of the Penal Settlement at Norfolk Island*. Melbourne: Hyland House, 1984.

Heney, Helen. *Dear Fanny: Women's Letters to and from New South Wales, 1788-1857*. Canberra: Australian National University Press, 1985.

Herman, Morton (editor). *Annabella Boswell's Journal*. Sydney: Angus and Robertson, 1965.

Hirst, John Bradley. *Convict Society and its Enemies: A History of Early New South Wales*. Sydney: Allen and Unwin, 1983.

Hoorn, Jeanette. *The Lycett Album: Drawings of Aborigines and Australian Scenery*. Canberra: National Library of Australia, c.1990.

Inglis, Kenneth. *The Australian Colonists: An Exploration of Social History, 1788-1870*. Carlton, Vic.: Melbourne University Press, 1974.

Irvine, Nance (editor) *The Sirius Letters*. Sydney: Fairfax Library, 1988.

Jackson, Robert V. *Australian Economic Development in the Nineteenth Century*. Canberra: Australian National University Press, 1977.

——— . *Population History of Australia*. Melbourne: McPhee Gribble, 1988.

Joel, Alexandra. *Best Dressed: Two Hundred Years of Fashion in Australia*. Sydney: William Collins, 1984.

Kerr, Colin. *'A Excelent Coliney': The Practical Idealists of 1836-1846*. Adelaide: Rigby, 1978.

Kerr, James Semple. *Design for Convicts: An Account of Design for Convict Establishments in the Australian Colonies During the Transportation Period.* Sydney: Library of Australian History, 1984.

Kerr, Joan, and Falkus, Hugh. *From Sydney Cove to Duntroon: A Family Album of Early Life in Australia.* Richmond, Vic.: Hutchinson, 1982.

Kiddle, Margaret. *Men of Yesterday: A Social History of the Western District of Victoria, 1834-1890.* Carlton, Vic.: Melbourne University Press, 1961.

King, Hazel. *Elizabeth Macarthur and Her World.* Sydney: Sydney University Press, 1980.

Kingston, Beverley. *My Wife, My Daughter, and Poor Mary Ann: Women and Work in Australia.* Melbourne: Nelson, 1975.

——— . (editor). *The World Moves Slowly: A Documentary History of Australian Women.* Stanmore, NSW: Cassell, 1977.

Levitt, Sarah. *Victorians Unbuttoned: Registered Designs for Clothing, their Makers and Wearers.* London: Allen and Unwin, 1986.

Linge, Godfrey. *Industrial Awakening: A Geography of Manufacturing, 1788-1890.* Canberra: Australian National University Press, 1979.

Lurie, Alison. *The Language of Clothes.* New York: Random House, 1981; 2nd edition, New York: Vintage Books, 1983.

McCarty, J. W., and Schedvin, C. B. (editors). *Australian Capital Cities: Historical Essays.* Sydney: Sydney University Press, 1978.

McCorkell, H. A. (editor). *The Diaries of Sarah Midgley and Richard Skilbeck: A Story of Australian Settlers, 1851-1864.* Melbourne: Cassell, 1967.

Macdonach, Oliver. *A Pattern of Government Growth, 1800-1860. The Passenger Acts and their Enforcement.* London: MacGibbon and Kee, 1961.

Mackay, David. *A Place of Exile: European Settlement of New South Wales.* Melbourne: Oxford University Press, 1985.

Madgwick, R. B. *Immigration into Eastern Australia, 1788-1851.* London: Longmans, Green and Co., 1937.

de Marly, Diana. *Fashion for Men.* London: Batsford, 1985.

——— . *Working Dress. A History of Occupational Clothing.* New York: Holmes and Meir, 1986.

Martin, Ged (editor). *The Founding of Australia: The Argument about Australia's Origins.* Sydney: Hale and Iremonger, 1978.

Mulvaney, Derek. *Encounters in Place: Outsiders and Aboriginal Australians, 1606-1905.* St Lucia: University of Queensland Press, 1989.

Murray, James. *Larrikins: Nineteenth-Century Outrage.* Melbourne: Lansdowne, 1973.

Neal, David. *The Rule of Law in a Penal Colony: Law and Power in Early New South Wales.* Melbourne: Cambridge University Press, 1991.

Nicholls, Mary (editor). *Traveller Under Concern: The Quaker Journals of Frederick Mackie on his Tour of the Australian Colonies, 1852-55.* Hobart: University of Tasmania, 1973.

Parker, Rozsika. *The Subversive Stitch: Embroidery and the Making of the Feminine.* London: Women's Press, 1984.

Patrick, Ross. *A History of Health and Medicine in Queensland, 1824-1960.* St Lucia: University of Queensland Press, 1987.

Perrott, Monica. *A Tolerable Good Success: Economic Opportunities for Women in New South Wales, 1788-1830.* Sydney: Hale and Iremonger, 1983.

Phillips, Jock. *A Man's Country? The Image of the Pakeha Male—A History.* Auckland: Penguin Books, 1987.

Plomley, Norman. *Friendly Mission: The Tasmanian Journals and Papers of George Augustus Robinson, 1829-1834.* Sydney: Halstead Press, 1966.

——— . *An Immigrant of 1824.* Hobart: Tasmanian Historical Research Association, 1973.

Pownall, Eve. *Mary of Maranoa: Tales of Australian Pioneer Women.* Carlton, Vic.: Melbourne University Press, 1964.

Quaife, G. R. (editor). *Gold and Colonial Society, 1851–1870*. Stanmore, NSW: Cassell, 1975.

Reekie, Gail. *Temptations: Sex, Selling and the Department Store*. Sydney: Allen and Unwin, 1993.

Ribeiro, Aileen. *Dress and Morality*. London: Batsford, 1986.

Ritchie, John Douglas. *The Evidence to the Bigge Reports*, vol. 1: *New South Wales Under Governor Macquarie*, vol. 2: *The Written Evidence*. Melbourne: Heinemann, 1971.

Robinson, Portia. *The Hatch and Brood of Time: A Study of the First Generation of Native-Born White Australians, 1788–1828*. Melbourne: Oxford University Press, 1985.

Robson, Leslie Lloyd. *The Convict Settlers of Australia: An Enquiry into the Origin and Character of the Convicts Transported to New South Wales and Van Diemen's Land, 1787–1852*. Carlton, Vic.: Melbourne University Press, 1965.

Rowley, C. D. *The Destruction of Aboriginal Society*. Harmondsworth: Penguin, 1978.

Ryan, Edna, and Conlan, Anne. *Gentle Invaders: Australian Women at Work, 1788–1974*. West Melbourne: Thomas Nelson, 1975.

Ryan, Lyndall. *The Aboriginal Tasmanians*. St Lucia: University of Queensland Press, 1981.

Salt, Annette. *These Outcast Women: The Parramatta Female Factory, 1821–1848*. Sydney: Hale and Iremonger, 1984.

Scandrett, Elizabeth. *Breeches and Bustles: An Illustrated History of Clothes Worn in Australia, 1788–1914*. Lilydale: Pioneer Design Studio, 1978.

Schaffer, Kay. *Women and the Bush: Forces of Desire in the Australian Cultural Tradition*. Melbourne: Cambridge University Press, 1988.

Sennett, Richard. *The Fall of Public Man*. London: Faber and Faber, 1986.

Serle, Geoffrey. *The Golden Age: A History of the Colony of Victoria, 1851–61*. Carlton, Vic.: Melbourne University Press, 1963.

——— . *The Rush to be Rich: A History of the Colony of Victoria, 1883–9*. Carlton, Vic.: Melbourne University Press, 1971.

de Serville, Paul. *Port Phillip Gentlemen and Good Society in Melbourne before the Gold Rushes*. Melbourne: Oxford University Press, 1980.

Shaw, A. G. L. *Convicts and the Colonies: A Study of Penal Transportation from Great Britain and Ireland to Australia*. London: Faber and Faber, 1966.

——— . *The Economic Development of Australia*. Melbourne: Longman Cheshire, 1980.

Smith, Babette. *A Cargo of Women: Susannah Watson and the Convicts of the 'Princess Royal'*. Kensington: University of New South Wales Press, 1988.

Smith, Bernard. *The Spectre of Truganini*. Sydney: ABC, 1980.

Stanner, W. E. H. *White Man Got No Dreaming: Essays, 1938–1973*. Canberra: Australian National University Press, 1979.

Statham, Pamela (editor). *The Tanner Letters: A Pioneer Saga of Swan River and Tasmania, 1831–1845*. Nedlands: University of Western Australia Press, 1981.

Steele, Valerie. *Fashion and Eroticism: Ideals of Feminine Beauty from the Victorian Era to the Jazz Age*. New York: Oxford University Press, 1985.

Stone, Sharman. *Aborigines in White Australia: A Documentary History of the Attitudes Affecting Official Policy and the Australian Aborigine, 1697–1973*. South Yarra, Vic.: Heinemann Educational, 1974.

Sturma, Michael. *Vice in a Vicious Society*. St Lucia: University of Queensland Press, 1983.

Thompson, Judith. *Bustles and Beaus: Fashion in South Australia, 1881–1981*. Adelaide: Art Gallery of South Australia, 1981.

Thomas, Evan (editor). *The Diary and Letters of Mary Thomas, 1836–1866*. Adelaide: Thomas and Co., 1983.

Thomas, Joan. *The Sea Journals of Annie and Amy Henning*. Sydney: Halstead Press, 1984.

Treborlang, Robert. *How to Survive Australia*. Sydney: Major Mitchell Press, 1985.

Veblen, Thorstein. *The Theory of the Leisure Class: An Economic Study of Institutions*. New York: Macmillan, 1912.

Ward, Russel. *The Australian Legend*. Melbourne: Oxford University Press, 1965.

———. *Finding Australia: The History of Australia to 1821*. Melbourne: Heinemann, 1987.

———. (editor). *The New Australia: Edmond Marin La Meslee*. London: Heinemann, 1973.

Weidenhofer, Maggie. *Colonial Ladies*. South Yarra, Vic.: Currey O'Neil Ross, 1985.

White, Richard. *Inventing Australia: Images and Identity, 1688–1980*. Sydney: Allen and Unwin, 1981.

Wilson, Elizabeth. *Adorned in Dreams: Fashion and Modernity*. London: Virago Press, 1985.

Woolcock, Helen. *Rights of Passage: Emigration to Australia in the Nineteenth Century*. London: Tavistock Publications, 1986.

Woolf, Virginia. *A Room of One's Own*. 1929; Harmondsworth: Penguin, 1973 (reprint).

Woolmington, Jean (editor). *Aborigines in Colonial Society, 1788–1850*. North Melbourne: Cassell, 1973.

## Later Articles and Papers

'A Letter from Melbourne'. Transcript of a letter from John Hadfield to his Mother. *LaTrobe Library Journal* (3) Oct 1972, pp. 25–30.

Alford, Katrina. 'Gilt-Edged Women: Women and Mining in Colonial Australia'. *Working Papers in Economic History* (64) Canberra: Australian National University, 1986.

———. 'Colonial Women's Employment as Seen by 19th Century Statisticians and 20th Century Economic Historians'. *Working Papers in Economic History* (65) Canberra: Australian National University, 1986.

———. 'The Drover's Wife and Her Friends: Women in Rural Society and Primary Production in Australia, 1850–1900'. *Working Papers in Economic History* (75) Canberra: Australian National University, 1986.

Amies, Marion. 'The Victorian Governess and Colonial Ideals of Womanhood'. *Victorian Studies* (31) 1988, pp. 537–65.

Attwood, Bain. 'Off the Mission Stations: Aborigines in Gippsland, 1860–1890'. *Aboriginal History* (10) 1986, pp. 131–51.

Auliciems, Andris, and Deaves, Stuart. 'Clothing, Heat and Settlement'. *The Australian Experience: Essays in Australian Land Settlement and Resource Management*, ed. R. L. Heathcote. Melbourne: Longman Cheshire, 1988.

Aveling, Marian. 'Gender in Early New South Wales Society'. *Push from the Bush* (24) April 1987, pp. 30–9.

Balls-Headley, Walter. 'Dress With Reference to Heat'. *Australian Health Society Lecture*, Melbourne, 1876.

Bartky, Sandra Lee. 'Foucault, Femininity, and the Modernization of Patriarchal Power'. *Feminism and Foucault: Reflections and Resistances*, ed. Irene Diamond and Lee Quinby. Boston: North Eastern University Press, 1988.

Bennett, Tony. 'Out of Which Past? Critical Reflections on Australian Museum Policy'. *Cultural Policy Studies*, Occasional Paper (3) 1988.

Benson, Susan P. 'Palace of Consumption and Machine for Selling: The American Department Store, 1880–1940'. *Radical History Review*, Fall 1979, pp. 199–221.

Blair, Sandra. 'The Felonry and the Free? Divisions in Colonial Society in the Penal Era'. *Labour History* (45) 1983, pp. 1–16.

Bolger, Peter. 'The Changing Image of Hobart'. *Australian Capital Cities*, ed. J. W. McCarty and C. B. Schedvin. Sydney: Sydney University Press, 1978.

Byrne, Paula-Jane. 'Women and the Criminal Law: Sydney, 1810–1821'. *Push from the Bush* (21) 1985, pp. 2–19.

Carisbrooke, Donald. 'Immigrants in the Bush'. *Push from the Bush* (5) 1979, pp. 31–54.

Carroll, John. 'Mateship and Egalitarianism'. *Intruders in the Bush. The Australian Quest for Identity*, ed. John Carroll. Melbourne: Oxford University Press, 1982.

Casteras, Susan. 'Victorian Images of Emigration Themes'. *Journal of Pre-Raphaelite Studies* (6) 1985, pp. 1-23.

Chaney, David. 'The Department Store as a Cultural Form'. *Theory Culture and Society* I, 1983, pp. 22-31.

Daniels, Kay. 'Prostitution in Tasmania during the Transition from Penal Settlement to "Civilized Society" '. *So Much Hard Work: Women and Prostitution in Australian History*, ed. Kay Daniels. Sydney: Fontana, 1984.

——. 'Feminism and Social History'. *Australian Feminist Studies* (1) Summer 1985, pp. 27-40.

Davison, Graeme. 'R. E. N. Twopeny and town life in Australia'. *Historical Studies* (16) 1974-5, pp. 292-305.

——. 'The Dimensions of Mobility in Nineteenth-century Australia'. *Australia 1888* (2) 1979, pp. 7-32.

Deacon, Desley. 'Political Arithmetic: The Nineteenth-century Australian Census and the Construction of the Dependent Woman'. *Signs* (11) Autumn 1985, pp. 27-47.

Dyster, Barrie. 'Public Employment and Assignment to Private Masters, 1788-1821'. *Convict Workers. Reinterpreting Australia's Past*, ed. Stephen Nicholas. Melbourne: Cambridge University Press, 1988.

Evans, Susanna. 'Kings without Kingdoms'. *Australian Connoisseur and Collector* (2) 1982, pp. 86-93.

Farrell, Frank. 'The Practical Politician'. *Australian Cultural History* (8) 1989, pp. 50-61.

de Fircks, Tatiana. 'Costume in the Early Years of Western Australia'. *Journal and Proceedings of the Royal Western Australian Historical Society* (9) 1988, pp. 27-38.

Fisher, Shirley. 'The Family and the Sydney Economy in the late Nineteenth Century'. *Families in Colonial Australia*, ed. Patricia Grimshaw, Chris McConville and Ellen McEwen. Sydney: Allen and Unwin, 1985.

Fox, Joan. 'Designing Differences'. *Making a Life. A People's History of Australia Since 1788*, ed. Verity Burgmann and Jenny Lee. Fitzroy, Vic.: McPhee Gribble, 1988.

Frost, Alan. 'The Conditions of Early Settlement: New South Wales 1788-1840'. *Intruders in the Bush. The Australian Quest for Identity*, ed. John Carroll. Melbourne: Oxford University Press, 1982.

——. 'Botany Bay: An Imperial Venture of the 1780s'. *English Historical Review* (100) April 1985, pp. 309-27.

——. 'Going Away, Coming Home'. *Studies from Terra Australis to Australia*, ed. John Hardy and Alan Frost. Canberra: Australian Academy of the Humanities, 1989.

Gillen, Mollie. 'The Botany Bay Decision, 1786: Convicts not Empire'. *English Historical Review* (98) October 1982, pp. 740-66.

——. 'Response to Alan Frost'. *English Historical Review* (100) April 1985, pp. 327-30.

Godden, Judith. 'A New Look at the Pioneer Woman'. *Hecate* (5) 1979, pp. 6-21.

Grimshaw, Patricia. 'Women and the family in Australian history—a reply to *The Real Matilda*'. *Historical Studies* (18) 1979, pp. 412-21.

——. ' "Man's Own Country": Women in Colonial Australian History'. *Australian Women. New Feminist Perspectives*, ed. Norma Grieve and Ailsa Burns. Melbourne: Oxford University Press, 1986.

Hagan, J. S. 'Employers, Trade Unions and the First Victorian Factory Acts'. *Labour History* (7) 1964, pp. 3-10.

Hirst, John Bradley. 'Egalitarianism'. *Australian Cultural History*, ed. S. L. Goldberg and F. B. Smith. Cambridge: Cambridge University Press, 1988.

Hodges, Eleanor. 'The Bushman Legend'. *Intruders in the Bush: The Australian Quest for Identity*, ed. John Carroll. Melbourne: Oxford University Press, 1982.

Hofmeyr, Isabel. 'Popularising History: The Case of Gustav Preller'. *African Studies Institute*. Johannesburg: University of the Witwatersrand, 1987.

Jones, Eric, and Raby, Geoffrey. 'The Fatal Shortage: Establishing a European Economy in New South Wales 1788-1805'. *Studies from Terra Australis to Australia*, ed. John Hardy and Alan Frost. Canberra: Australian Academy of the Humanities, 1989.

Kennedy, Richard. 'Charity and Ideology in Colonial Victoria'. *Australian Welfare History. Critical Essays*, ed. Richard Kennedy. South Melbourne: Macmillan, 1982.

Kidwell, Claudia Brush. 'Transformation of the Women's Wear Industry into the Fashion Industry; Gender and the Ready-Made Industry in the United States'. *Per Una Storia della Moda Pronta.* Milan: CISST, 1990.

Kingston, Beverley. 'The Lady and the Australian Girl: Some Thoughts on Nationalism and Class'. *Australian Women: New Feminist Perspectives*, ed. Norma Grieve and Ailsa Burns. Melbourne: Oxford University Press, 1986.

Knight, Roger. 'The First Fleet: Its State and Preparation, 1786-1787'. *Studies from Terra Australis to Australia*, ed. John Hardy and Alan Frost. Canberra: Australian Academy for the Humanities, 1989.

Lake, Marilyn. 'The politics of respectability: identifying the masculinist context'. *Historical Studies* (22) 1986, pp. 116-17.

Lee, Jenny, and Fahey, Charles. 'A Boom for Whom? Some Developments in the Australian Labour Market, 1870-1891'. *Labour History* (50) 1986, pp. 1-27.

Lemire, Beverley. 'Developing Consumerism and the Ready-Made Clothing Trade in Britain 1750-1800'. *Textile History* (15) Spring 1984, pp. 1-42.

——— . 'Consumerism in Pre-industrial and Early Industrial England: The Trade in Secondhand Clothes'. *Journal of British Studies* (27) 1988, pp. 1-24.

——— . 'The Theft of Clothes and Popular Consumerism in Early Modern England'. *Journal of Social History* (24) 1990-1, pp. 255-76.

Liebenberg, Mare. 'Voortrekkers Kleredrag'. *Die Huisgenoot* 1931, pp. 69-77.

London, H. Stanford. 'The Broad Arrow as a Government Badge'. *Heraldry Today* (3) 1954, pp. 135-6.

McBryde, Isabel. ' "To Establish a Commerce of this Sort"—Cross Cultural Exchange at the Port Jackson Settlement'. *Studies from Terra Australis to Australia*, ed. John Hardy and Alan Frost. Canberra: Australian Academy of the Humanities, 1989.

McCarty, J. W. 'Australian Capital Cities in the Nineteenth Century'. *Urbanization in Australia in the Nineteenth Century*, ed. C. B. Schedvin and J. W. McCarty. Sydney: Sydney University Press, 1974.

McConville, Chris. 'Outcast Children in Marvellous Melbourne'. *The Colonial Child*, ed. Guy Featherstone. Melbourne: Royal Historical Society of Victoria, 1981.

McEwen, Ellen. 'Family History in Australia: Some Observations on a New Field'. *Families in Colonial Australia*, ed. Patricia Grimshaw, Chris McConville and Ellen McEwen. Sydney: Allen and Unwin, 1985.

Martin, Biddy. 'Feminism, Criticism and Foucault'. *Feminism and Foucault. Reflections and Resistances*, ed. Irene Diamond and Lee Quimby. Boston: North Eastern University Press, 1988.

Maynard, Margaret. 'A Form of Humiliation: Early Transportation Uniforms in Australia'. *Costume* (21) 1987, pp. 57-66.

——— . 'Dress and the Urban Experience'. *Brisbane in 1888: The Historical Perspective*. Brisbane History Group Papers (8) 1989.

——— . 'Civilian Clothing and Fabric Supplies: The Development of Fashionable Dressing in Sydney, 1790-1830'. *Textile History* (21) 1990, pp. 87-100.

——— . 'Terrace Gowns and Shearer's Boots: Rethinking Dress in Public Collections'. *Culture and Policy* (3) 1992, pp. 77-84.

Moorhouse, Frank. 'Australian Mythologies. The Australian Legend and R. M. Williams—Male Costume and Accoutrement'. *Island* (9/10) 1982, pp. 24-8.

Nicholas, Stephen. 'The Care and Feeding of Convicts'. *Convict Workers, Reinterpreting Australia's Past*, ed. Stephen Nicholas. Melbourne: Cambridge University Press, 1988.

Otzen, Roslyn. 'Recovering the Past for the Present: the History of Victorian Calisthenics'. *Lilith* (5) 1988, pp. 96-112.

Perrot, Philippe. 'A Different Approach to the History of Dress'. *Diogenes* (114) 1981, pp. 157-76.

Plomley, N. J. B. 'Pictures of the Tasmanian Aborigines'. *Art Bulletin of Tasmania* (44) 1983, pp. 36-47.

Rayner, Tony. 'The Female Factory at Cascades, Hobart'. *National Parks and Wildlife Service, Tasmania, Occasional Paper* (3) April 1981.

Reece, Bob. 'Laws of the White People: The Frontier of Authority in Perth in 1838'. *Push from the Bush* (17) 1984, pp. 2-28.

Reece, R. H. W. 'Feasts and Blankets: The History of Some Early Attempts to Establish Relations with the Aborigines of New South Wales, 1814-1846'. *Archaeology and Physical Anthropology in Oceania* (2) 1967, pp. 190-206.

Reynolds, Henry. 'Racial Thought in Early Colonial Australia'. *Australian Journal of Politics and History* (20) 1974, pp. 45-53.

———. Aborigines and European Social Hierarchy'. *Aboriginal History* (7) 1983, pp. 124-33.

Ribeiro, Aileen. 'Provision of Ready-made and Second-hand Clothing in the Eighteenth Century in England'. *Per Una Storia della Moda Pronta*. Milan: CISST, 1990.

Richards, E. S. 'The Genesis of Secondary Industry in the South Australian Economy to 1876'. *Australian Economic History Review* (15) 1975, pp. 107-35.

Roberts, Helene. 'The Exquisite Slave: The Role of Clothes in the Making of the Victorian Woman'. *Signs* (2) 1977, pp. 554-69.

Rowland, E. C. 'Simeon Lord. A Merchant Prince of Botany Bay'. *Journal of the Royal Australian Historical Society* (30) 1944, pp. 157-95.

Rowley, Sue. 'Inside the Deserted Hut: The Representation of Motherhood in Bush Mythology'. *Westerly* (4) 1989, pp. 76-96.

Rowse, Tim. ' "Interpretive Possibilities": Aboriginal Men and Clothing'. *Cultural Studies* (5) 1991, pp. 1-13.

Ruddell, David-Thiery. 'The Domestic Textile Industry in the Region and City of Quebec, 1792-1835'. *Material History Bulletin* (17) Fall 1983, pp. 95-125.

Rush, Anita. 'Changing Women's Fashion and its Social Context, 1870-1905'. *Material History Bulletin* (14) 1982, pp. 37-45.

Russell, Penny. 'The Relationship Between Family Life and Class Formation in Nineteenth-century Melbourne'. *Lilith* (5) Spring 1988, pp. 113-26.

Sawchuk, Kim. 'A Tale of Inscription/Fashion Statements'. *Canadian Journal of Political and Social Theory* (11) 1987, pp. 51-67.

Shrimpton, Jayne. 'Dressing for a Tropical Climate: The Role of Native Fabrics in Fashionable Dress in Early Colonial India'. *Textile History* (23) 1992, pp. 55-70.

Sinclair, W. A. 'The Tariff and Manufacturing Employment in Victoria 1860-1900'. *Economic Record* May 1955, pp. 100-4.

———. 'Women and Economic Change in Melbourne, 1871-1921'. *Historical Studies* (20) 1982-3, pp. 278-91.

Stephen, Ann. 'The Mail-Order Catalogue: From Family Bible to Junk Mail'. *West* (3) 1991, pp. 30-5.

Steven, Margaret. 'The Changing Pattern of Commerce in New South Wales, 1810-1821'. *Business Archives and History*, Aug 1963, pp. 139-55.

Sturma, Michael. 'Eye of the Beholder: The Stereotype of Women Convicts, 1788-1852'. *Labour History* (34) 1978, pp. 3-10.

de Teliga, Jane. 'Twentieth-century Costume: A Focus for Australian Art Museums'. *Art and Australia* (19) 1982, pp. 343-8.

Thompson, Judith. 'Lifestyle and Fashion in Nineteenth-century South Australia'. *Australasian Antique Collector* (20) 1980, pp. 107-13.

Tregenza, John. 'Two Notable Portraits of South Australian Aborigines'. *Journal of the Historical Society of South Australia* (12) 1984, pp. 22-31.

Walsh, G. P. 'Factories and Factory Workers in New South Wales, 1788–1900'. *Labour History* (21) 1971, pp. 1–16.

Williams, Glyndwr. 'Reactions on Cook's Voyages'. *Seeing the First Australians*, ed. I. and T. Donaldson. Sydney: Allen and Unwin, 1985.

Windschuttle, Elizabeth. 'The New Science of Etiquette'. *Push from the Bush* (7) 1980, pp. 58–77.

——. 'The New Science of Etiquette'. *Supplement to the Historic Houses Trust Newsletter* (6) 1985, pp. 2–8.

——. 'Feeding the Poor and Sapping their Strength: The Public Role of Ruling Class Women in Eastern Australia 1788–1850'. *Women, Class and History: Feminist Perspectives on Australia 1788–1978*, ed. Elizabeth Windschuttle. Melbourne: Fontana/Collins, 1980.

Winkworth, Kylie. 'Marsden Family Costume'. *A Companion to the Mint Collections.* Sydney: Museum of Applied Arts and Sciences, 1982.

——. 'Provenance "A Guarantee of Paternity"'. *Australian Antique Collector* July/Dec 1984, pp. 78–81.

Wood, S. 'The British Gorget in North America'. *Waffen und Kostum Kunde* (1) 1984, pp. 4–12.

Woolmington, Jean. 'The Civilisation/Christian Debate and the Australian Aborigines'. *Aboriginal History* (10) 1986, pp. 90–8.

Wright, Richard. 'A Modicum of Taste: Aboriginal Cloaks and Rugs'. *Australian Institute of Aboriginal Studies Newsletter*, New Series 1979, pp. 51–68.

Young, Linda. 'The Experience of Convictism: Five Pieces of Convict Clothing from Western Australia'. *Costume* (22) 1988, pp. 70–84.

**Unpublished—Theses and Lectures**

Reekie, Gail. 'Sydney's Big Stores, 1880–1930: Gender and Mass Marketing'. Ph.D. diss., University of Sydney, 1987.

Russell, Penny. 'Significant Pauses: The Language of Class and Femininity in Nineteenth Century Melbourne 1860–80'. Roger Joyce Lecture, University of Melbourne, 1988.

Stenning, Eve. 'Textile Manufacturing in New South Wales, 1788–1851'. M.A. diss., University of Sydney, 1986.

# Index